IMAGES
of America

DONALDSONVILLE

On the Cover: The flooding of the Mississippi River is a natural occurrence and happens every spring due to snowmelts and rainfall. So, the industrious people of Donaldsonville built levees to protect their homes, businesses, and farms from the overwhelming amounts of water traveling to the Gulf of Mexico. In this photograph, one can see that the levees are only a few feet high. Today, they have been moved away from the buildings and are much higher and wider. In the background is Bayou Lafourche. At this time, it was still open to the Gulf and was a bustling transportation lane. The logs in the water are not there by chance. Notice the rope that is stretched over them. When the rain falls and the river water rises, everything in the path of the Mississippi is taken with it. Photographed on their journey south, these logs will be dried and used for timber by whoever finds them—finders, keepers. (Courtesy of the Marchand family.)

IMAGES
of America

DONALDSONVILLE

Will LeBlanc

ARCADIA
PUBLISHING

ISBN 978-0-7385-9168-1

Published by Arcadia Publishing
Charleston, South Carolina

Printed in the United States of America

Library of Congress Control Number: 2011945037

For all general information, please contact Arcadia Publishing:
Telephone 843-853-2070
Fax 843-853-0044
E-mail sales@arcadiapublishing.com
For customer service and orders:
Toll-Free 1-888-313-2665

Visit us on the Internet at www.arcadiapublishing.com

This book is dedicated to the works, the laughter, the struggles, and the memory of Kirk Paul Landry.

Contents

ACKNOWLEDGMENTS

I would gratefully like to acknowledge the assistance and contributions of the residents and families of Donaldsonville. In particular, thanks go to the following: Kirk Landry, Missy Martinez, Brent Landry, Andrew Capone, Glen Falgoust, Charlie Sotile, Kathy Hambrick Jackson, Sidney Marchand, Paul Marchand, Larry Lassere, Missy Jandura, Stevie Graugnard, the Lemman family, Charles Thibaut, the Kocke family, the Donaldsonville Library staff, and everyone who contributed to the collection of photographs and stories of our past.

I would also like to thank my wife, Ellen, for her inspiration and understanding when I kept saying, "This won't take much longer."

For more information on Donaldsonville's history, visit us at www.Dville.org

INTRODUCTION

Donaldsonville's history is a storybook full of tales of pirates, battles, plantations, commerce, and cultures. From the Native Americans who traded with the French settlers in the early 1700s to the influx of slaves, Acadians, Isleños, Jews, and Italians; from the Civil War to Reconstruction; and from the churches to synagogues, Donaldsonville has seen it all.

In 1682, Sieur de La Salle explored the Mississippi River Valley and claimed it for France and King Louis XIV. In honor of the king, he called it Louisiana. At the junction of the river and a bayou, he found the Chetimaches Indians. La Fourche des Chetimaches became the name of the stream. *La fourche* means "the fork." It was later changed to Bayou Lafourche.

Jesuit priests frequently led expeditions up and down the river, and in 1704, Fr. John Buissin de St. Cosme camped on the riverbank below Bayou Lafourche; the Chetimaches Indians slaughtered his party. Governor Sieur Jean Baptiste Lemoyne de Bienville used competing Indian tribes to wage war on the Chetimaches Indians until they were all but extinct and forced to move north to Bayou Goula. Most of the early settlers were Canadian hunters, French fortune-seekers, and French criminals who chose relocation over jail. Most were uninterested in farming as they found it to be hard work with little reward.

In 1755, the British deported the French settlers from Acadia (the original name of Nova Scotia) and scattered them throughout the colonies along the Eastern Seaboard with only the possessions they could carry. Many of the colonies did not welcome them; Louisiana, with its French rule, French language, and Catholic faith, became the promised land. In 1763, the new immigrants were shocked to learn that France had ceded Louisiana to Spain, but were well received by the Spanish governors who were kind and sympathetic to them. The new Acadian immigrants were given land along the river and food for the first year in return for constructing and maintaining levees and roads along the fronts of their properties.

Louisiana prospered under Spanish rule but continued to cost the Spanish government over $300,000 per year. In 1800, Spain ceded the territory to France under the secret Treaty of San Ildefonso. The treaty was not made public for about two years. On November 3, 1803, at the Cabildo in New Orleans, Spain publicly transferred Louisiana to France. On December 20, 1803, the French turned Louisiana over to the United States under the Louisiana Purchase. It became a state on April 30, 1812.

Pierre Landry received a Spanish land grant for the property bordered by the Mississippi River and La Fourche des Chetimaches in 1775. William Donaldson, a young merchant from New Orleans, selected the Landry farm as the site for his new town and purchased it for $12,000 on February 10, 1806. He commissioned Bartholomew Lafon to draw a plan for La Ville de Donaldson. The plan included a crescent-shaped park to welcome river traffic and to lead to the Place de La Louisiane, a park that the future county seat and state capitol would face. Donaldson Town was formally dedicated on April 27, 1806. La Ville de Donaldson was incorporated on March 25, 1813. William Donaldson died in September 1813.

The post office was established in June 1808. Mail came from New Orleans by stagecoach and was then transported across the river by skiff to Mrs. A.P. LeBlanc or Landry's store for local distribution. The journey took 35 hours. By 1831, mail was delivered twice a week by riders on horseback. Later, mail was delivered by riverboat, which still required a minimum of 24 hours to and from New Orleans. It was only when the railroad came in 1871 that news and mail could reach Donaldsonville in only four hours.

On January 1, 1845, the Sisters of Charity of St. Joseph arrived from Emmitsburg, Maryland, to establish a school. They became the Daughters of Charity of St. Vincent De Paul in 1850. The legislature had allowed the Church of Ascension to donate a portion of land to the sisters. A small, four-room cottage served as both a convent and school. Life was difficult, but they soon enrolled 30 students. Some controversy arose because they insisted on teaching English instead of French, which was commonly taught in the area, but they proved themselves as educators through several displays of the talents of their students, and the school grew rapidly.

William Donaldson donated two lots on the corner of Chetimaches and Attakapas Streets to be used for a county courthouse and jail. After several fires and the Civil War, a new jail was built at this location in 1867. A new courthouse was built in 1887 but burned in 1889. The next year, another courthouse, designed by James Freret, was built on the same site. It has solid masonry load-bearing walls and a wooden frame interior. Though wings have been added, the original structure stands today.

William Donaldson died before seeing his dream of having his town become the state capital. In 1825, Donaldsonville was selected to become the "Capital City of the Commonwealth of Louisiana." The legislature appropriated $30,000 for a statehouse and authorized five commissioners to select the site. Antoine Peytavin was contracted to build a 150-by-100-foot statehouse. The state purchased from Francois Lefort the entire square of ground bounded by Cabahanosse, Opelousas, Houmas, and Claiborne Streets.

In February 1825, the general assembly jointly resolved that the state government would move to Donaldsonville on or before January 21, 1826. Legislators who traveled to inspect the new statehouse were not impressed. It was poorly constructed, the roof leaked, the streets were not paved, and there were no sidewalks. Donaldsonville also did not offer the same level of entertainment and comfort that the legislature was afforded in New Orleans. On January 8, 1831, the legislature was moved back to New Orleans.

Louisiana seceded from the United States to join the Confederate States of America in 1861. Although New Orleans was captured early, Donaldsonville's men continued to fight during the entire war. In 1833, the Louisiana legislature passed an act and formed Les Cannoniers de Donaldson with the help of Numa Augustin. They departed for Virginia on September 18, 1862, to join the forces of Capt. Victor Maurin. The company fought gallantly at Yorktown, Williamsburg, and many other battles in that area until the South surrendered.

In Donaldsonville, the wharves became the site for guerilla attacks on Union ships, which caused Adm. D.G. Farragut to attack the city. On August 9, 1862, federal gunboats opened fire on the city for a few hours, and then, parties were sent to torch the remaining buildings. Except for Solomon Weinschenck's home (now Ferris's Store), the city was burned from the bayou to the church grounds. Late in 1862, 5,000 Union troops were sent to build a star-shaped, dirt fort at the mouth of Bayou Lafourche opposite Donaldsonville. It was named Fort Butler.

As in many places in the South after the Civil War, Donaldonsville's agriculture-based economy was destroyed. Slowly, Donaldsonville's sugar industry started to recover, the infrastructure was rebuilt, and Donaldsonville become a center for commerce once again.

One

Donaldson Town

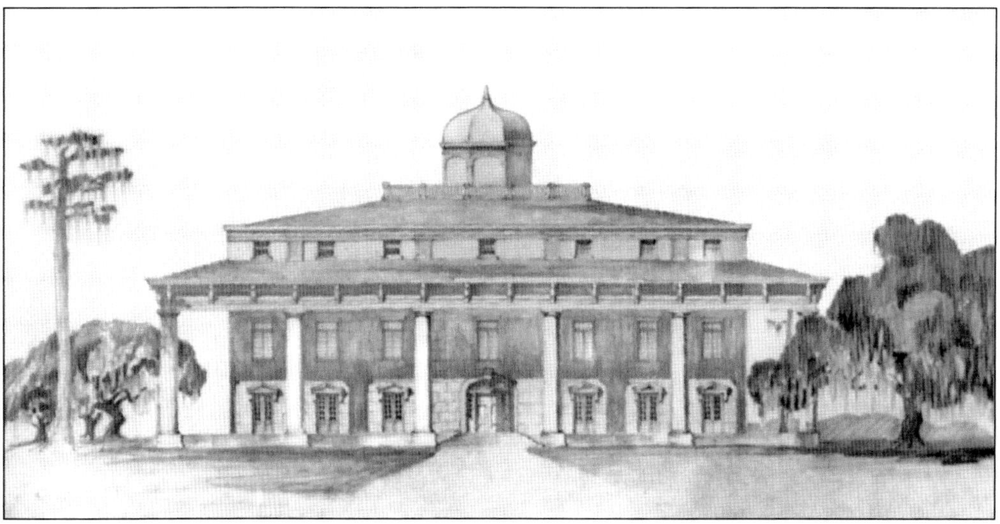

This was the capitol of the state of Louisiana when it was located in Donaldsonville from 1830 to 1831. The original sketch was done by Sydney A. Marchand Jr. when he was in the ninth grade at Donaldsonville High School. He obtained the directions for his sketch from a translation made by Dr. Percy H. LeBlanc who was teaching French at the time. The translation was obtained from the French records of the building contract found at the Ascension Parish Courthouse. (Courtesy of the Marchand family.)

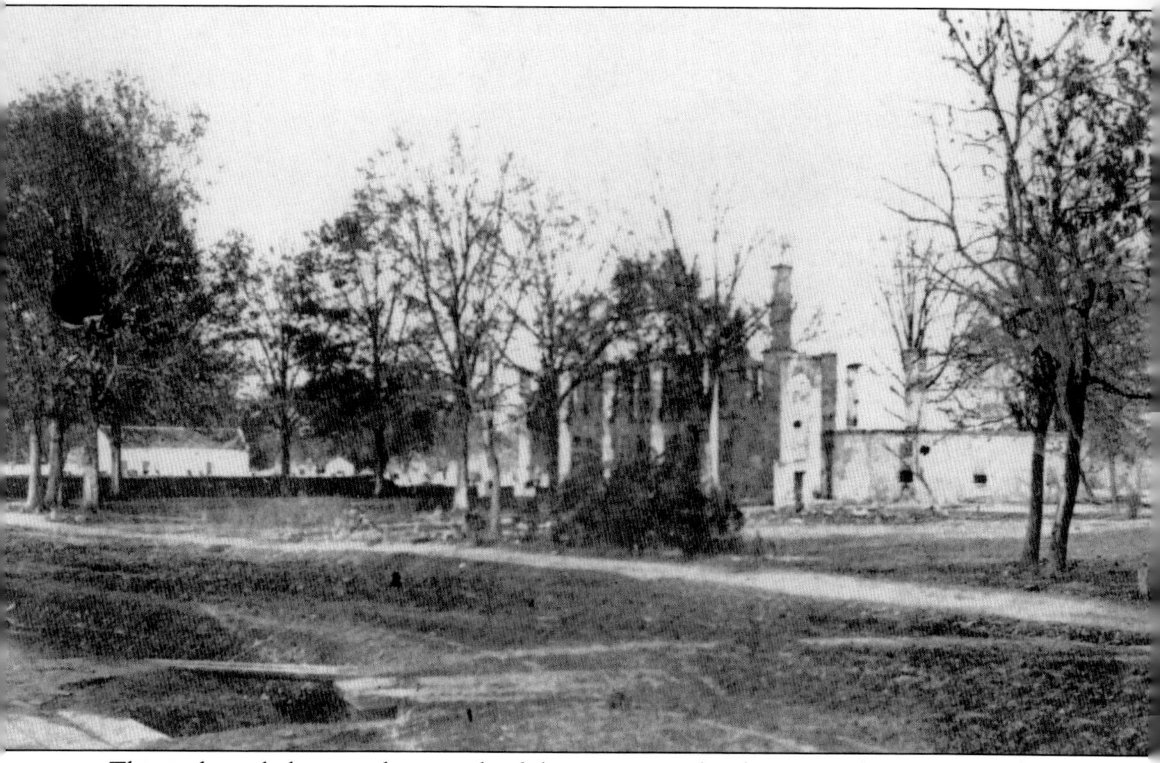

This is the only known photograph of the state capitol, taken around 1863. It cost $30,000 to build but was plagued with problems from the beginning. The state's general assembly was supposed to move from New Orleans to Donaldsonville on January 21, 1826, but upon inspection of the statehouse, the legislators were not impressed. The streets were not paved, there were no sidewalks, and the level of entertainment was dreadful. While there were sessions held here, on January 8, 1831, the legislature was adjourned to New Orleans. Abandoned for years and then dismantled, the wood was used to shore up the bayou levee on the Donaldsonville side. (Courtesy of the Capone family.)

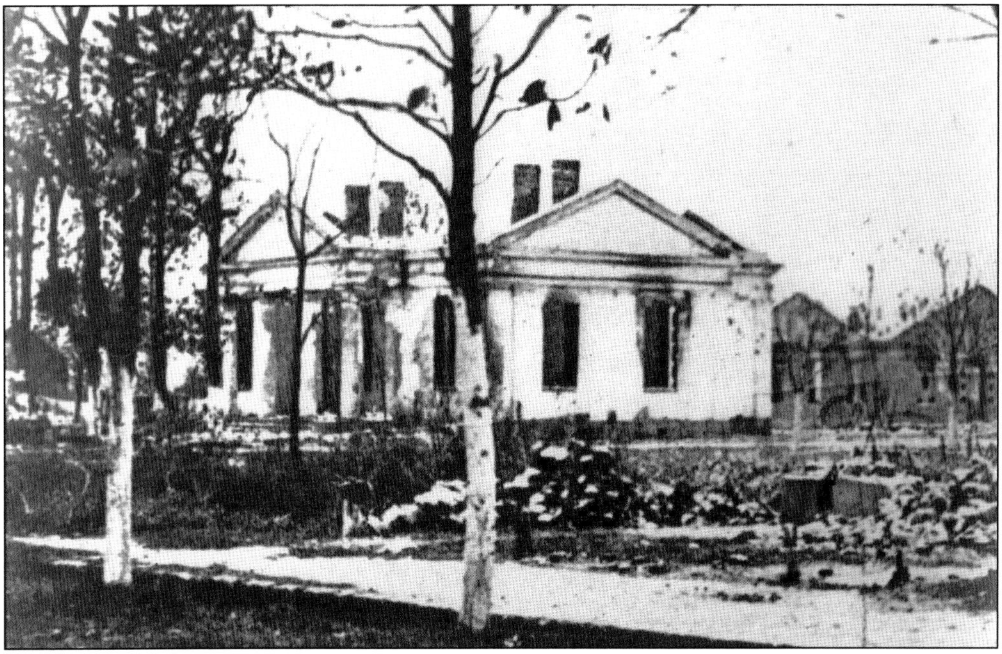

After relentless, harassing assaults from local rebels during the Civil War, Adm. David G. Farragut sent warships to Donaldsonville and delivered the following decree: "To the people of Donaldsonville, Louisiana, Every time my boats get fired upon, I will burn a portion of your town." (Courtesy of the Landry family.)

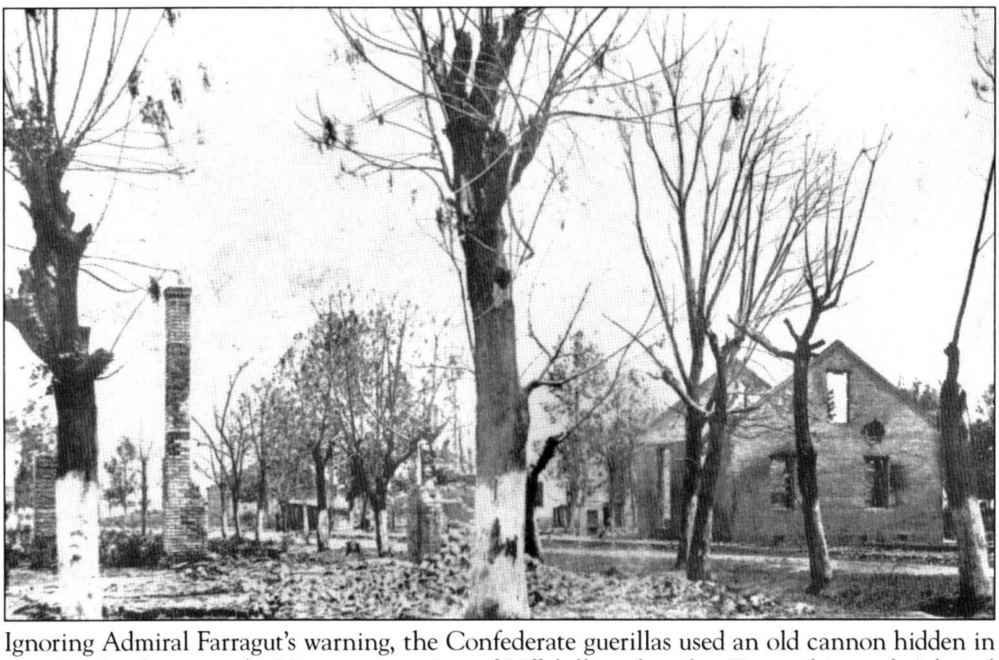

Ignoring Admiral Farragut's warning, the Confederate guerillas used an old cannon hidden in the wharf to fire upon the Union steamer *Laurel Hill*, killing the pilot. True to his word, Admiral Farragut's gunboats opened fire on Donaldsonville on August 9, 1862, for a few hours, and then, parties were sent in to burn the city. Notice the cannonball hole in the wall of the house on the right. (Courtesy of the Capone family.)

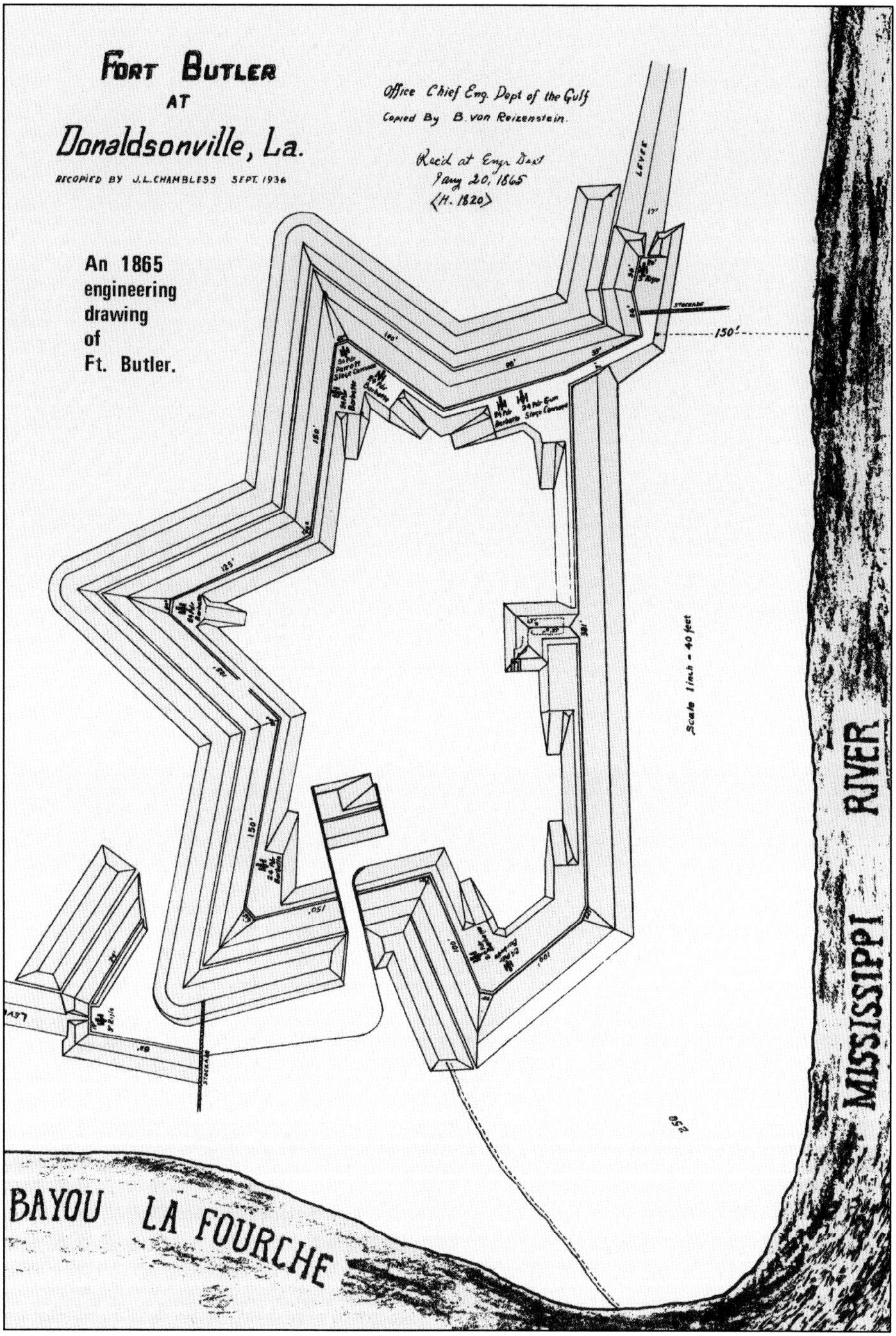

An 1865 engineering drawing of Ft. Butler.

Late in 1862, about 5,000 Union troops were sent to build a star-shaped, dirt fort at the mouth of Bayou Lafourche opposite Donaldsonville. It was finished in January 1863 and named Fort Butler. On June 27, 1863, Confederate troops under the command of Gen. Thomas Green marched all night from Thibodaux to a campsite within nine miles from Fort Butler. To distract the Union army, Green dispatched one regiment across the bayou to advance on the Donaldsonville side. Intelligence reported that 500–600 soldiers were in the fort with five gunboats in the river. (Courtesy of the Marchand family.)

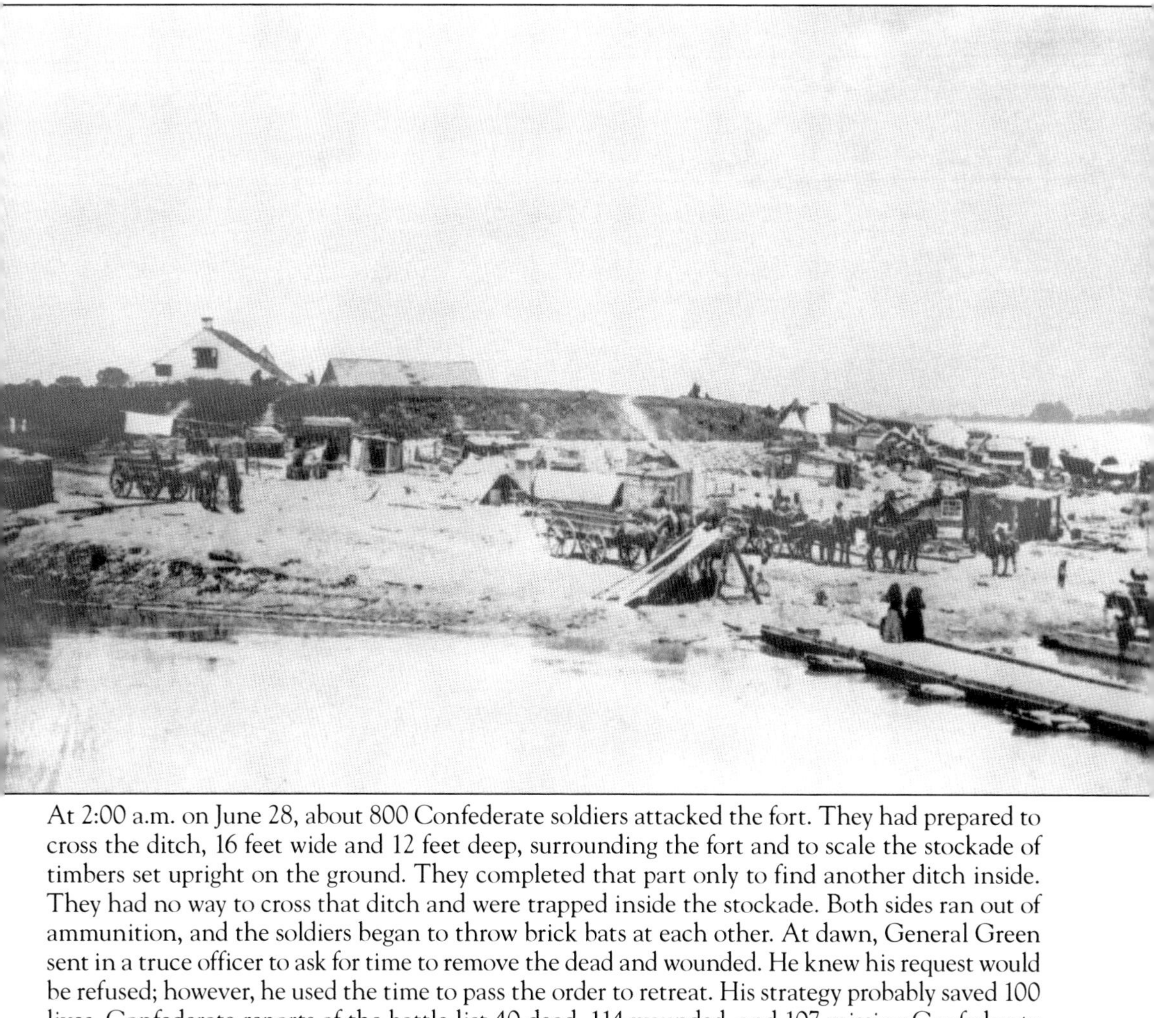

At 2:00 a.m. on June 28, about 800 Confederate soldiers attacked the fort. They had prepared to cross the ditch, 16 feet wide and 12 feet deep, surrounding the fort and to scale the stockade of timbers set upright on the ground. They completed that part only to find another ditch inside. They had no way to cross that ditch and were trapped inside the stockade. Both sides ran out of ammunition, and the soldiers began to throw brick bats at each other. At dawn, General Green sent in a truce officer to ask for time to remove the dead and wounded. He knew his request would be refused; however, he used the time to pass the order to retreat. His strategy probably saved 100 lives. Confederate reports of the battle list 40 dead, 114 wounded, and 107 missing Confederate troops. Union reports list Confederate losses at 350 dead and wounded and 130 taken prisoner. Union files list their own losses at "five or six dead and a few wounded." This is the only known photograph of Fort Butler. (Courtesy of the Marchand family.)

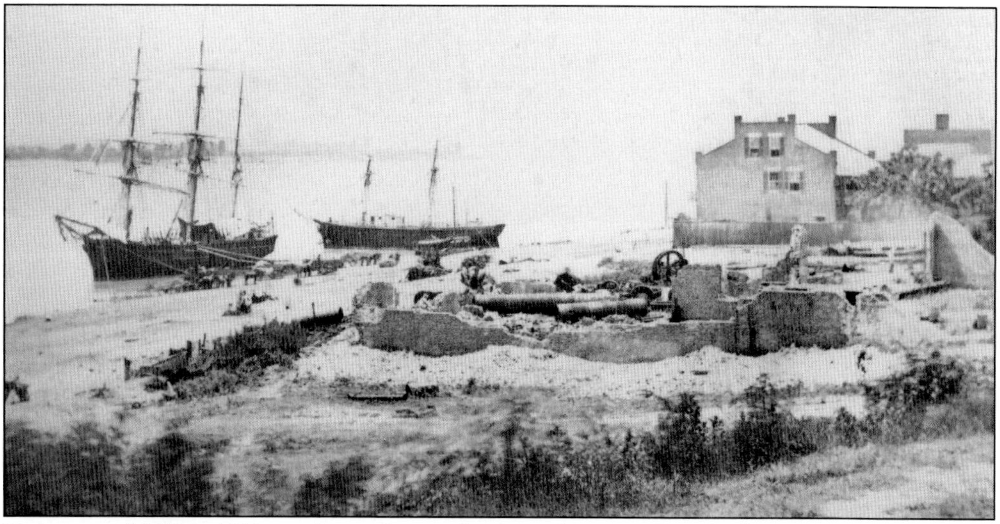

Here, two of Admiral Farragut's warships unload supplies near Fort Butler. Notice the destroyed wharf in the foreground. This was the wharf that Confederate rebels used to fire upon ships passing up and down the river. (Courtesy of the Capone family.)

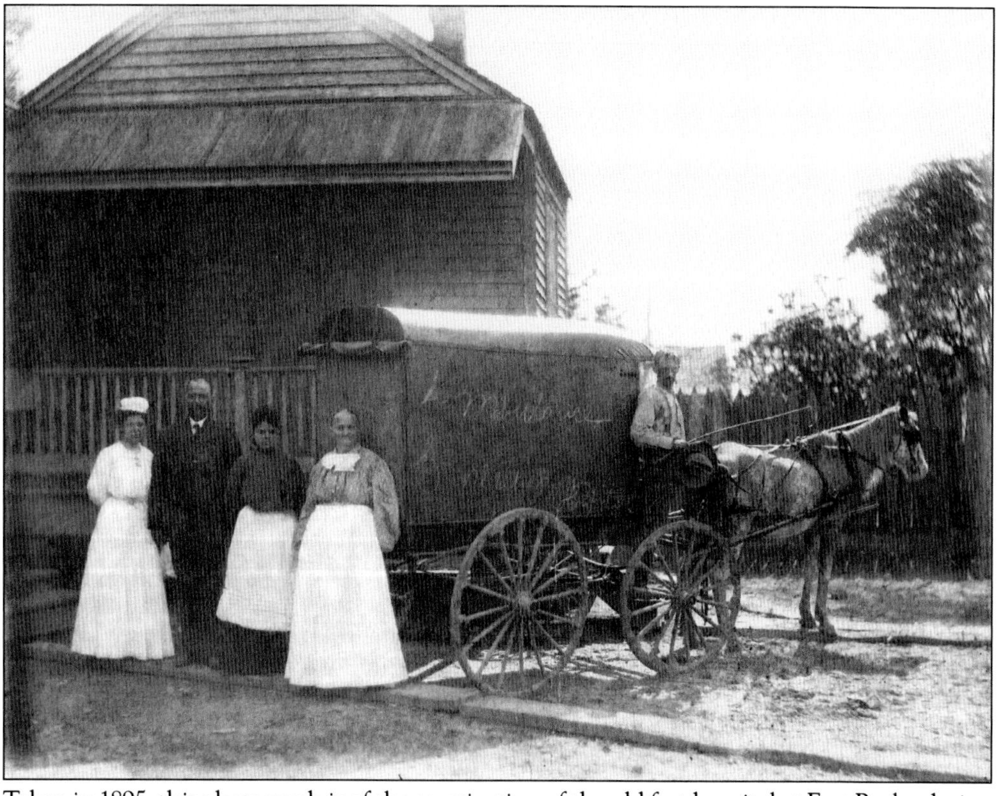

Taken in 1895, this photograph is of the reactivation of the old fort hospital at Fort Butler during the Spanish-American War. The people in the photograph were local historian and photographer August Bradford's family members, including, from left to right, his wife Mary Dudenheffer, his grandfather Millard Philmore Bradford, his niece Laura Bradford; Mrs. Dudenheffer, driver Charlie Rodriguez, and the horse, Yellow. (Courtesy of the Marchand family.)

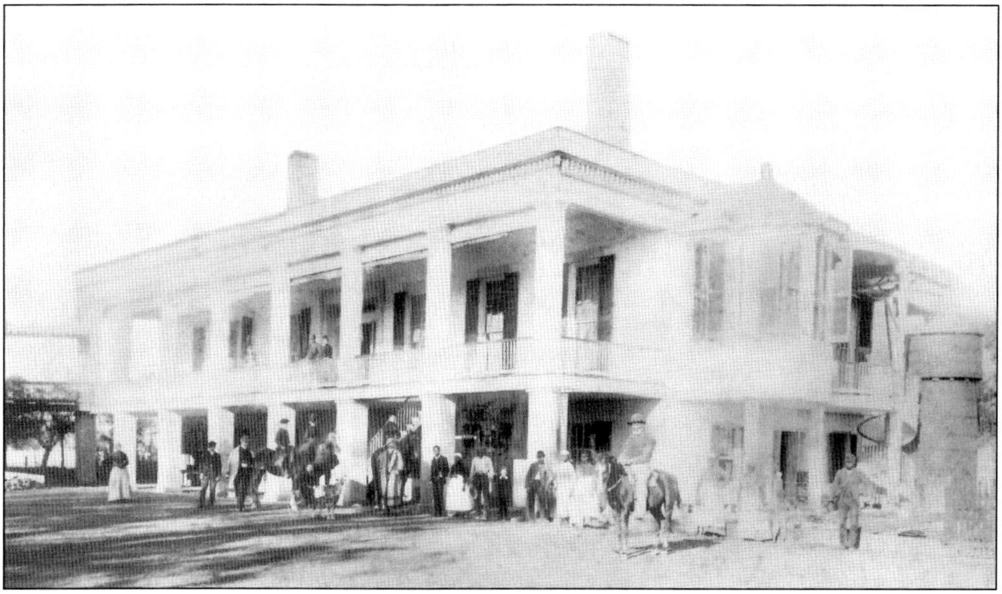

Evan Hall Plantation is situated on the Mississippi River in Ascension Parish just above the town of Donaldsonville. The main line of the Texas & Pacific railway became an important factor in the state's sugar industry. Evan Hall contains a total of 3,577 acres, including 260 acres of woodland, with a fine drainage system. It is also well equipped with everything that appertains to a first-class sugar plantation. This photograph shows the "Big House" and some of its residents and employees. (Courtesy of the Thibaut family.)

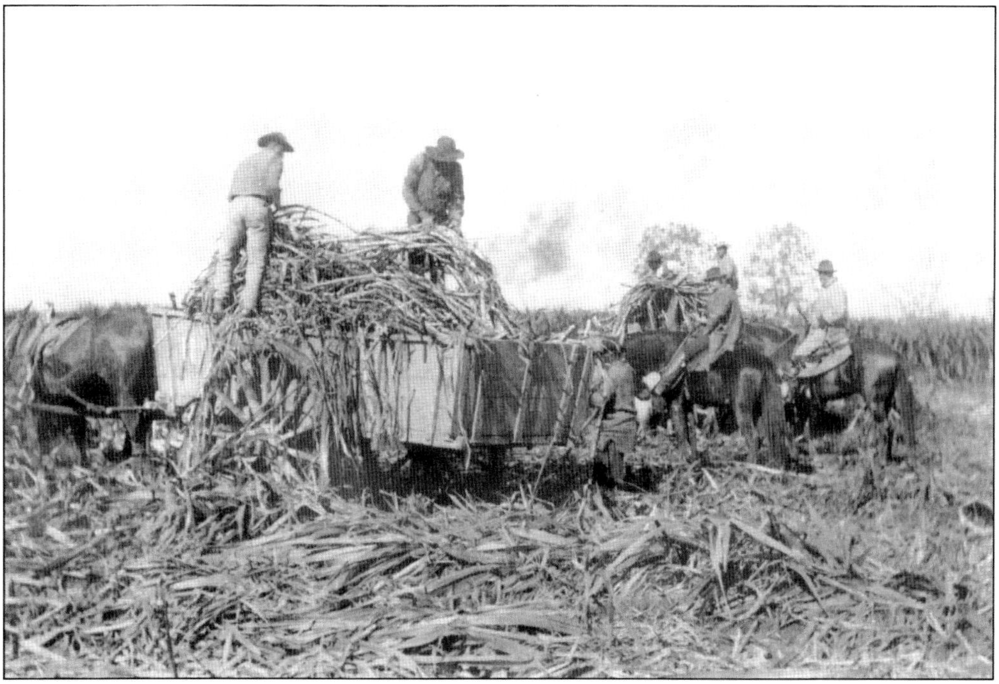

Work on the plantation was hard and slow. The plantation was mostly self-contained, with quarters for workers and staff, stables, barns, blacksmith and woodworking shops, a public store, and a post office. (Courtesy of the Thibaut family.)

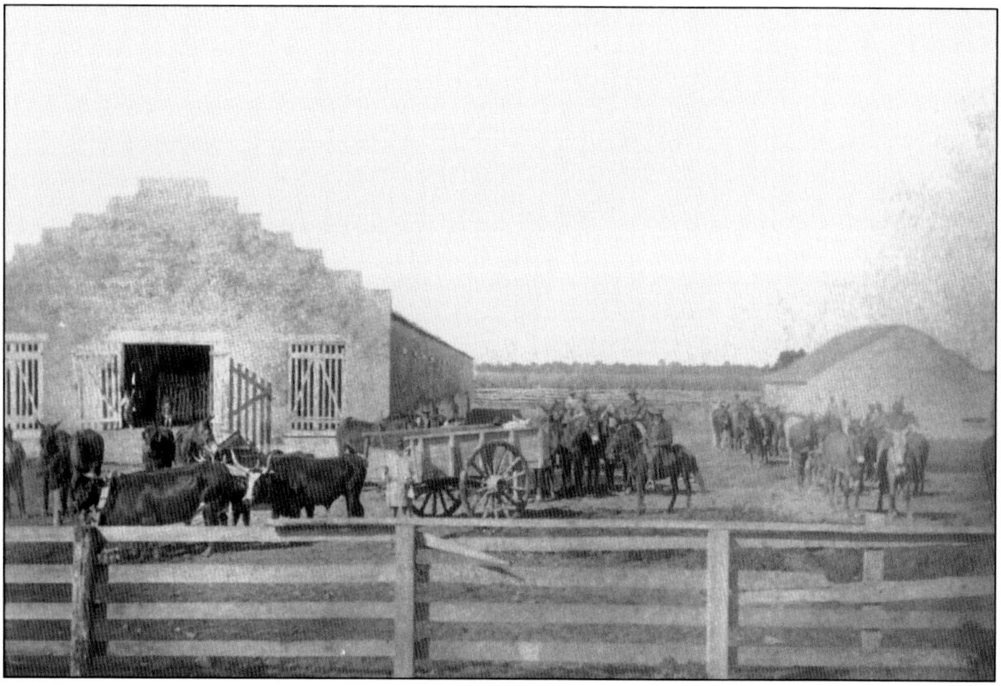

Everyone worked on the plantation. The women did most of the housework, and there were always chores for the kids. The cattle supplied the milk and meat, and the horses pulled the sugarcane carts and were the main mode of transportation. (Courtesy of the Thibaut family.)

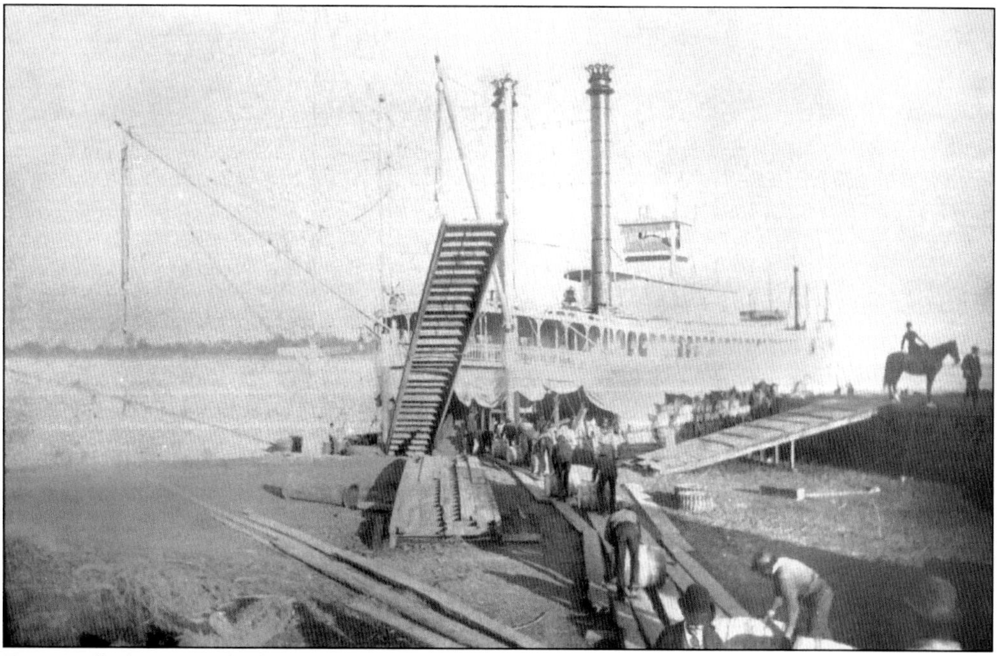

Evan Hall Plantation had property along the Mississippi River, which was used to load and ship sugar around the world. This photograph shows barrels of sugar being loaded onto a steamboat. Notice the supervisor on horseback on the right. This was a common way of transporting sugar until the railroad lines crossed Bayou Lafourche. (Courtesy of the Thibaut family.)

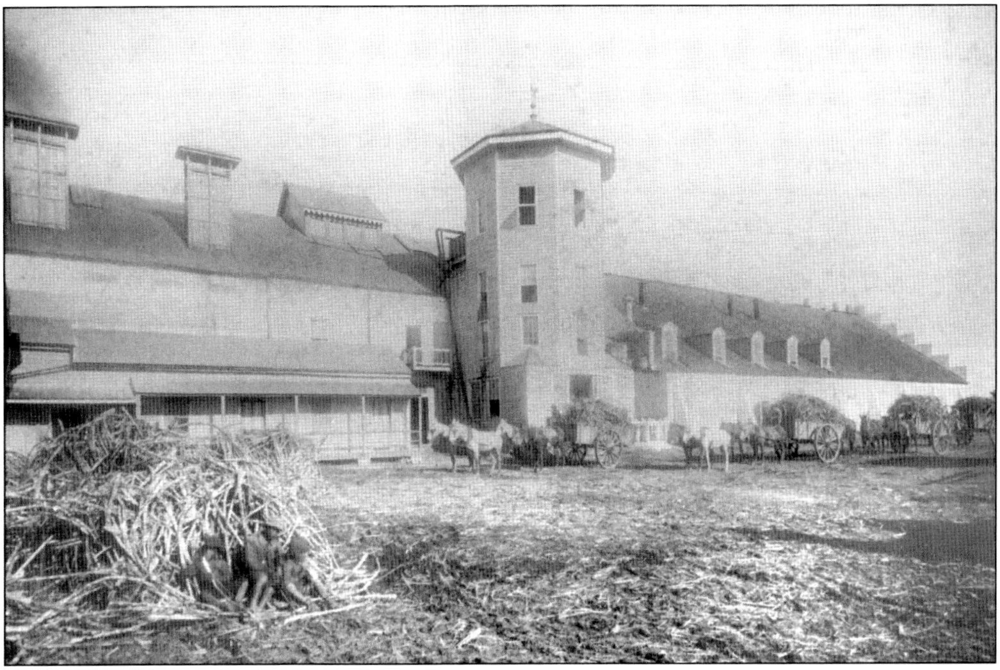

A sugarcane farmer, as he is known in South Louisiana, must have double the amount of land that any other farmer would need. This is because of the long nine-month growing season of sugarcane. A good sugarcane farmer should have two crops in the ground at the same time: one ready for harvest and one that has been planted just prior to harvest for the following year. Cultivation of the land in the early years of farming was done with a plow and a mule. Larger cultivators, which had large iron wheels, were later manufactured to open rows for planting. The cane was planted in big rows about six feet apart. Cane was grown by putting short pieces of cane in the ground and covering them with dirt; after a short period of time, new stalks would grow from the joints of the old cane. If the farmer was lucky, a new stalk would grow from each joint of the cane that was planted. (Courtesy of the Thibaut family.)

Grinding, as it is called in South Louisiana, or the harvest, took place in early October and lasted until late December. Grinding was the most pressure-packed time of the year for the sugarcane farmer, as it was very important to get the entire cane crop out before the first freeze. Most farmers tried to have their crops harvested before Christmas. Some farmers waited a little bit longer to harvest their cane, because the longer they waited the sweeter their cane would be; however, if an early freeze came along before the cane was cut, they could lose a lot of it. (Courtesy of the Thibaut family.)

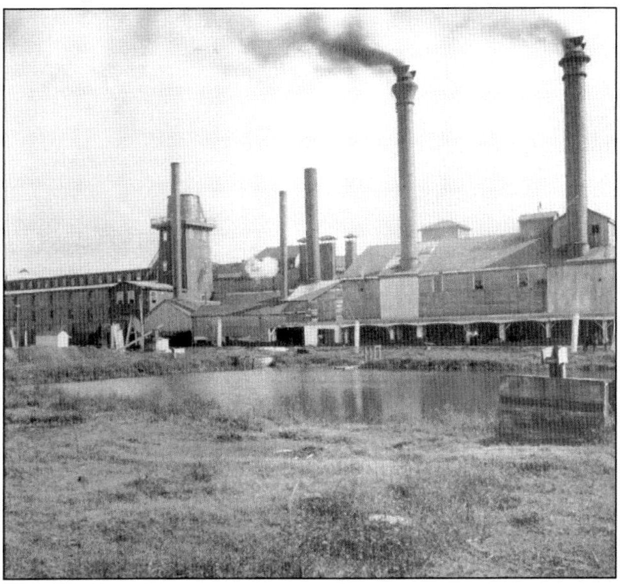

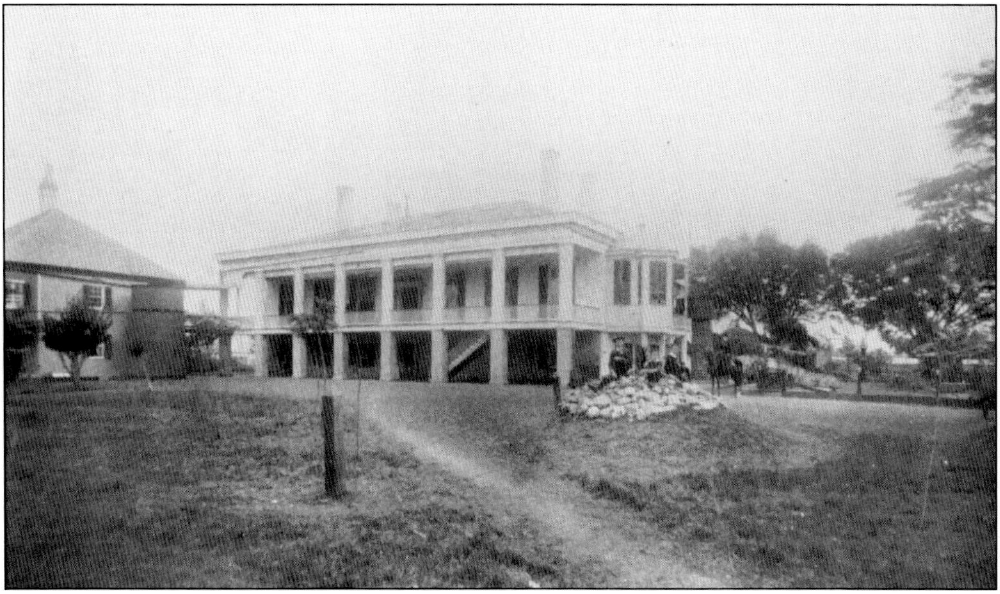

Here is another view of the Big House at Evan Hall. It offers a better view of the kitchen, to the left of the main house. A cistern collects rainwater for cooking and cleaning. (Courtesy of the Thibaut family.)

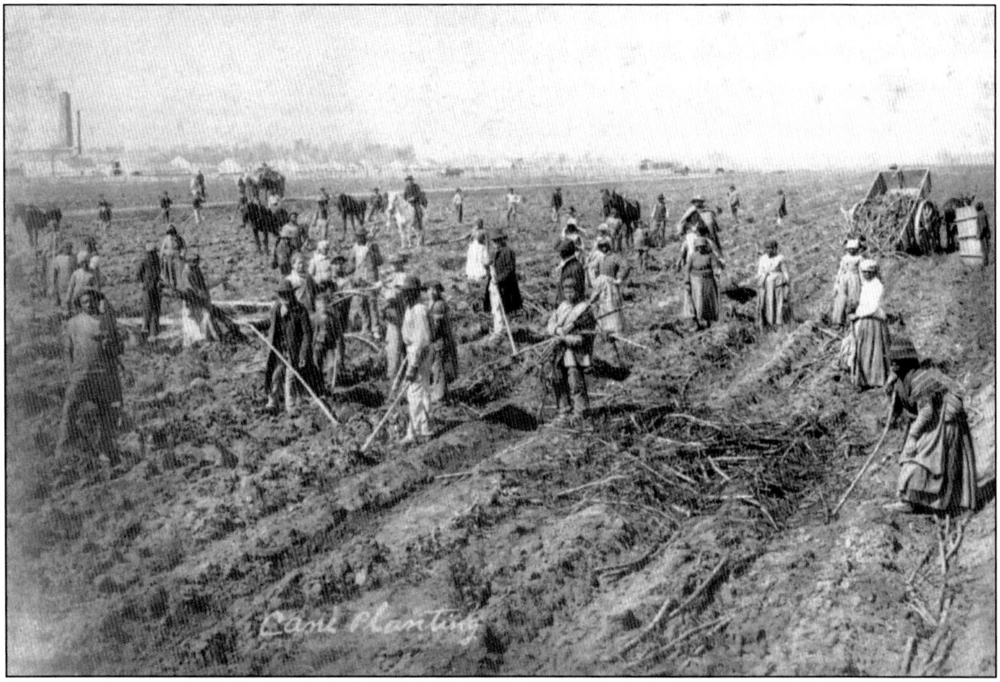

Nearby, Palo Alto Plantation was also a major sugar producer in the Donaldsonville area. Palo Alto, which translates to "tall trees," was once a wedding gift from the wealthy Spanish plantation owner Oscar Ayraud to his daughter Rosalie. The property was later purchased by Jacob Lemann. Since his purchase in 1865, the plantation has been home to every crop native to Louisiana's rich soil. The plantation has grown considerably in its 150-year existence to encompass more than 6,000 acres of sugarcane, pasture land, woodlands, and ponds. (Courtesy of the Lemann family.)

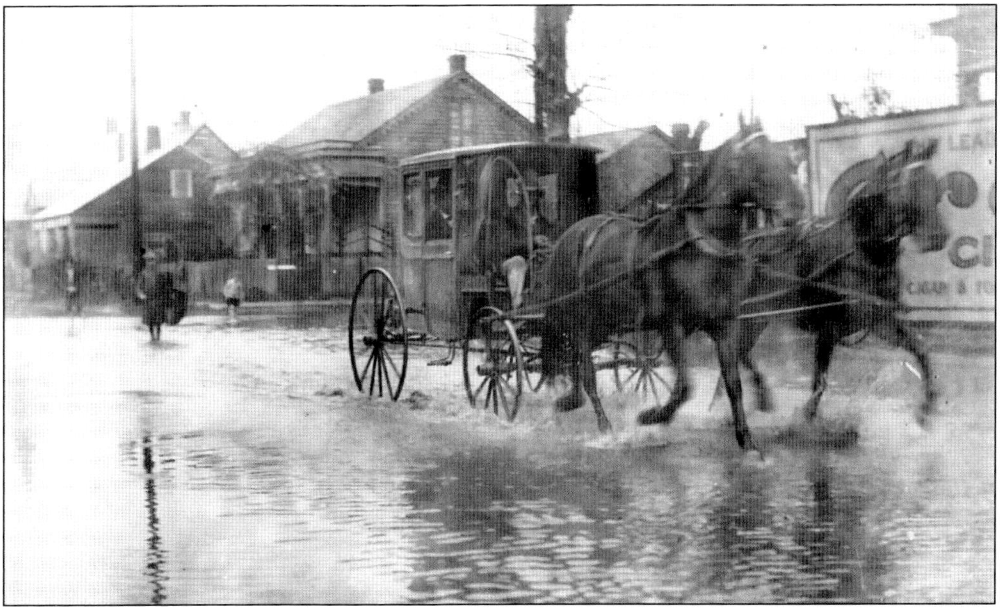

A horse and carriage makes its way down Railroad Avenue in 1911 Donaldsonville. The water in the streets is from the spring flooding of the Mississippi River that topped the levees. Until the levees were raised to protect the city and the local industries, the streets would stay flooded for months at a time. (Courtesy of the Landry family.)

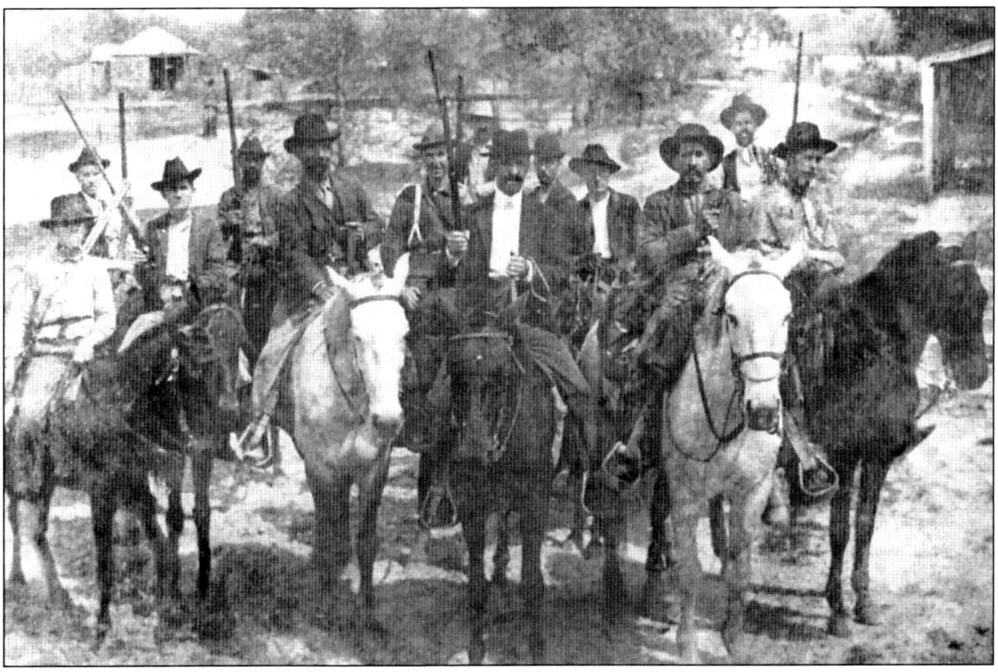

Levees were built on both sides of the Mississippi River to control spring flooding. During very high river stages, members of communities along the river would travel upstream looking for a place to breach the levee to relieve the pressure on their area. When this happened, thousands of acres around the breached area would flood. Towns soon began forming levee posses to patrol their levees and protect their communities from sabotage. (Courtesy of the Marchand family.)

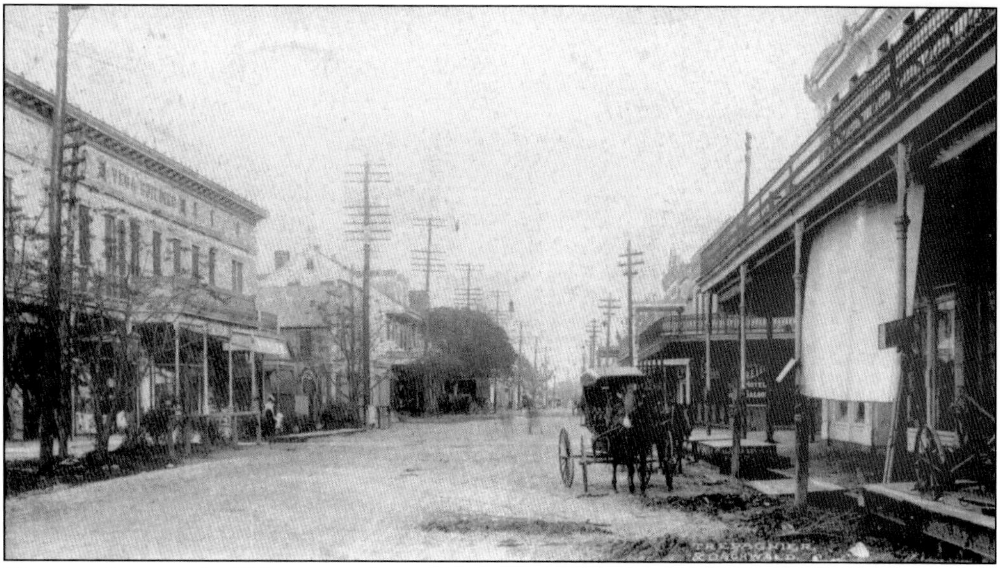

This is a photograph of Mississippi Street, looking east. The river is just behind the buildings on the left. The first building on the left is the Vega Building, built in 1898 by Antoine D. Vega. He was a Civil War veteran who became a dry goods salesman after the war. Vega was notorious for undercutting his competition, which earned him the nickname "Cheap Tony." The building just past the Vega Building is the Nicholls Hotel. (Courtesy of the Landry family.)

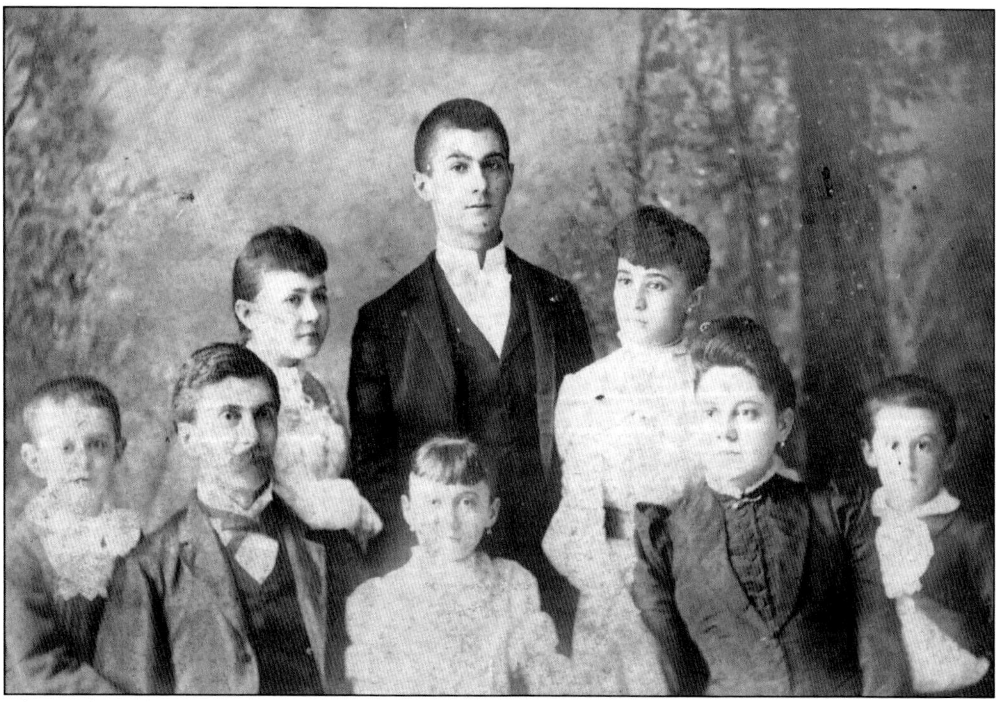

This is the only known photograph of Civil War veteran and local businessman Antoine D. Vega and his family. His nickname, Cheap Tony, became the brand name he used in advertising in the local paper and on signage. (Courtesy of the Hanson family.)

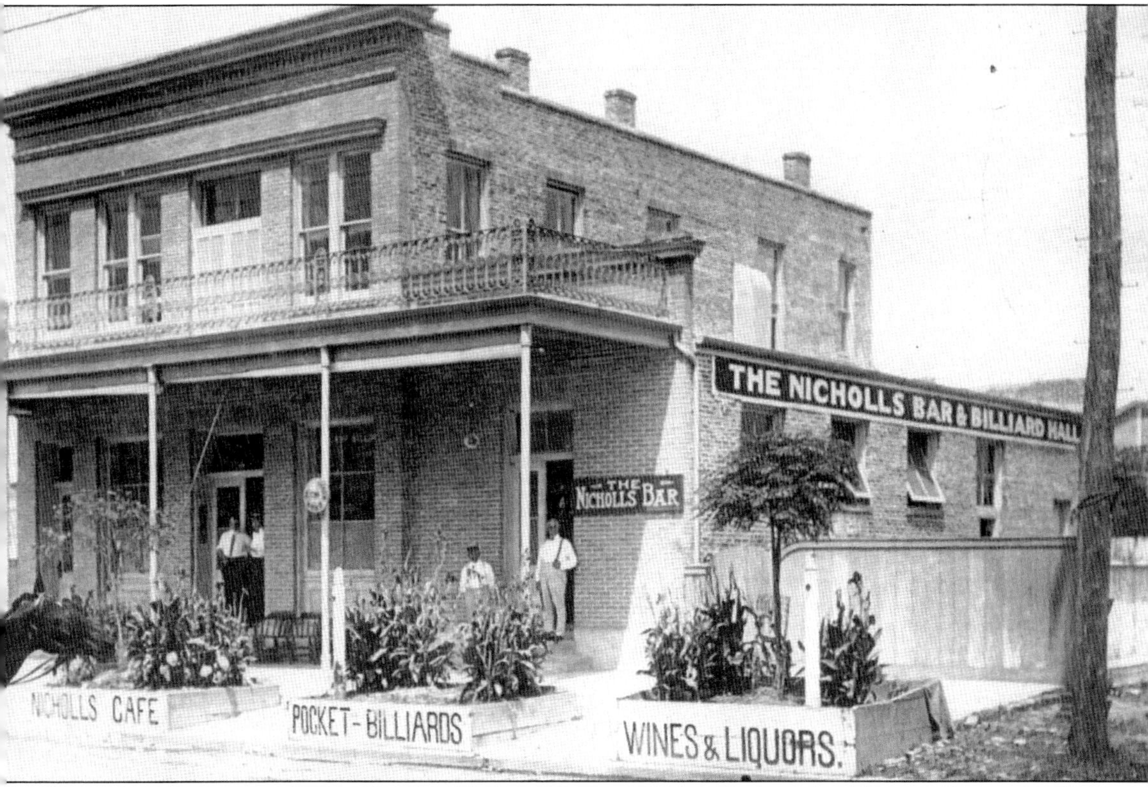

Fred Rogge owned the Nicholls Bar and Billiard Hall on the 400 block of Mississippi Street, once the site of the renowned Nicholls Hotel. Rogge operated the Nicholls Hotel, which was named after Civil War hero, governor, chief justice of the Supreme Court, and Donaldsonville native Francis T. Nicholls. The hotel was consumed by fire on February 22, 1911, along with a major portion of the downtown area. Rogge rebuilt the Nicholls Bar in its place. The building is still standing today. (Courtesy of the Landry family.)

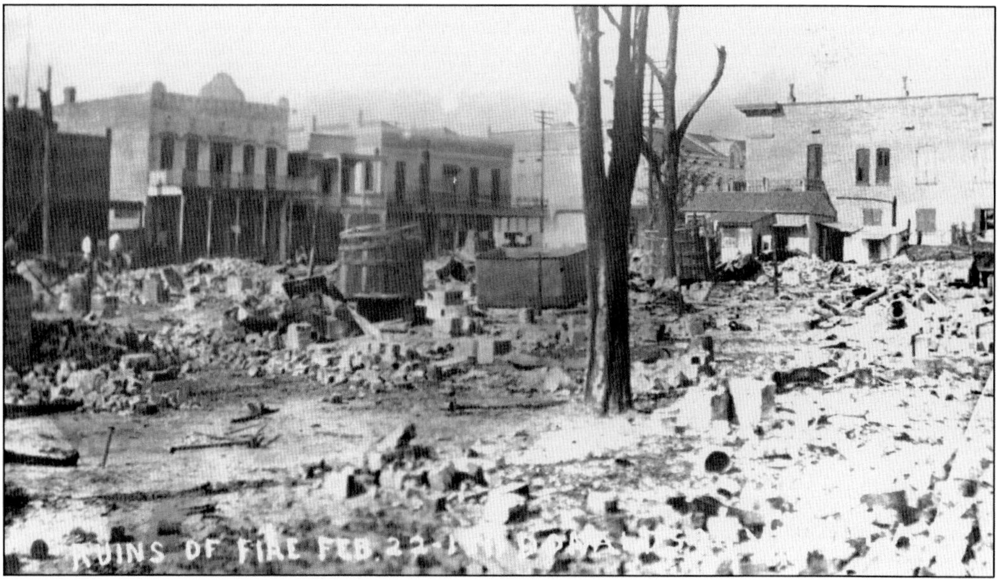

This is one of the only known photographs of the great fire of 1911. The following is part of the story as reported by local newspaper *Donaldsonville Chief*: "Business block wiped out – Donaldsonville swept by most disastrous fire in history of the city – property worth $250,000 destroyed – flames originate in Nicholls Hotel kitchen – Neighboring towns render valuable aid. The most disastrous fire in the history of Donaldsonville visited this city on Wednesday last, the 22nd wiping out nearly a score of buildings in the heart of the business and residence sections of the community and causing a property loss estimated at approximately a quarter of a million dollars. Starting from a defective flue in the kitchen of the Nicholls Hotel at bout 10:30 o'clock a.m., the flames, fanned by a high north wind, soon got beyond control of the firemen and swirled through the doomed district with great velocity, consuming frame buildings as though they were a pile of shavings and devouring the most substantially constructed brick structures with seemingly equal ease and rapidity." (Courtesy of the Landry family.

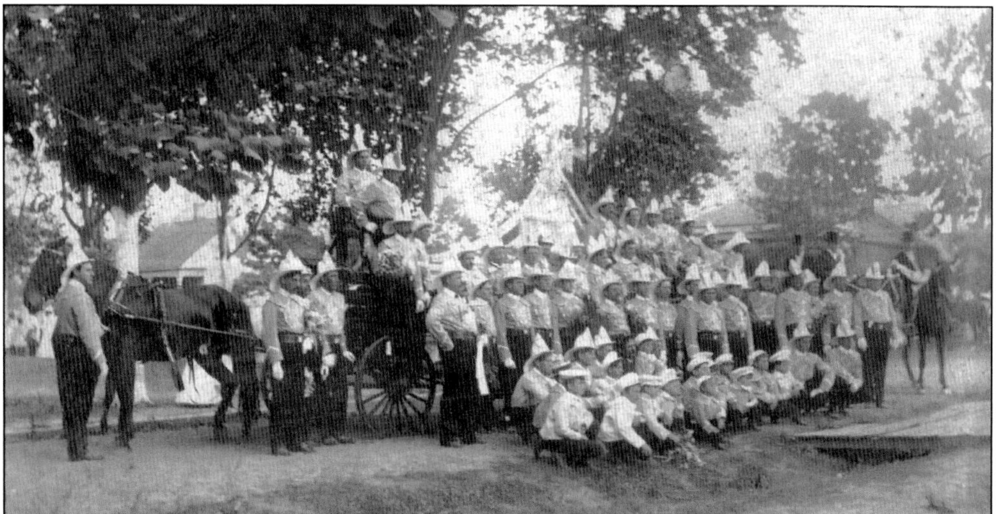

Donaldsonville had several fire departments at the turn of the century, but they were no match for the great fire of 1911. (Courtesy of the Landry family.)

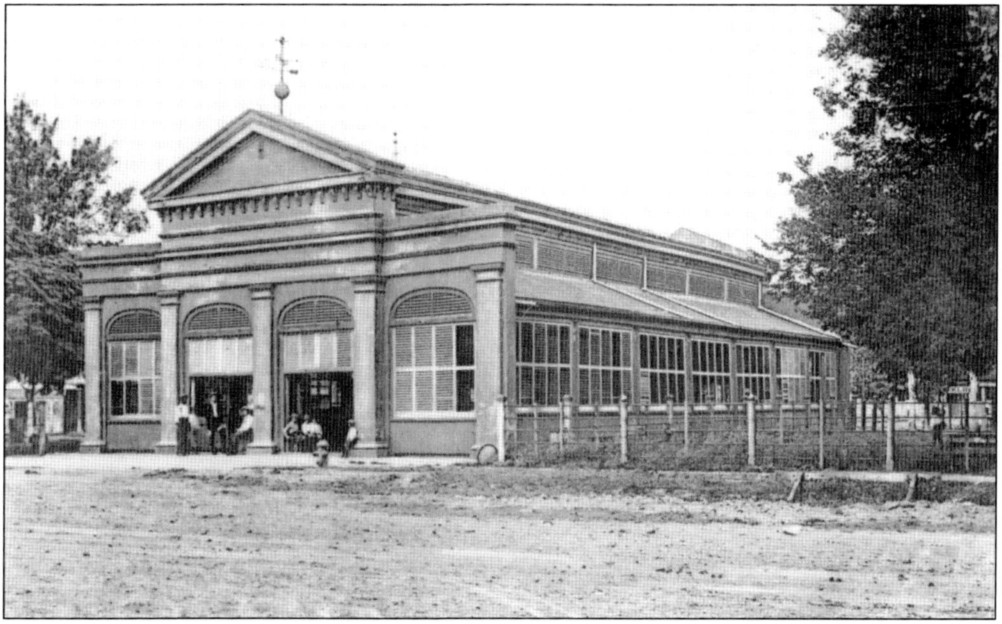

John Belson of Assumption Parish constructed the old market in 1853 for $6,000. Although damaged, it survived Admiral Farragut's bombardment of the city in August 1862. During Reconstruction, it was used to disperse goods to the local residents. During this time, it was nicknamed "Butler's Market" after Union general Benjamin "Beast" Butler. In 1918, Elray Kocke Service tore down the old market, which was in disrepair. (Courtesy of the Landry family.)

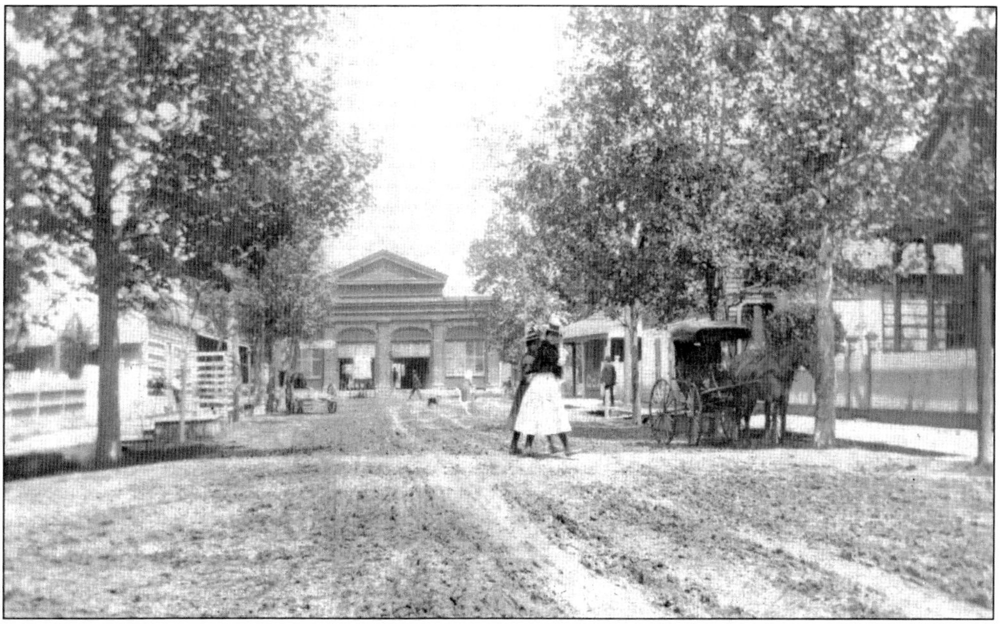

This is Houmas Street around 1900, looking toward the Mississippi River. The building in the middle is the old market, a common destination for residents and neighbors from the surrounding area. The river is just on the other side of the building. The old market was located where the gazebo in Crescent Park is now. Fresh food and produce were shipped in daily to meet the demands of this bustling town. (Courtesy of the Hanson family.)

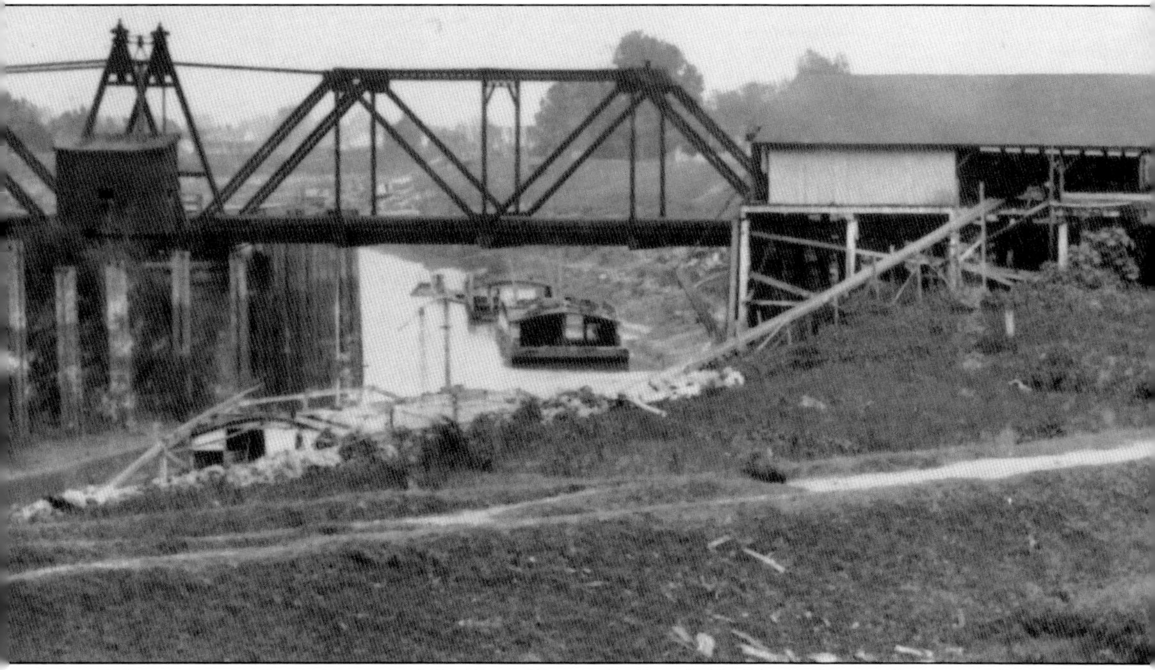

This is a view from the roof of the Donaldsonville Rice Mill. To the left is the turnstile railroad bridge over Bayou Lafourche. Below it are two barges. The trail that goes along the bayou is the

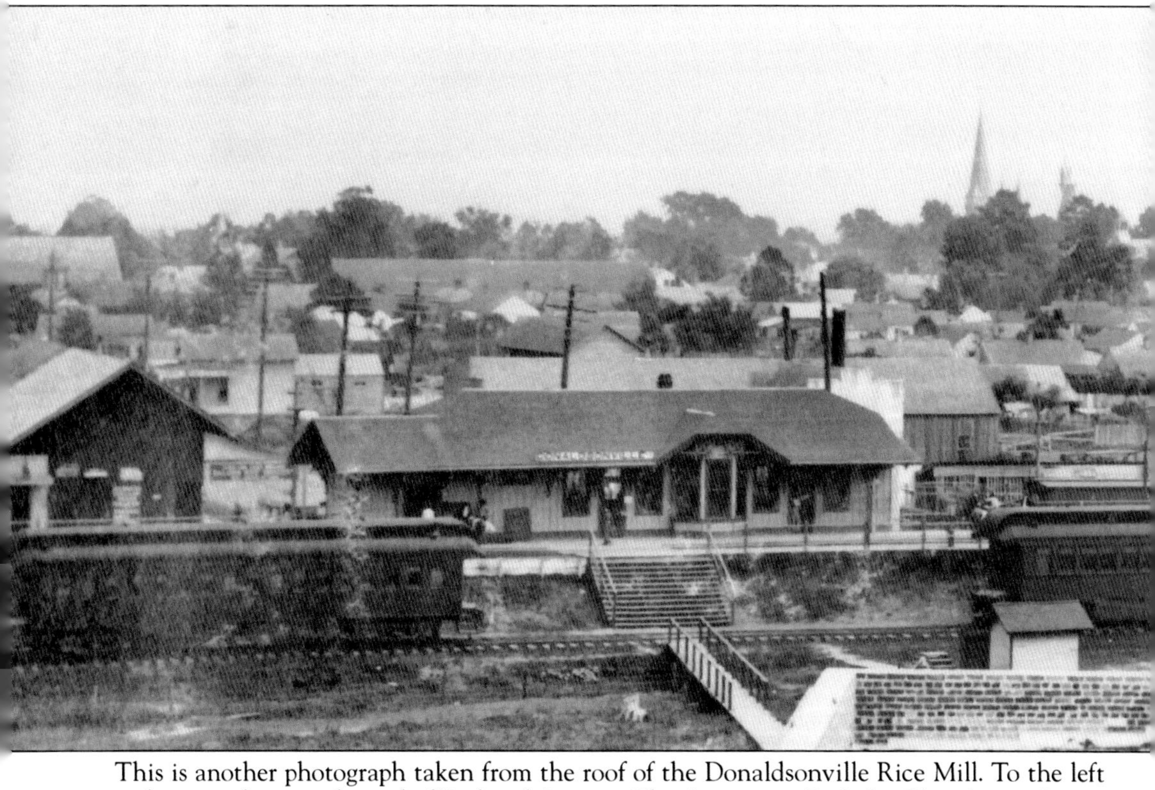

This is another photograph taken from the roof of the Donaldsonville Rice Mill. To the left is the train depot at the end of Railroad Avenue. The Ascension Catholic Church steeple can

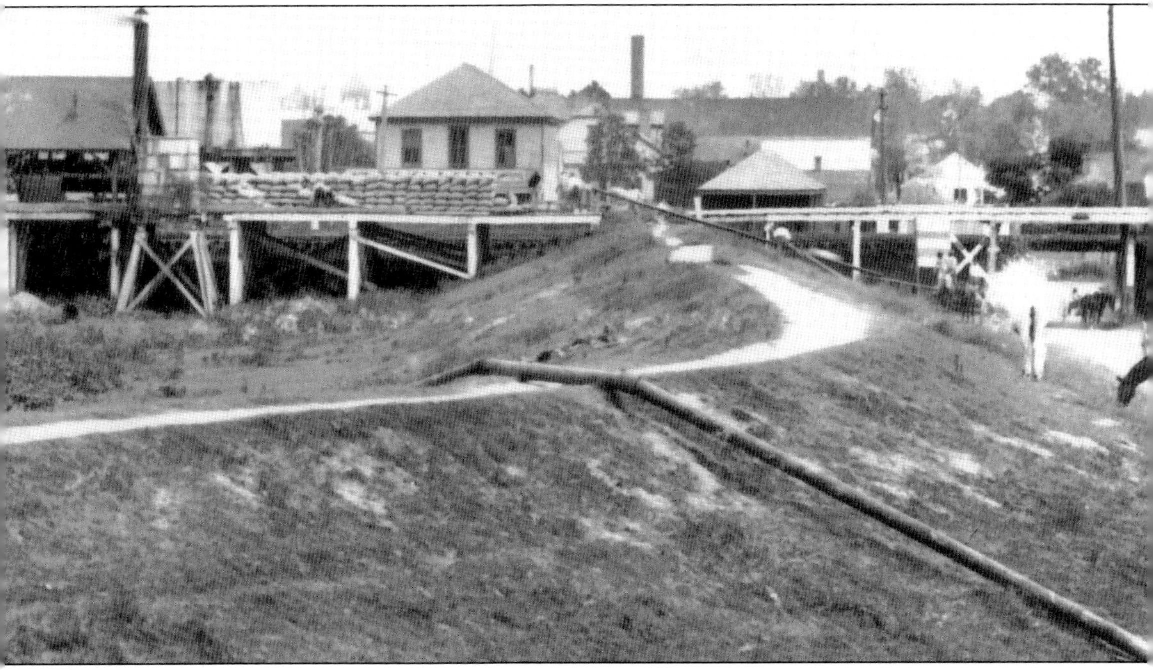
path that donkeys would walk as they pulled barges upstream toward the river. (Courtesy of the Capone family.)

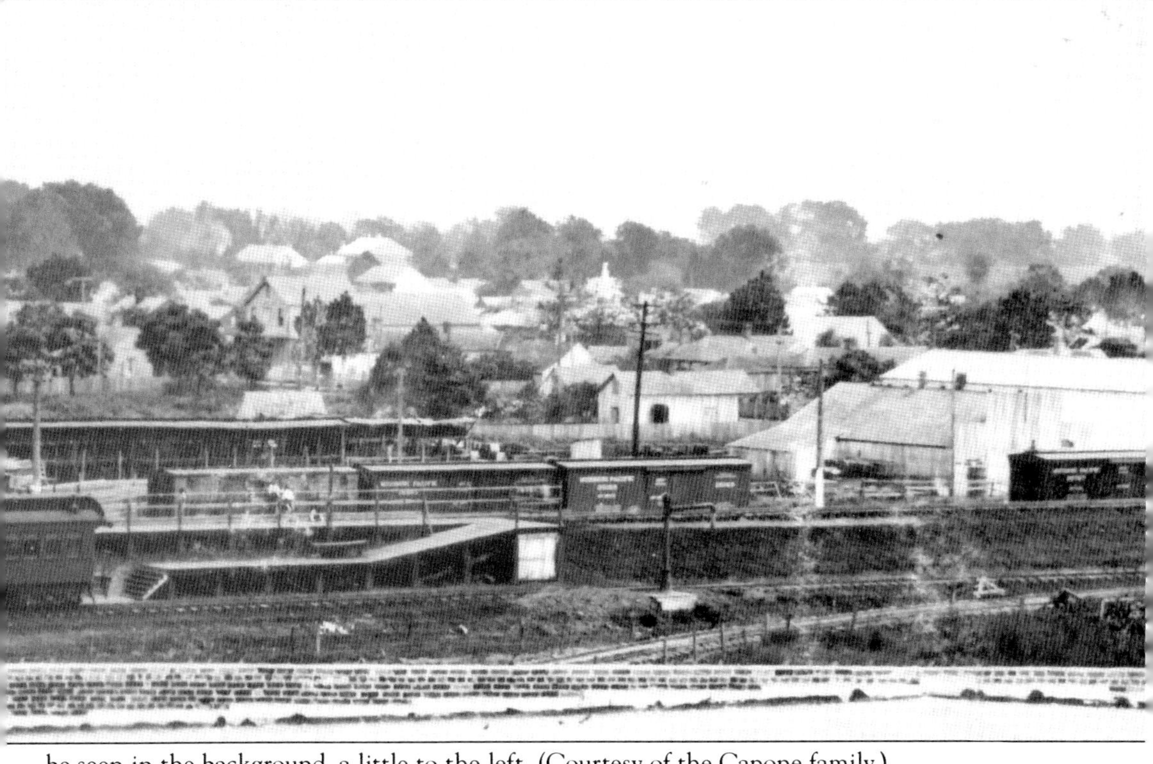
be seen in the background, a little to the left. (Courtesy of the Capone family.)

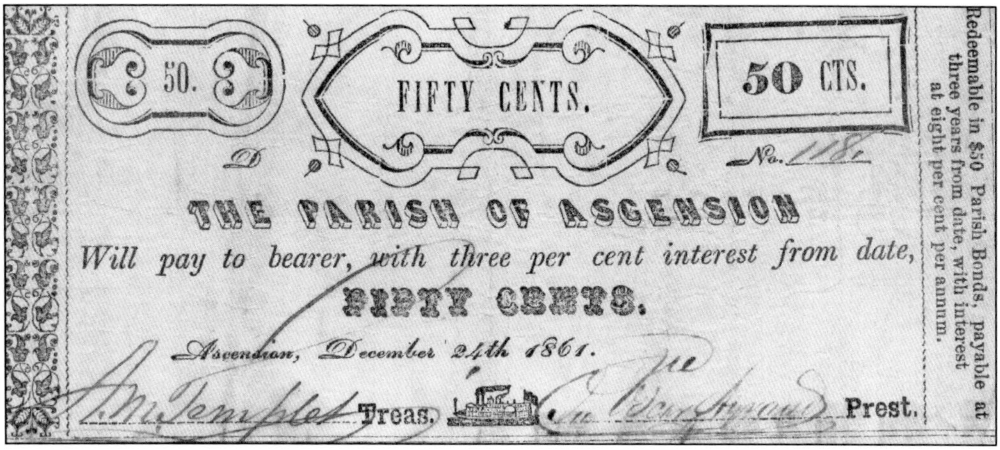

The Town of Donaldsonville and the Parish of Ascension printed their own money in the 1860s. Pictured here are an Ascension Parish 50¢ bill (above) and a Donaldsonville 25¢ bill (below). Notice that each bill is numbered. (Both, courtesy of the Landry family.)

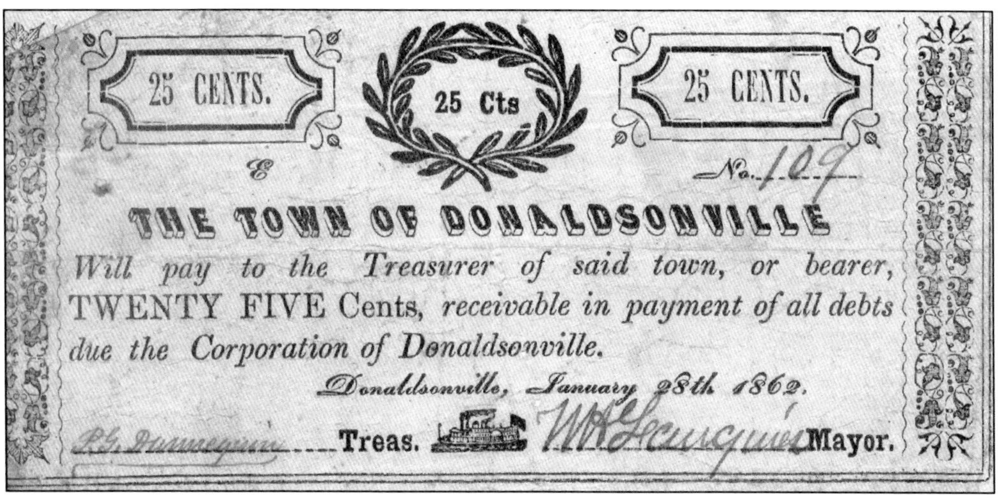

Two

Main Street

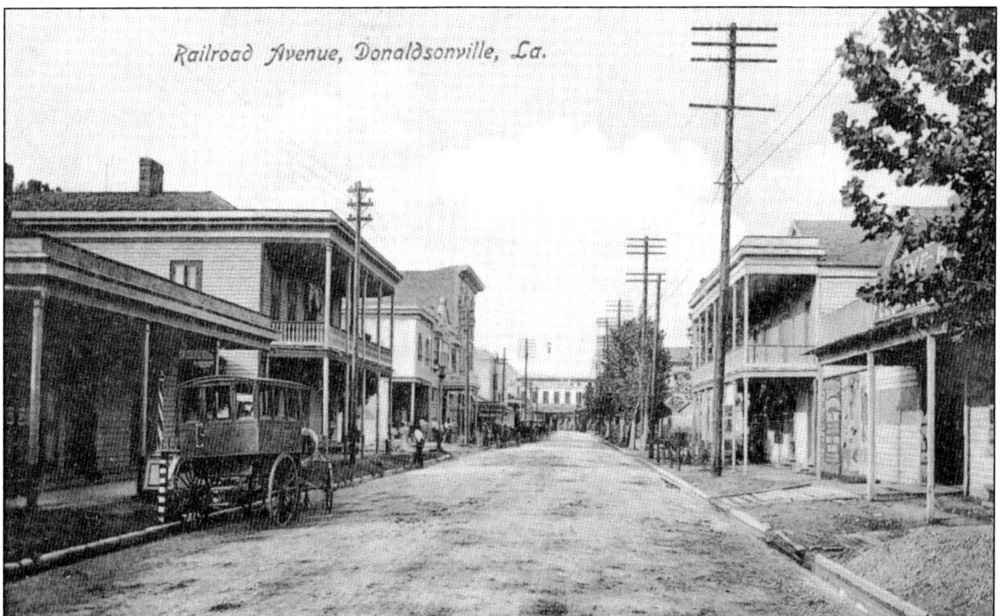

This image is looking down Railroad Avenue toward the Mississippi River. Donaldsonville was a trading destination for people traveling to and from New Orleans on the river or up and down Bayou Lafourche. The train tracks stopped at Bayou Lafourche, and cargo had to be loaded onto barges to cross or travel down the bayou. (Courtesy of the Landry family.)

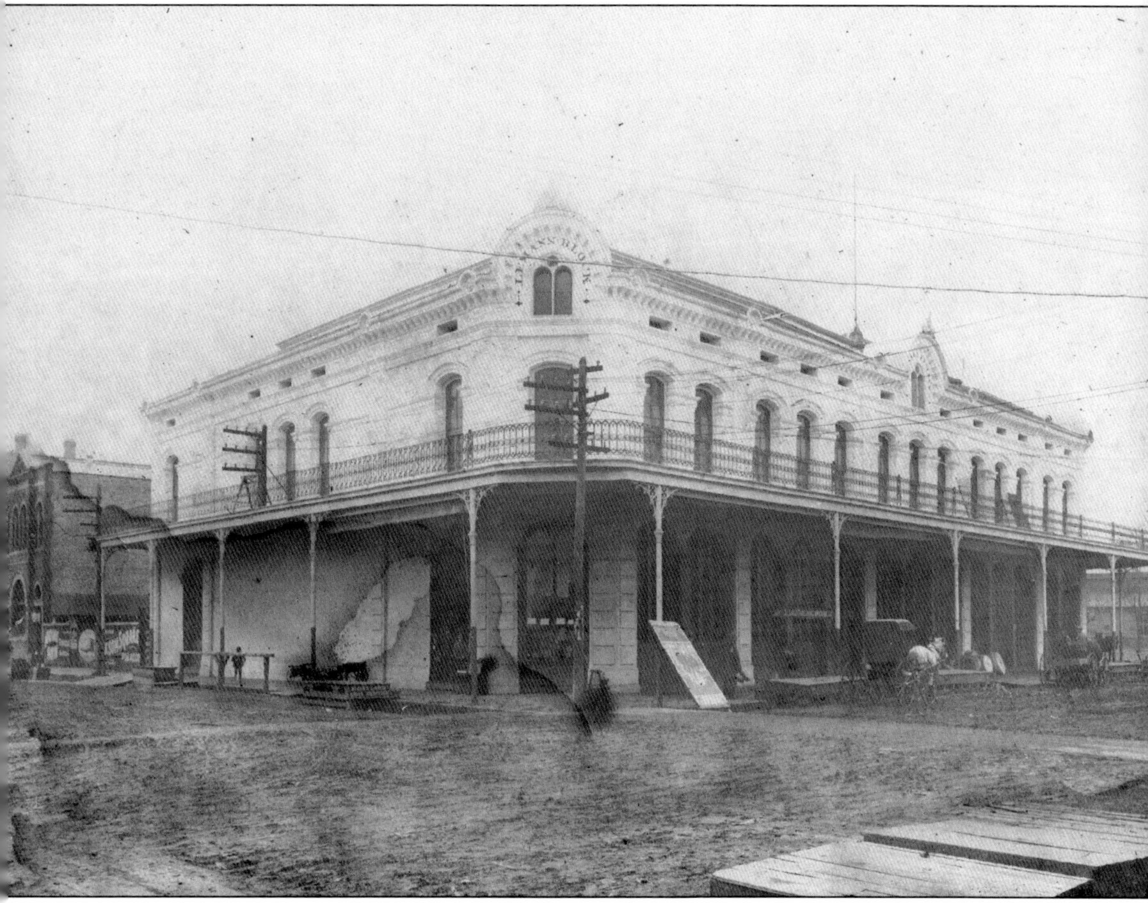

Once the oldest family-operated department store in Louisiana, Jacob Lemann's business was founded in 1836 after he spent years selling goods from a horse-drawn cart. Notice the old market building behind and to the right of the Lemann Building. Built in the Italianate style, this commercial building has the characteristic arched windows and brackets. It is constructed of brick and stucco, with heavily molded pilasters and window details. On the first floor, the stucco resembles stone. The main entrance faces the corner and is defined by a raised rounded parapet with a pair of dormer windows. This is repeated at the center of each side. The cast-iron storefront follows the curve of Cresent Park, and the fluted cast-iron colonettes with leaf capitals support the gallery, which extends the width of the sidewalk on three sides. (Courtesy of the Lemann family.)

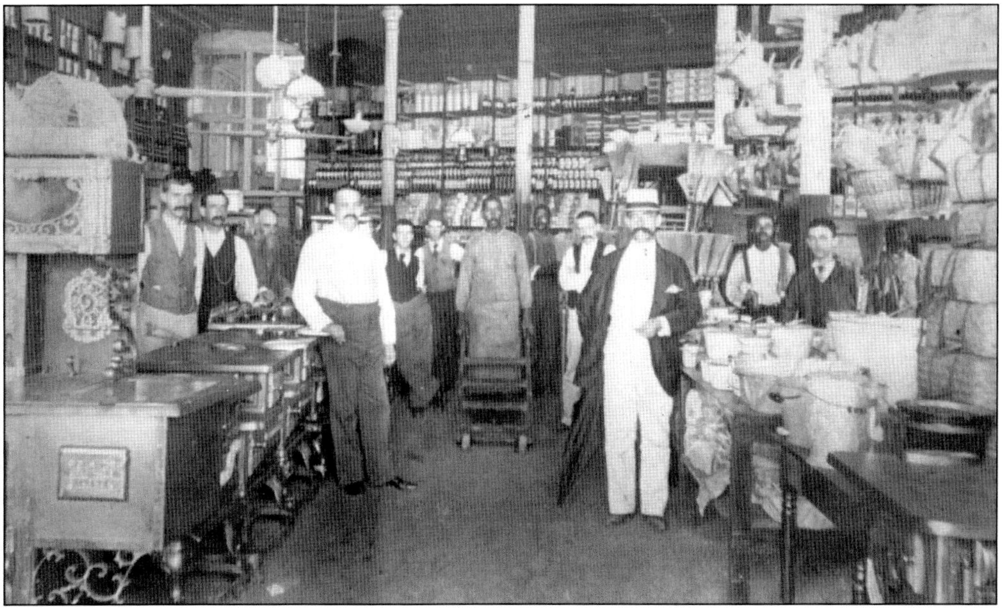

The motto of J. Lemann & Son Department Store was "fair dealing, courteous treatment, and money refunded if goods are not satisfactory." People came from all over South Louisiana to shop at the largest retail establishment in the state. One could find anything from agriculture supplies and implements to buggies, carriages, saddlery, hardware, paints, dry goods, and groceries. (Courtesy of the Lemann family.)

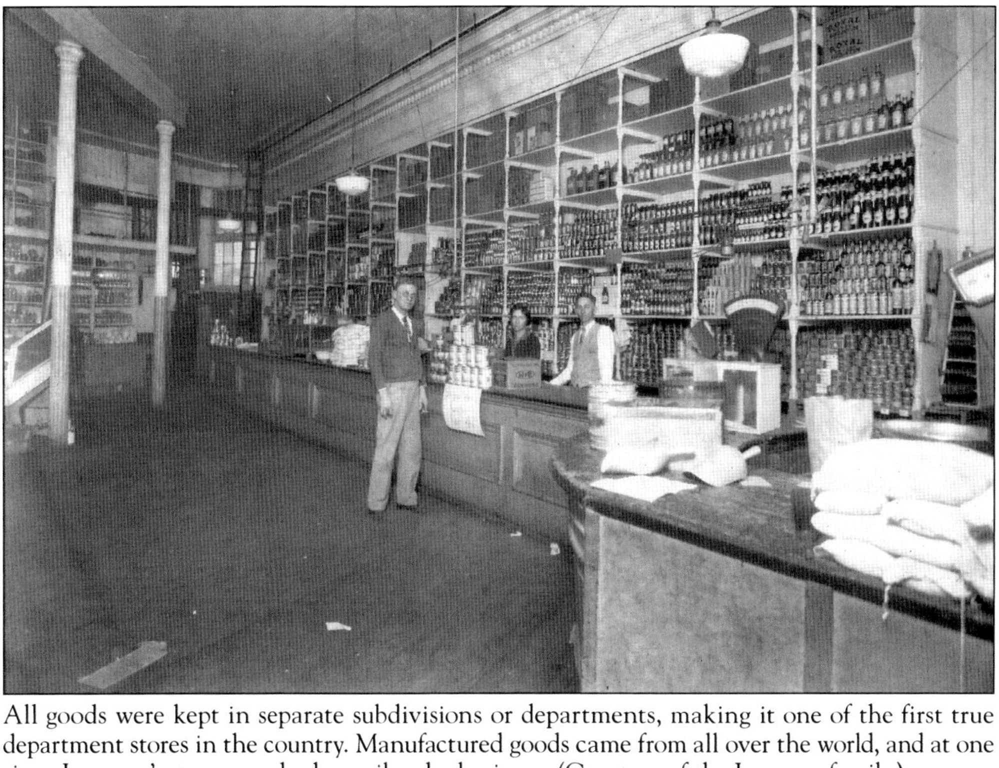

All goods were kept in separate subdivisions or departments, making it one of the first true department stores in the country. Manufactured goods came from all over the world, and at one time, Lemann's store even had a mail-order business. (Courtesy of the Lemann family.)

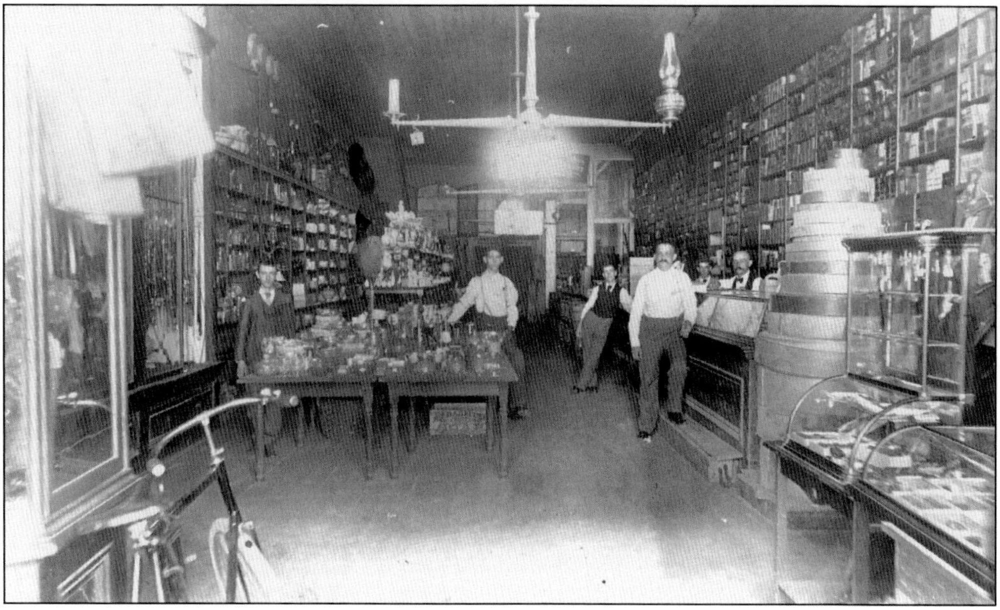

As the years progressed, Lemann's stock would change to fit the needs and wants of its customers. Coming to Donaldsonville was an ordeal, but it was the largest store in the area outside of New Orleans. (Courtesy of the Lemann family.)

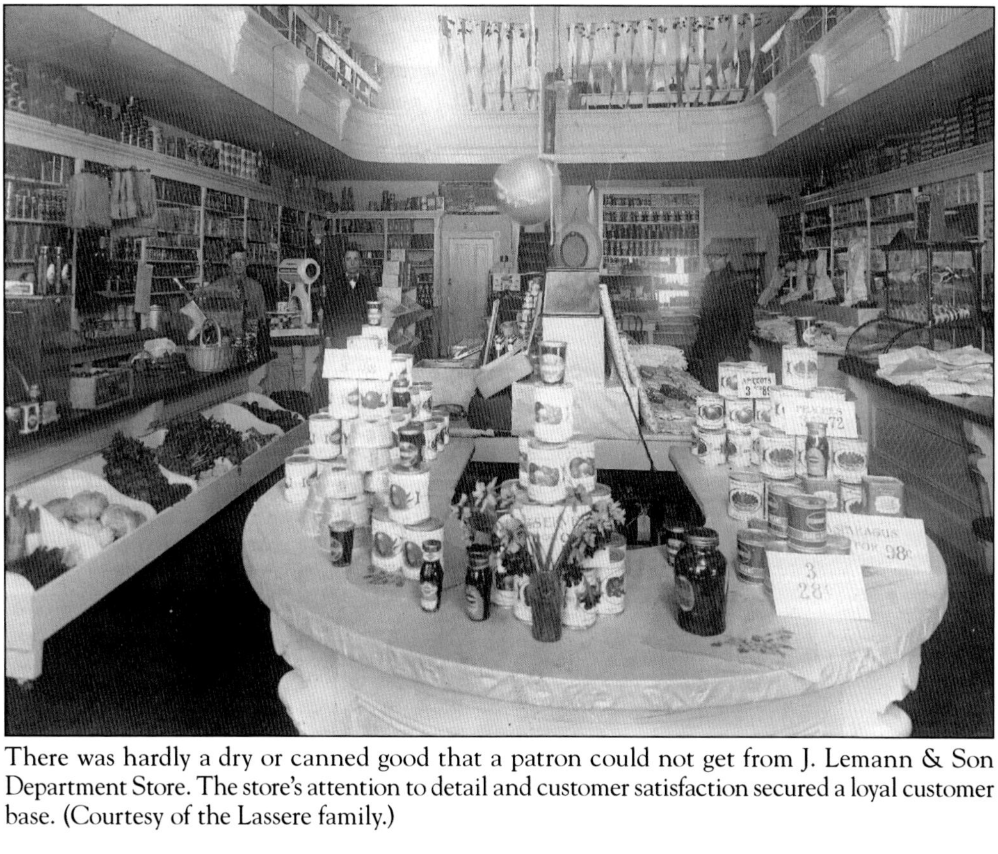

There was hardly a dry or canned good that a patron could not get from J. Lemann & Son Department Store. The store's attention to detail and customer satisfaction secured a loyal customer base. (Courtesy of the Lassere family.)

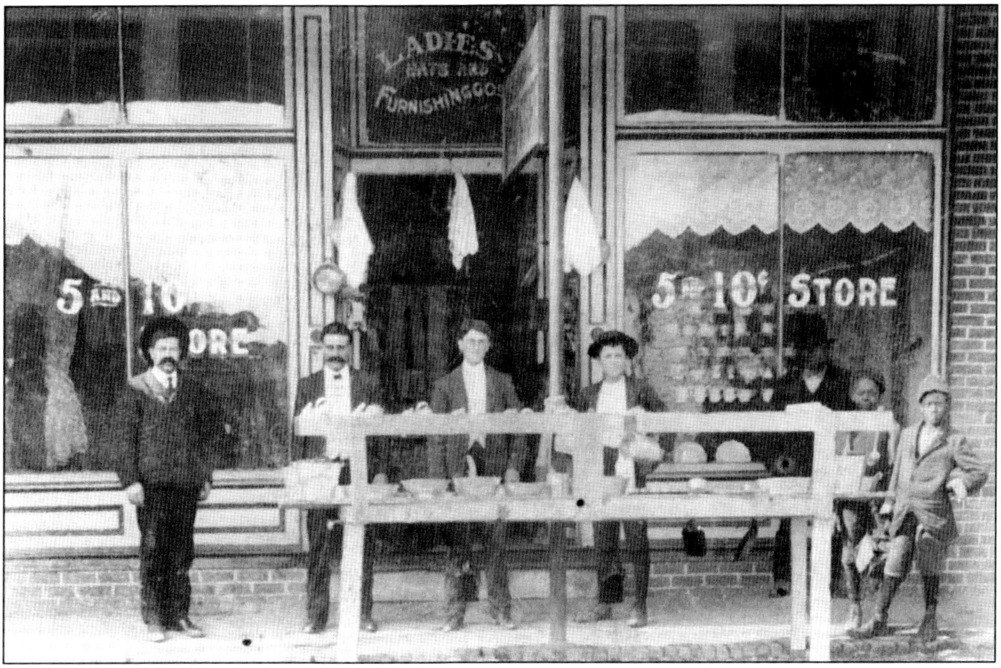

In the late 1800s, immigrants from near Beirut, Lebanon, migrated from New York to New Orleans, to Raceland, Louisiana, and eventually to Donaldsonville. Among these families were the Ferrises and Shaheens. Habib Shaheen started out as a peddler, eventually opening a store in Donaldsonville on Railroad Avenue at its current location. Pictured in this photograph are, from left to right, Habib Shaheen, Aneen Shaheen, Jimmy Shaheen, Joe Shaheen, and three unidentified people. (Courtesy of the Shaheen family.)

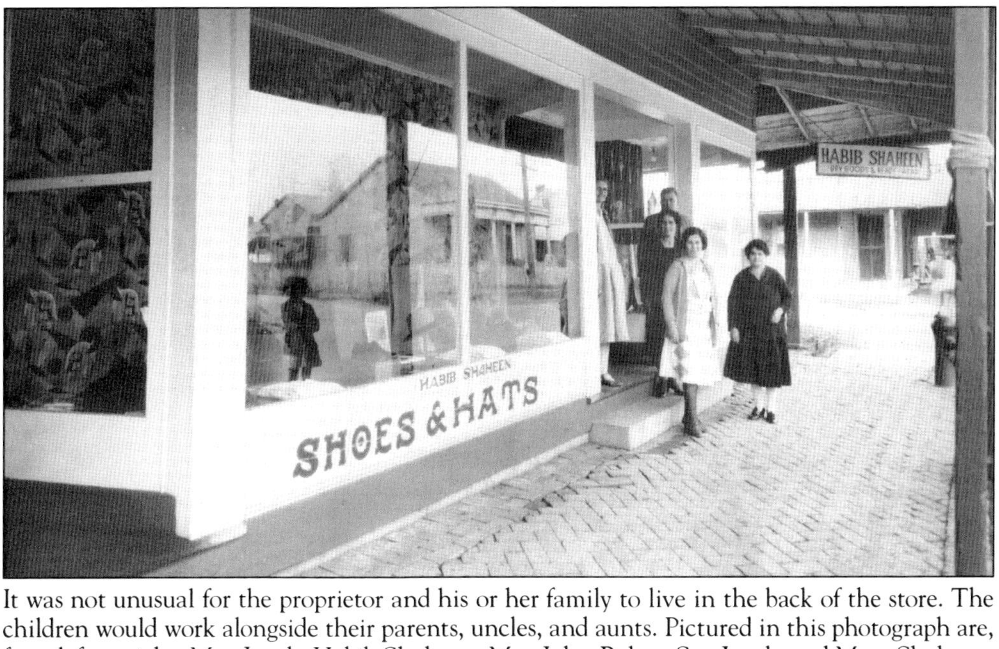

It was not unusual for the proprietor and his or her family to live in the back of the store. The children would work alongside their parents, uncles, and aunts. Pictured in this photograph are, from left to right, Mrs. Jacob, Habib Shaheen, Mrs. John Bahry, Sue Jacob, and Mary Shaheen. (Courtesy of the Shaheen family.)

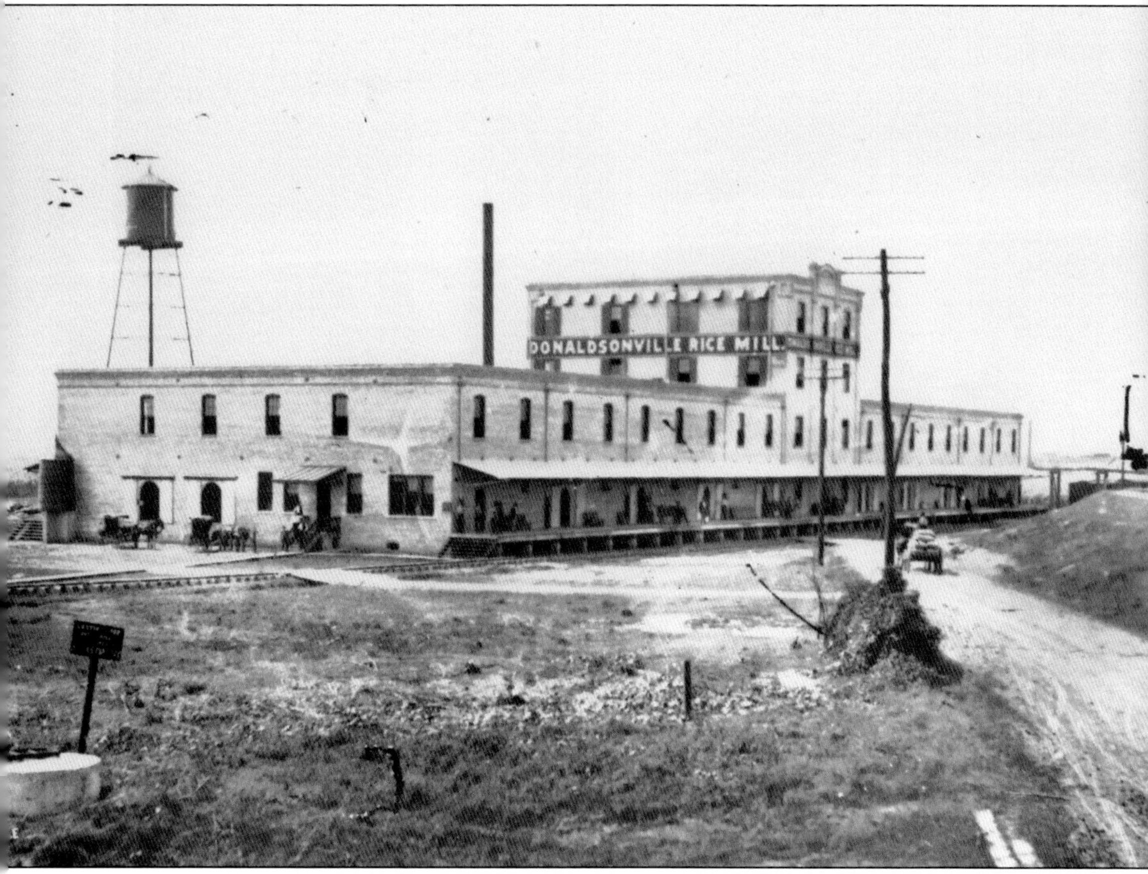

Built in 1898, the Donaldsonville Rice Mill was being touted as the largest operating rice mill in the world by the year 1903. It was built by a number of area planters, including R.N. Sims. In 1914, the mill was closed; however, it was back in operation by 1916. In 1927, the Moro Manufacturing Co. leased and operated the building as a garment factory. (Courtesy of the Capone family.)

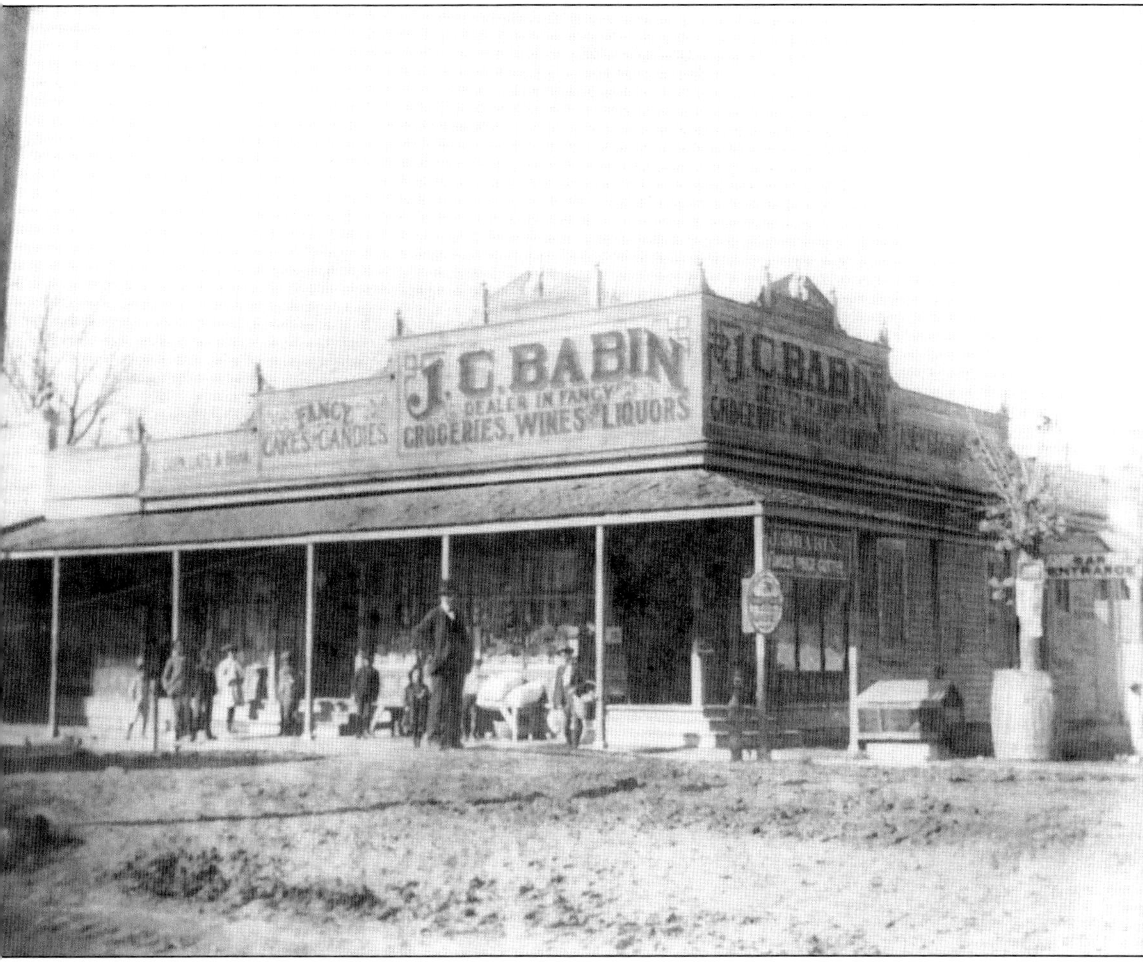

The J.C. Babin store was a landmark on Railroad Avenue in Donaldsonville. Customers could get their dry goods, candies, groceries, and liquors at this one location. There was even a separate entrance to the bar on the right side of the building. Notice the small cage on the right, near the barrel. This was where the chickens were stored until they were sold. Customers would purchase a chicken, then walk outside and retrieve it as they left. Also, the old state building that hosted the state legislature was located directly behind the store until it was torn down. (Courtesy of the Rodrigue family.)

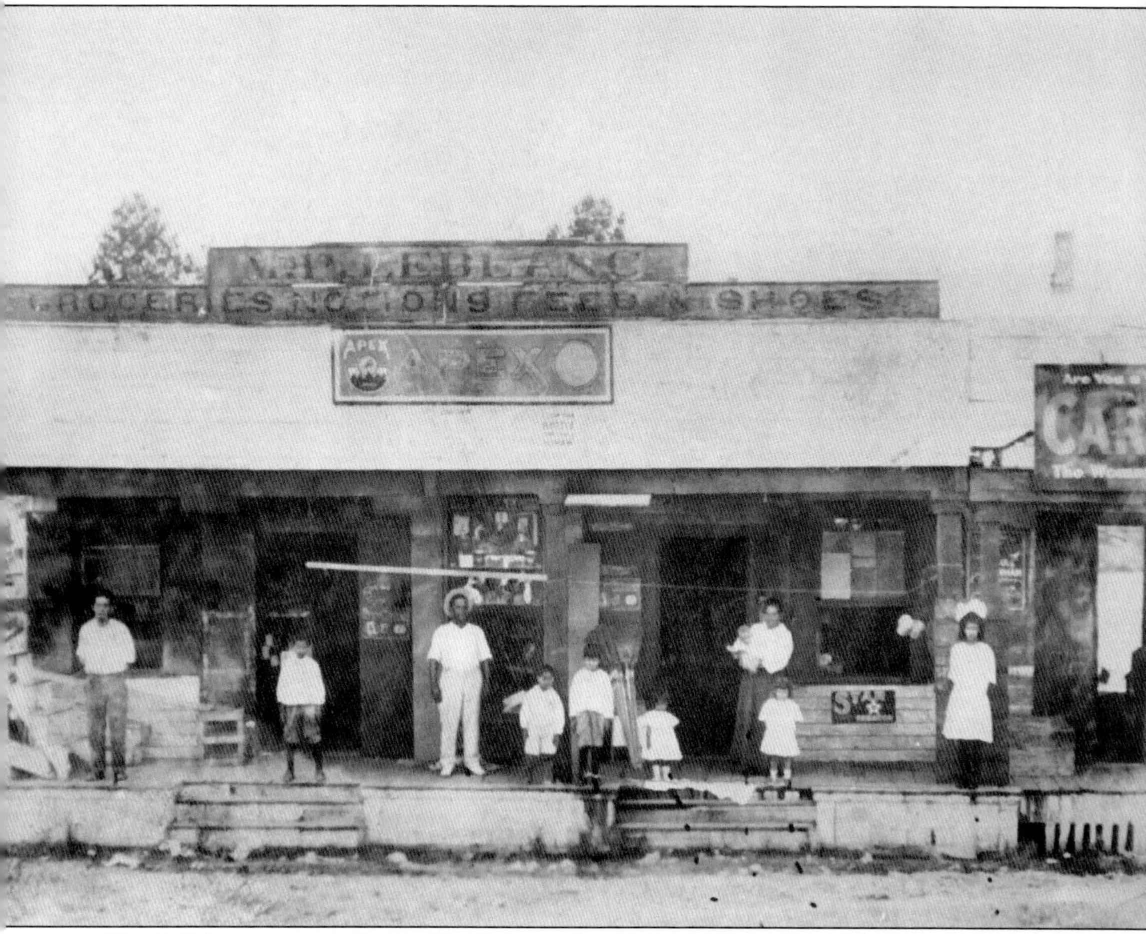

The LeBlanc stores in Smoke Bend, located just upriver from Donaldsonville, were the last upriver stores in Smoke Bend. At one time, there was a small chain of three LeBlanc general stores in Smoke Bend, selling farm equipment, clothing, feed, gunpowder, and other dry goods. The whole family was involved in the retail business, and Leonard LeBlanc went on to start the Payless grocery chain. The Smoke Bend Post Office was located in the LeBlanc store until the early 1960s, when the building was demolished. The mailbag was put on a pole next to the train track, and when the train passed by, it would catch it with a special hook at full speed. One had to be careful because the train would also throw the mail being delivered on the ground nearby, again, at full speed. (Courtesy of the Marchand family.)

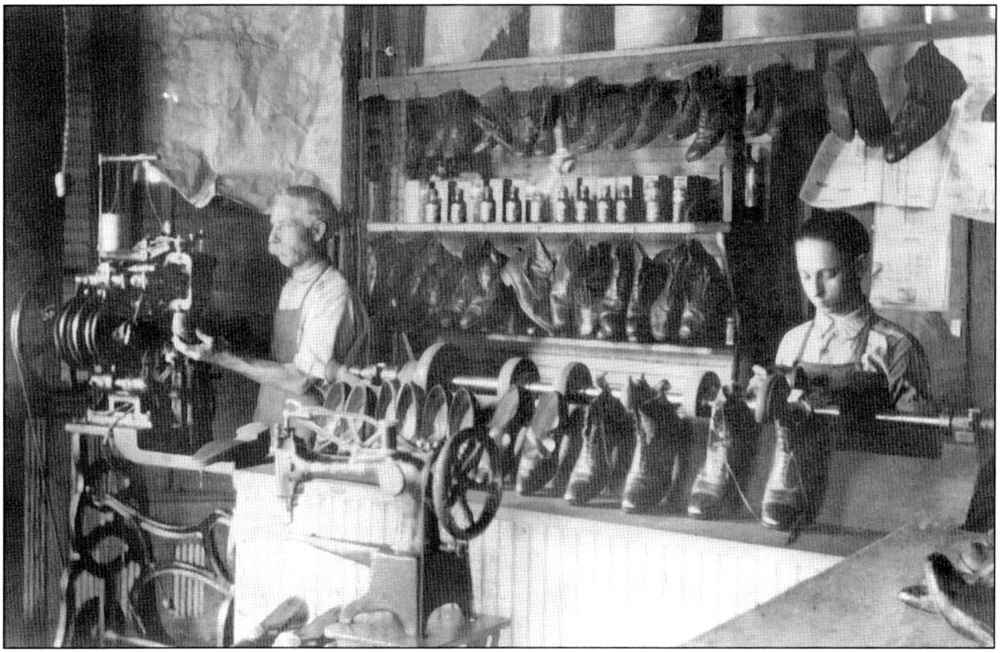

Paul's Shoe Shop is pictured with its original owner, Brasse, and 13-year-old Paul "Polo-Breezy" Divencenzo. Divencenzo would spend his entire working career in the shoe repair business. In his later years, he was known for his colorful language and his refusal to work on customers' shoes if they waited in the store. The business was located at the corner of Railroad Avenue, which is now Marchand Drive. (Courtesy of the Lassere family.)

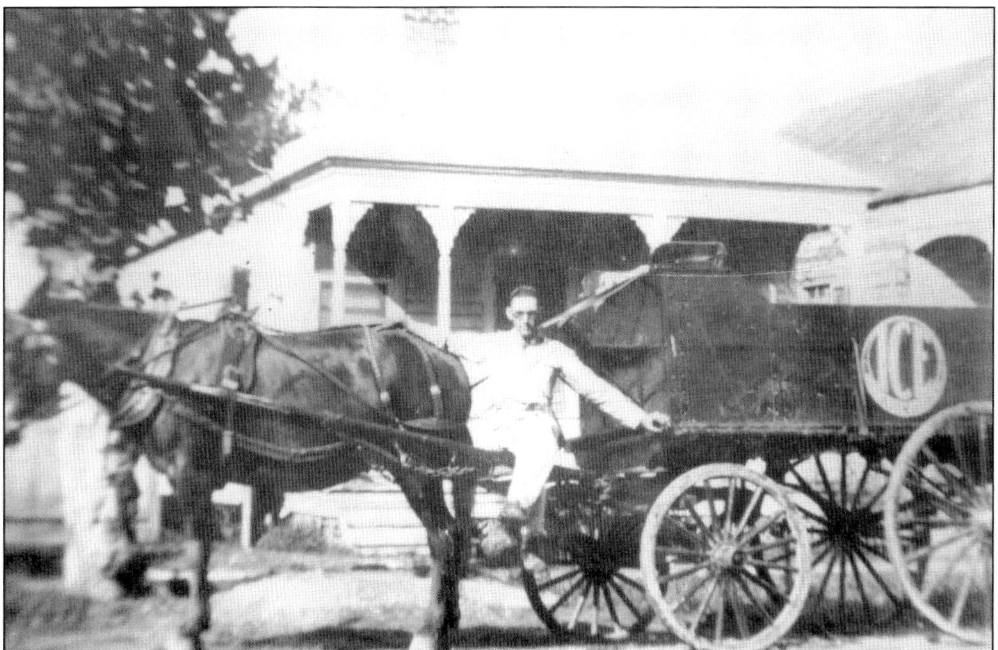

Service was a part of everyday life in Donaldsonville. Pictured above is Ernest F. Morris, with his horse and carriage, making a home ice delivery. (Courtesy of the Lemann family.)

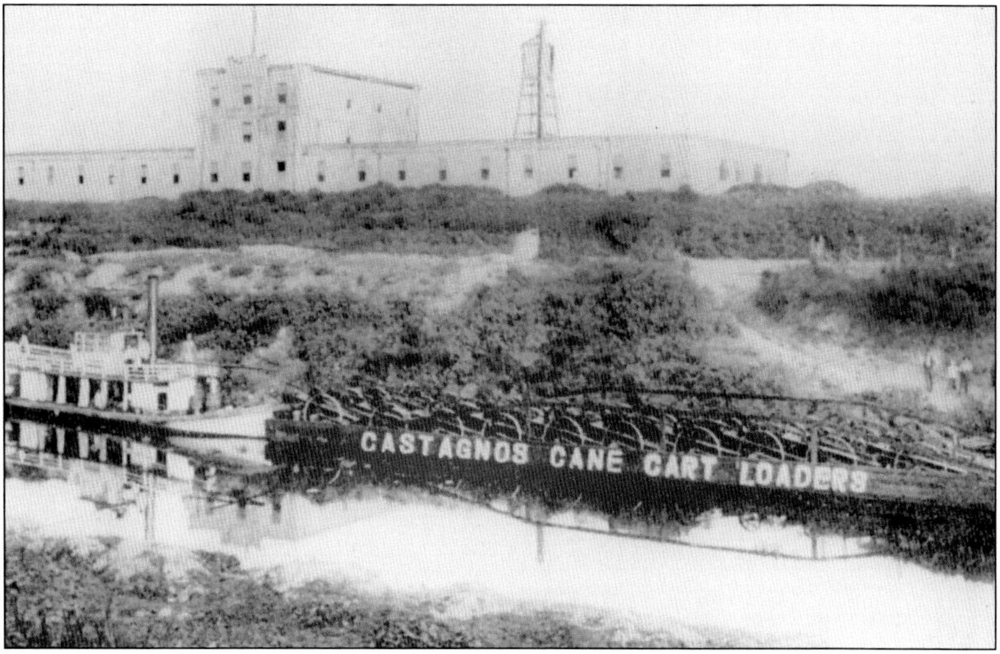

J.B. Castagnos, a native of France, learned the trade of machine blacksmith in one of the largest railroad yards in Paris before immigrating to Louisiana where he immediately began working at a sugar plantation. During the rainy season, the farmers would gather around the blacksmith shop and talk of the need for a mechanized sugarcane loader. It was suggested that he might try to design one. In 1908, Castagnos erected a new factory in Donaldsonville where he started producing the world's first gasoline engine sugarcane loader. The above photograph is of a barge full of cane loaders ready to be shipped down Bayou Lafourche. (Courtesy of the Castagnos family.)

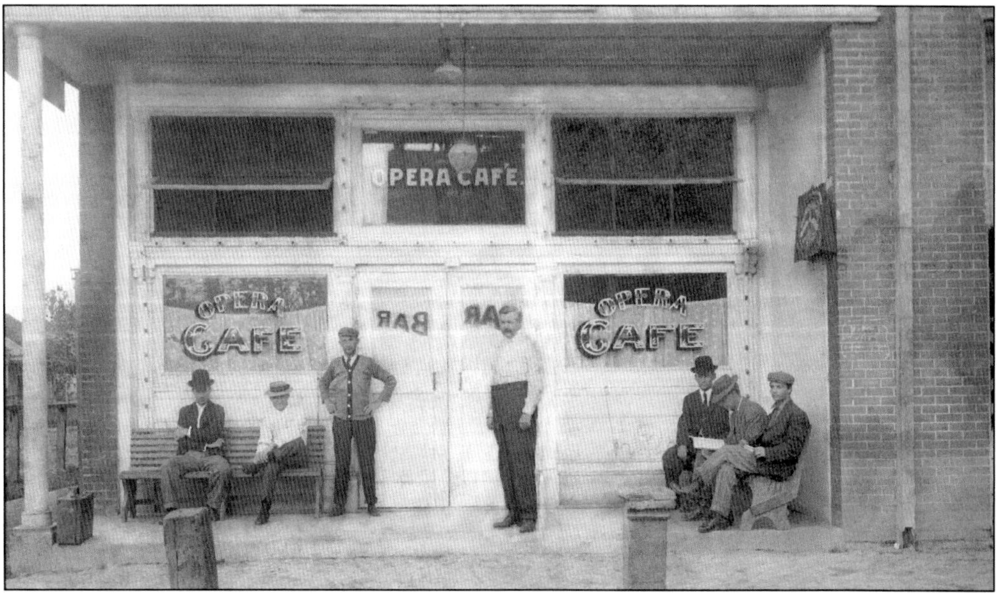

The Montero and Brande's Opera Café was next door to the Gondran Theatre, which was a venue for plays, vaudeville acts, and lectures before its debut of motion pictures in January 1914, two years after it became the Grand Theatre. (Courtesy of the Marchand family.)

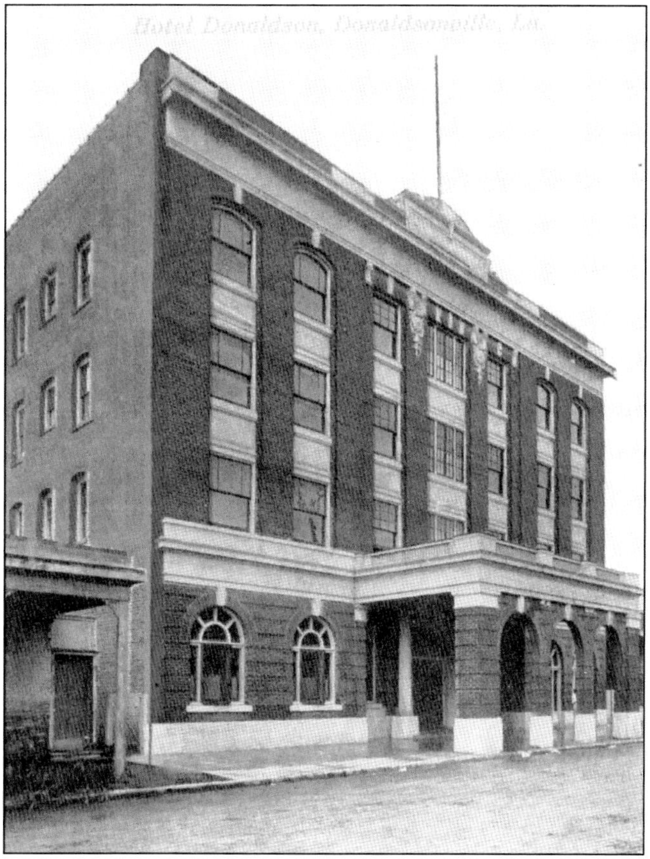

The Hotel Donaldson was a four-story, 44-room hotel constructed by the Donaldsonville Hotel Association in 1912. The hotel was constructed due to the great fire of 1911, which destroyed the Nicholls Hotel, arguably Donaldsonville's most renowned destination. The hotel, which was located on the 500 block of Mississippi Street, was torn down in 1964. (Courtesy of the Landry family.)

Harry's Place was owned by Harry and Novela Dugas and was located at the four-way intersection of Highway 1, Albert Street, and Highway 18. The building was later remodeled to include a restaurant. It is located where CVS is today. (Courtesy of the Dugas family.)

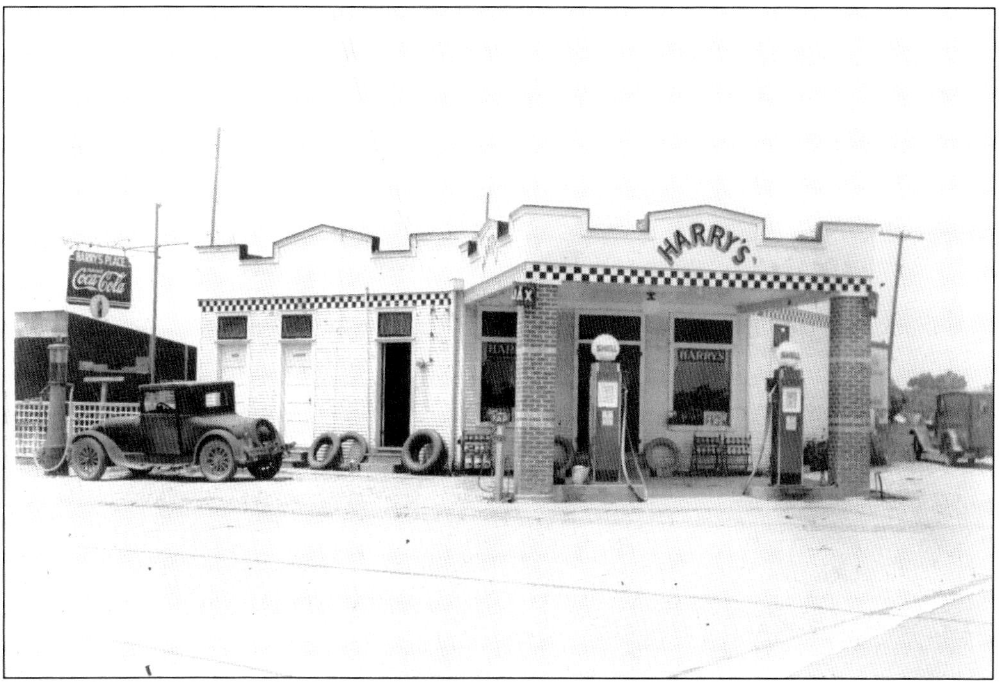

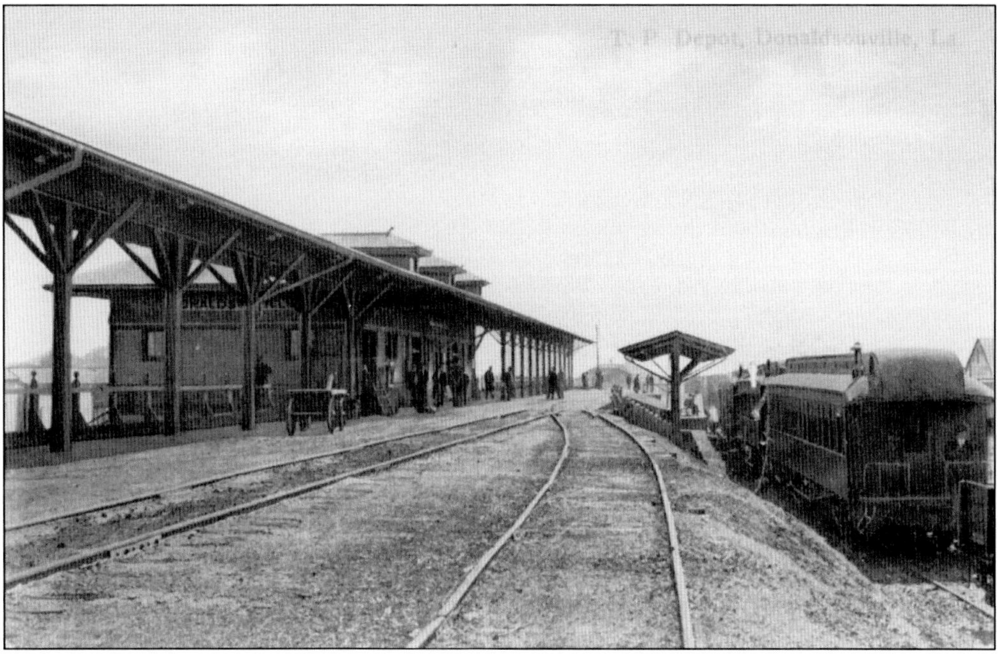

The railroad came to Donaldsonville in 1871, providing service to New Orleans. The rail service was certainly an asset to the city's economy. In 1873, the city council decided to change the name of the main street from the Indian name, Cabahanosse, to Railroad Avenue. The following is a quote from the *Donaldsonville Chief* about the matter on November 11, 1871: "Now that the street leading to the railroad has been transformed from almost an impassible road to a beautiful thoroughfare, would it not be well for the council to bestow upon it a more appropriate and sensible title than 'Cabahanosse,' that polysyllabic monstrosity of ancient origin, fearful orthography and doubtful pronunciation? Call it Broadway, First Avenue or Depot Street – anything but Cabahanosse." The above photograph was taken around 1917; shown below is a passenger ticket to Gretna, Louisiana, just outside of New Orleans. (Both, courtesy of the Landry family.)

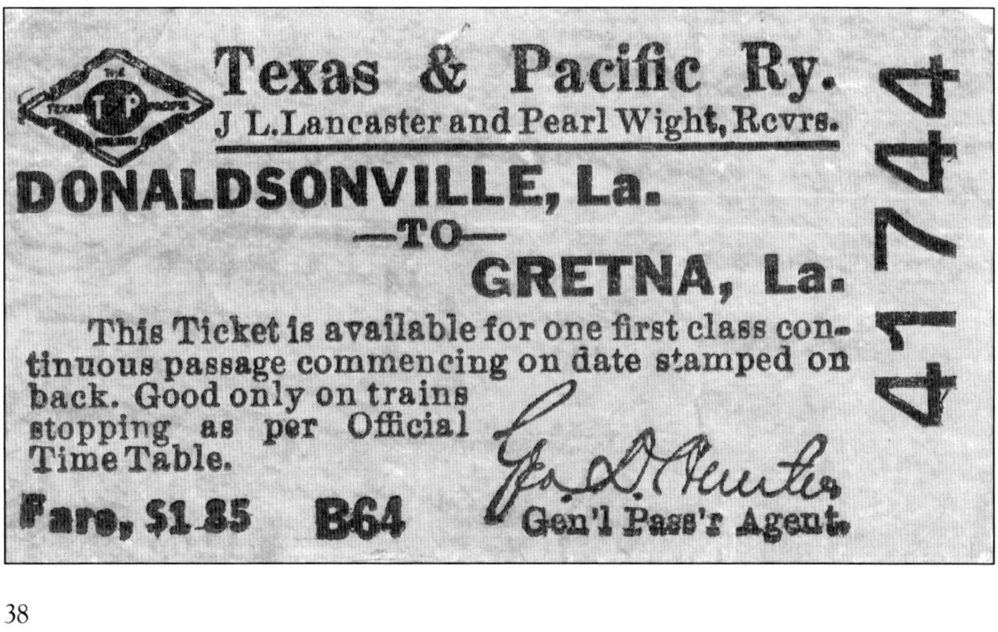

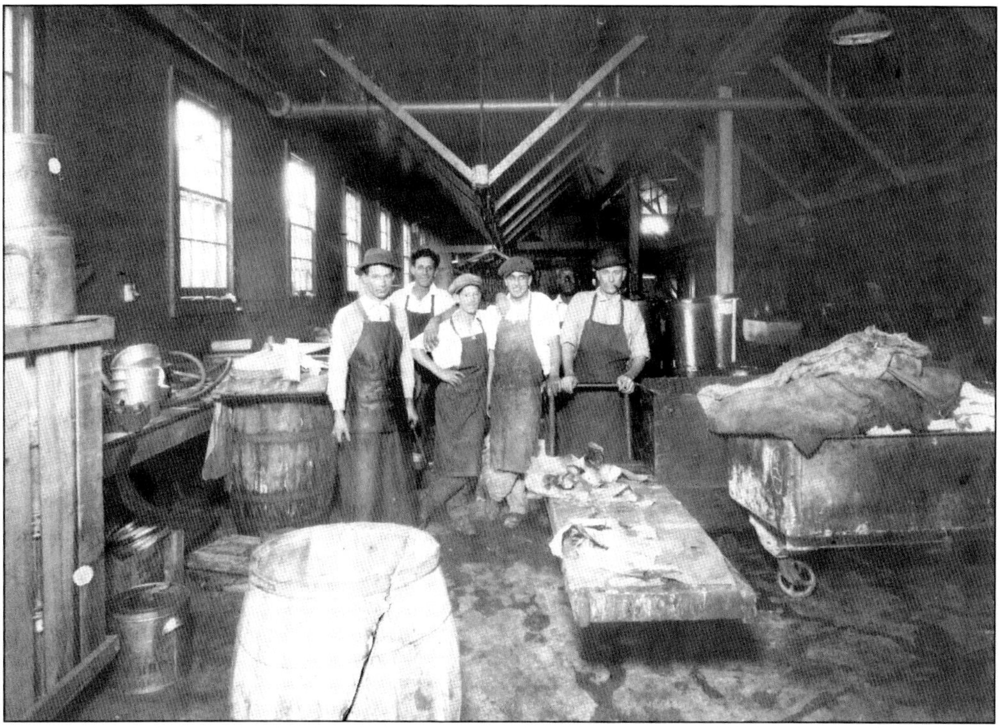

This is an inside view of the Frey Brothers meatpacking plant in Donaldsonville. From left to right are Dominick Regira, LaLa Regira, and Nace Giambrone. LaLa Regira would eventually own his own restaurant/club and become mayor of Donaldsonville. (Courtesy of the Regira family.)

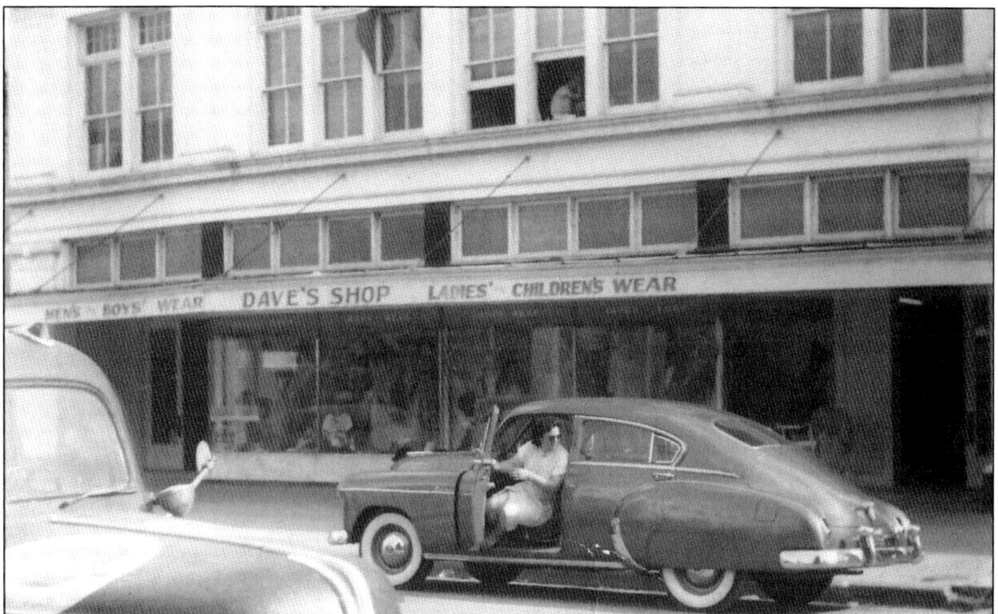

Dave's Shop offered the finest clothing and styles in Donaldsonville at the time. Dave's wife, Yvonne, was the sister of Gaston Hirsh, who came to Donaldsonville and opened a very successful men's store after being held in a concentration camp in Germany. (Courtesy of the Regira family.)

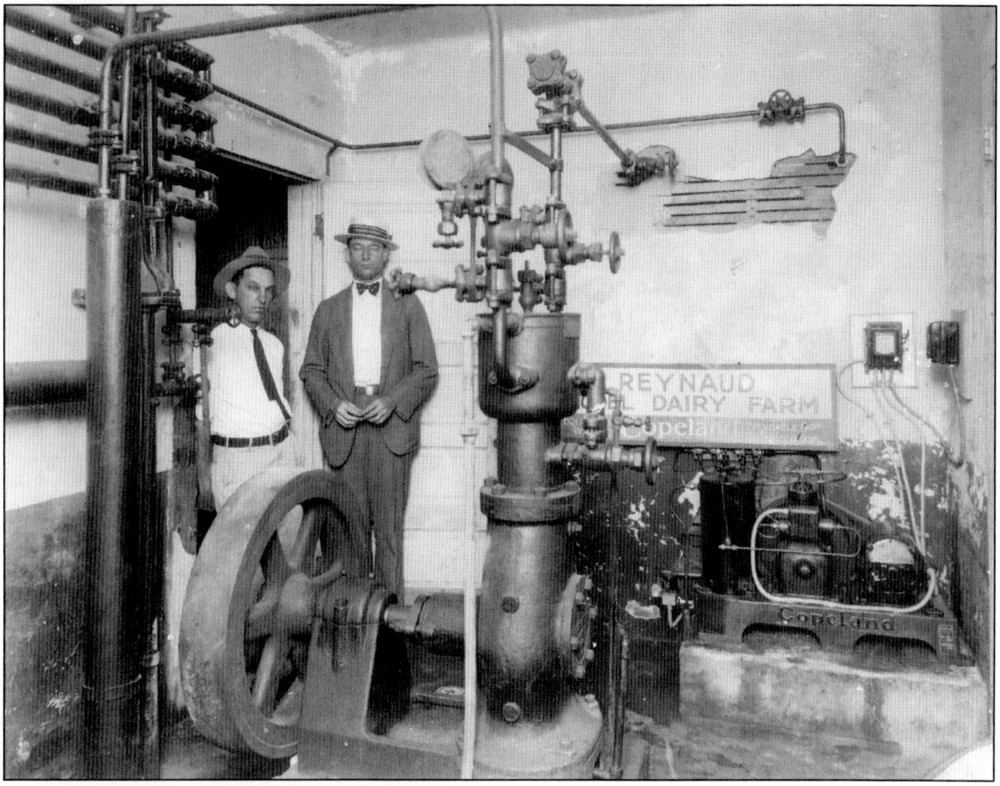

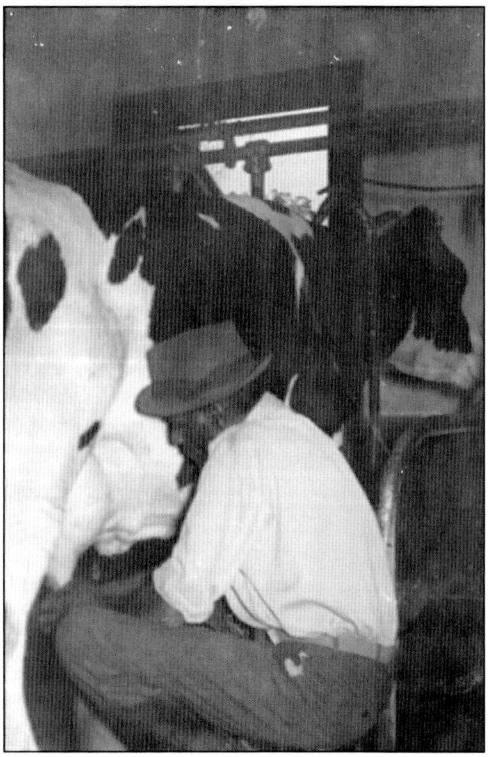

Albert Reynaud, shown on the left with an unidentified client, and his brother bought 365 acres in 1930 and started the Reynaud Dairy Farm just south of Donaldsonville on Bayou Lafourche. The property had been a dairy before but had fallen into disrepair. Their dairy stock included Jersey cows, which supplied very rich milk, and Holstein cows, which supplied a higher volume of milk. Cows were milked twice a day, first at 3:00 a.m. and again at 3:00 p.m. Reynaud Dairy Farm was a full-service dairy. The milk was pasteurized, bottled, and delivered to homes and grocery stores as far as Houma, Louisiana. Eventually, they stopped delivering their milk and sold it in bulk to another dairy. The business was closed in 1949, and the property was leased for sugarcane fields. (Courtesy by the Reynaud family.)

Louis "Razoo" Welfort is shown milking a cow at the Reynaud Dairy Farm. Louis was a fixture at the dairy and capable of doing any of the jobs, filling in wherever he was needed. (Courtesy by the Reynaud family.)

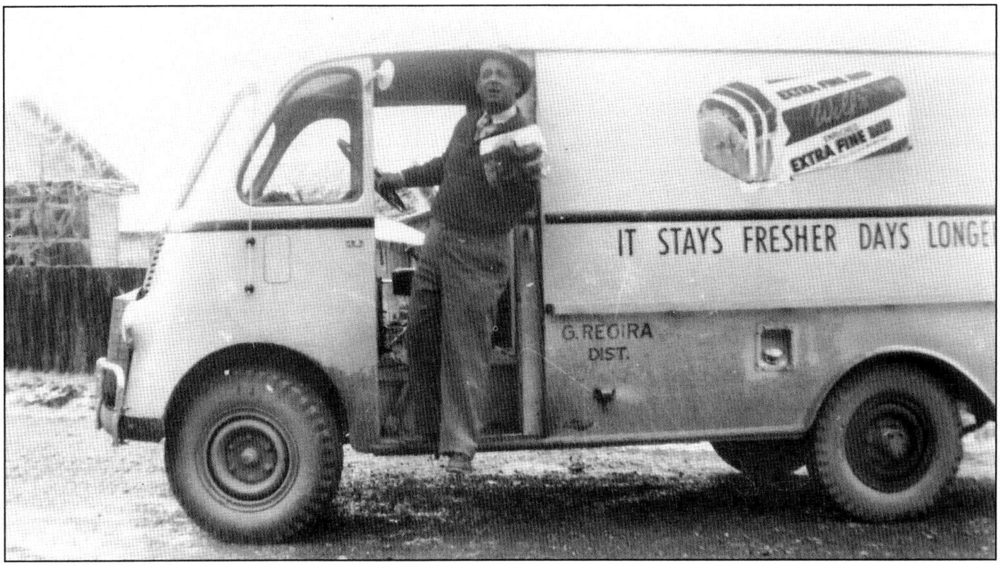

George Regira delivered bread for Wolf"s Bakery. He was a self-employed distributor, which was very unusual. Almost everyone else was a paid employee, but George had a warehouse and would get a fresh shipment every morning. Harry Smith, his competitor, sold Evangeline bread from Napolonville. Even though George and Harry competed for customers in the grocery stores, they were fishing buddies and friends. When Harry Smith Jr. got married, George drove the bride and groom to the wedding in his car. (Courtesy of the Regira family.)

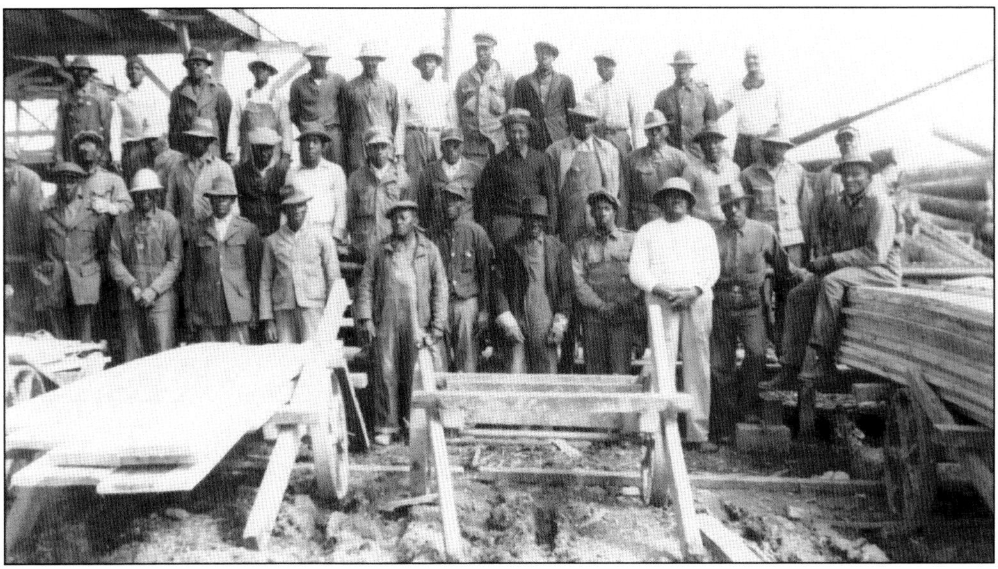

As Donaldsonville's economy boomed, the need for building material and skilled labor increased. This undated photograph is of the employees of the Donaldsonville Sawmill, located just outside of town. (Courtesy of the Marchand family.)

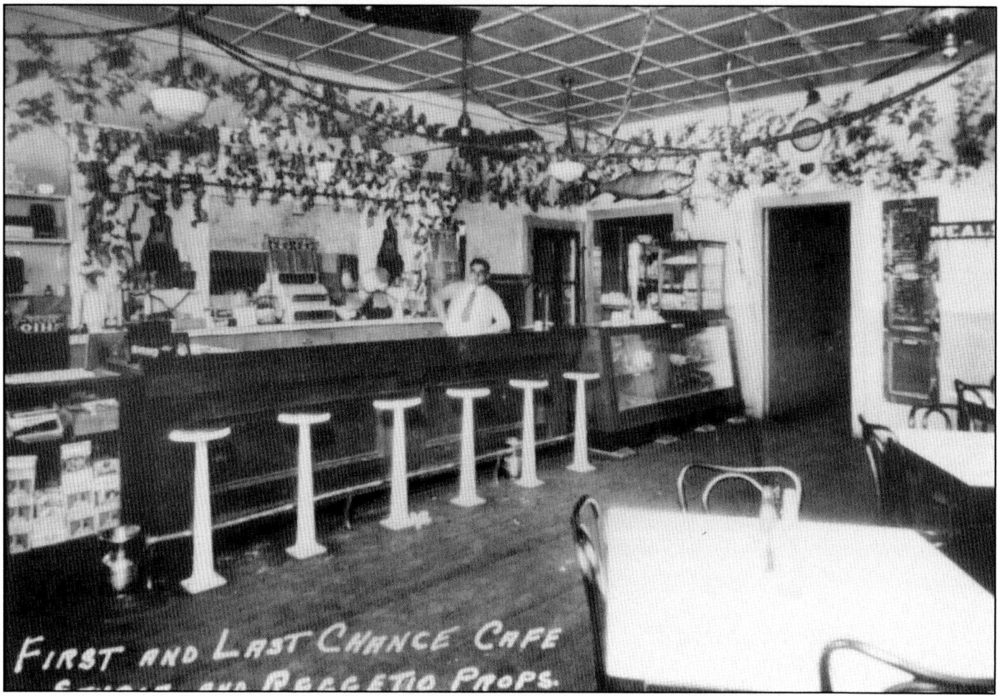

Charles Collie Savoia poses at the bar of the original First and Last Chance, which burned down in 1930. Travelers would stop for food and drinks as they waited for the train to arrive just across the street. (Courtesy of the Savoia family.)

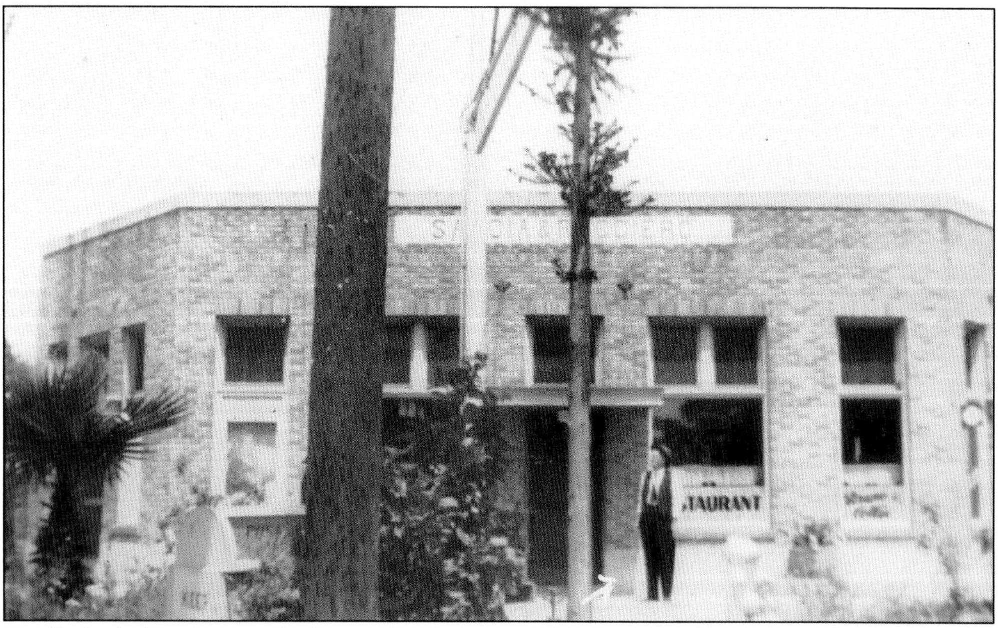

Cyrille Rodeillat, a bartender for years at the First and Last Chance, takes a break out front. The Chance had curb service at the back door. One could pull up to the back door and blow the horn, and a waiter would come outside and take the order. (Courtesy of the Rodeillat family.)

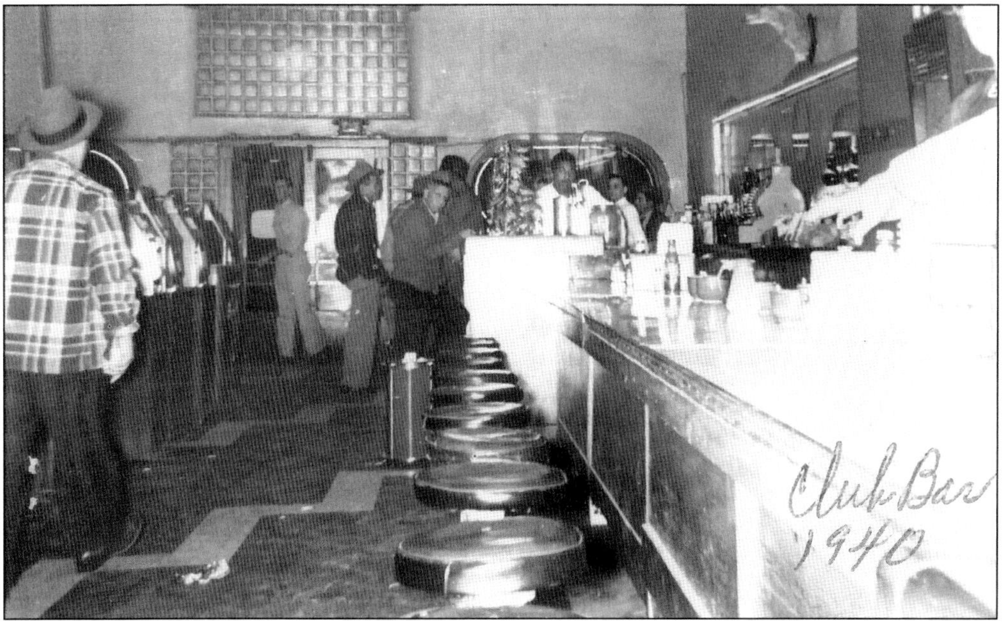

Here is the Club Bar in 1940. Soon-to-be mayor LaLa Regira owned and operated the Club Bar on Mississippi Street for years. Notice the slot machines, which were legal at the time, just inside the front door. The Club Bar was also a restaurant that had a reputation for great chicken fried steak. Pictured below are, from left to right, LaLa Regira (behind bar), Lange Casso, unidentified, and James Caillet. (Courtesy of the Regira family.)

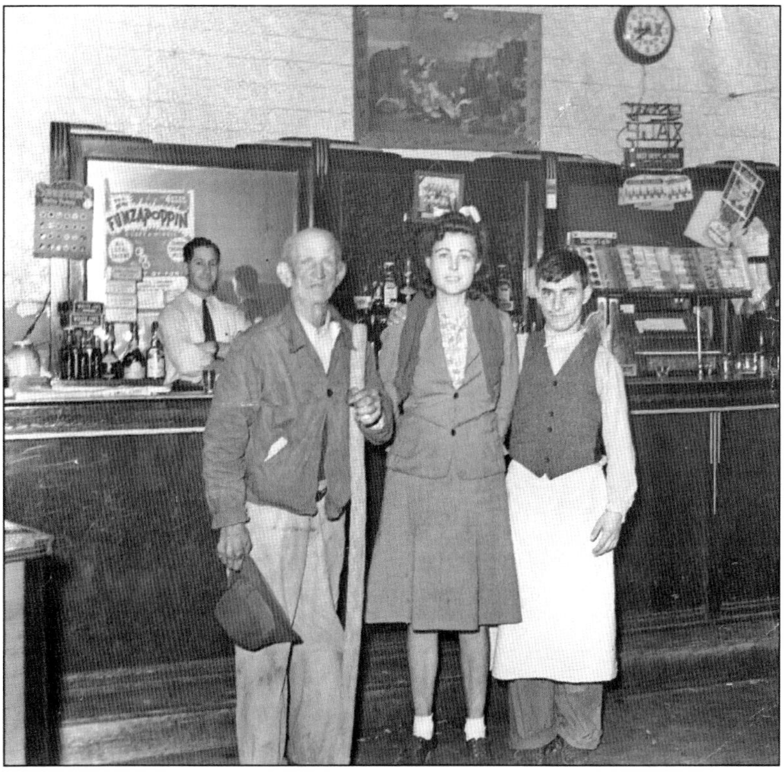

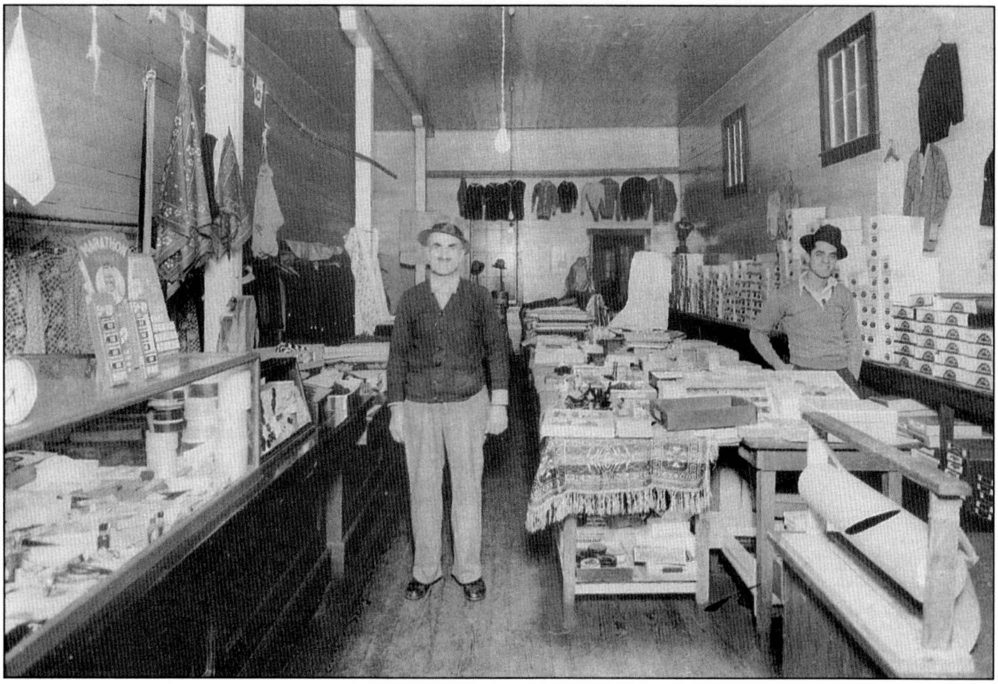

John Bahry (left) and Ede Bahry are seen in Cheap John's, later Bahry's Department Store, at 602 Railroad Avenue. (Courtesy of the Bahry family.)

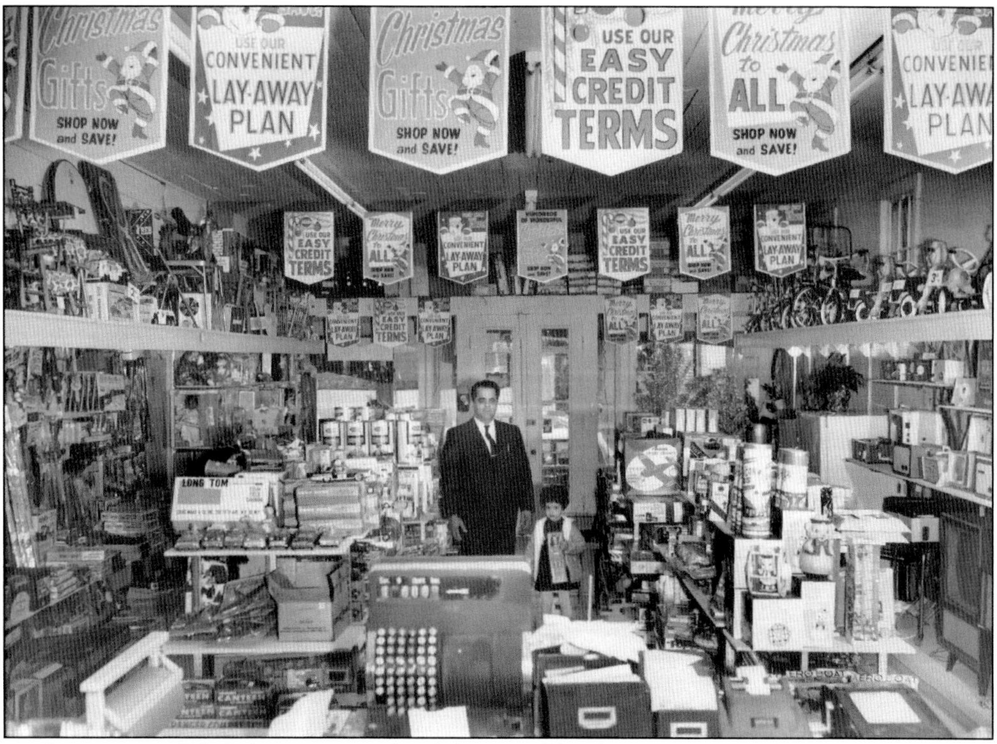

In a later picture, Ede Bahry is pictured with his granddaughter Dana Caballero in his department store. (Courtesy of the Bahry family.)

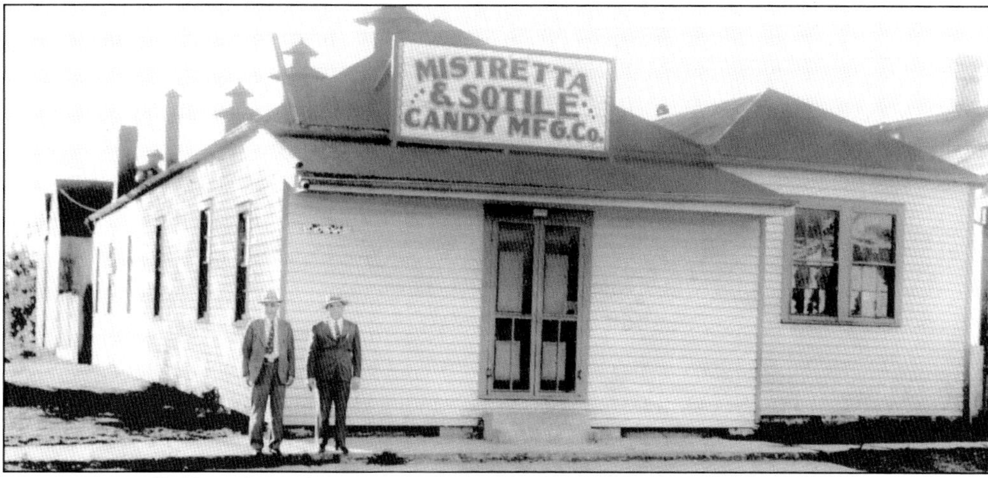

Joe Mistretta (left) and Frank Sotile (right) were boyhood friends. They went into the Army together in World War I and saw action in Europe. When they returned home to Donaldsonville, they established the Mistretta & Sotile Candy Mfg. Co. and went into the candy business, making 1¢ and 5¢ peppermint sticks and 5¢ peanut and coconut bars. They employed approximately 20 people at the height of their business. Eventually, the large candy companies were too much for them to compete with, and they closed the business in 1970. (Courtesy of the Sotile family.)

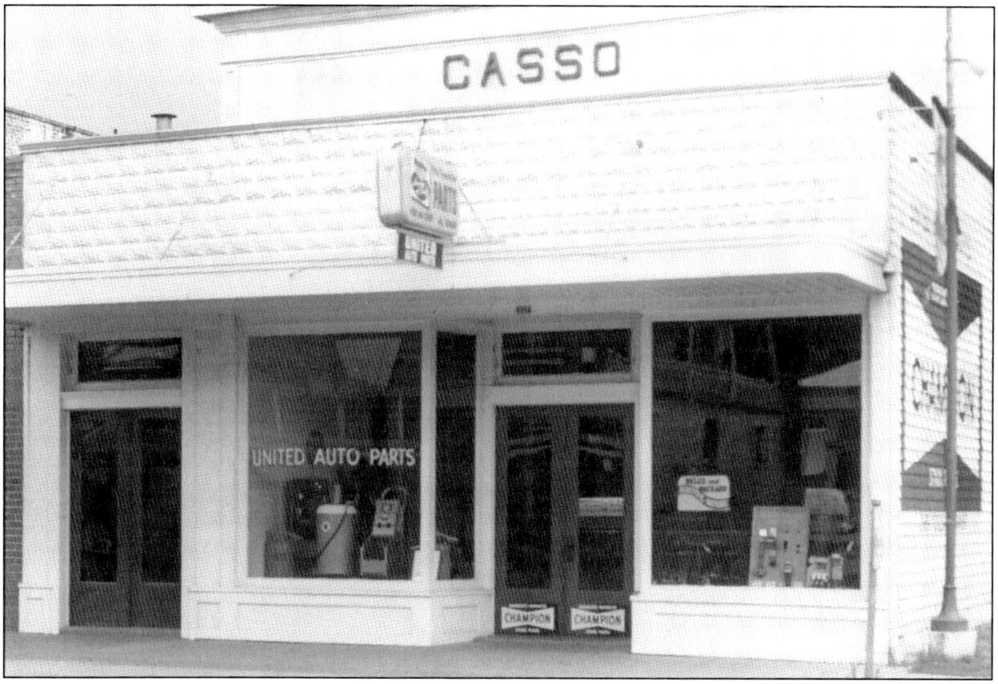

Having left his motherland of Italy during the turbulent years when Garibaldi was waging civil war across the land, Lorenzo Casso found himself caught up in the American Civil War soon after his arrival in the United States. He became Ascension Parish's first Italian immigrant, settling in Donaldsonville, where he married a Louisianan Creole and founded the Casso family in Louisiana. His descendants now total almost 500. Pestilence, flood, crop failure, civil strife, death, destruction, and disappointment, the age-old elements in man's struggle for existence, are all part of the Casso family's life on the Louisianan frontier. (Courtesy of the Casso family.)

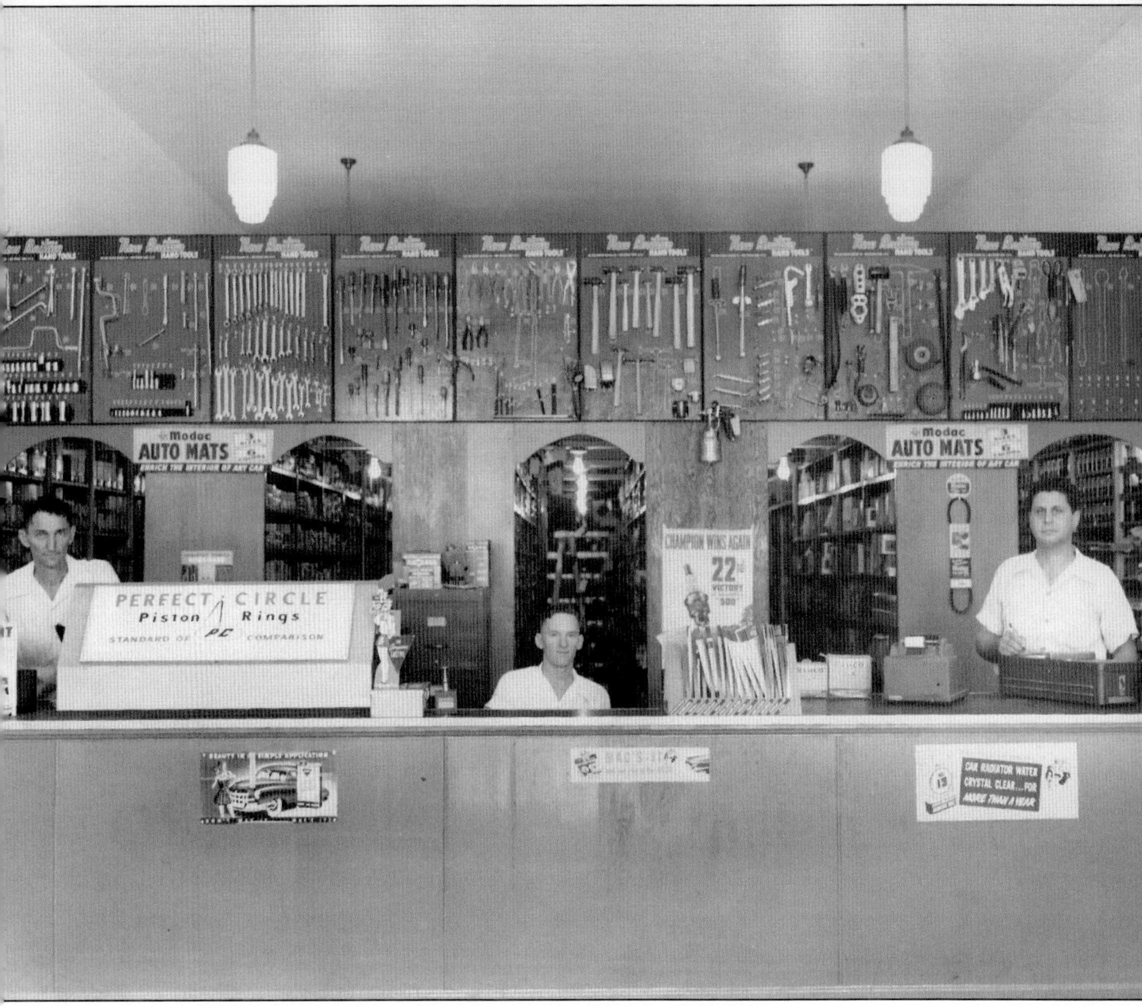

The United Auto Parts store was a staple business on Railroad Avenue for years. From left to right, Bullie Casso, Red Naquin, and Mr. Bouquet are pictured. (Courtesy of the Casso family.)

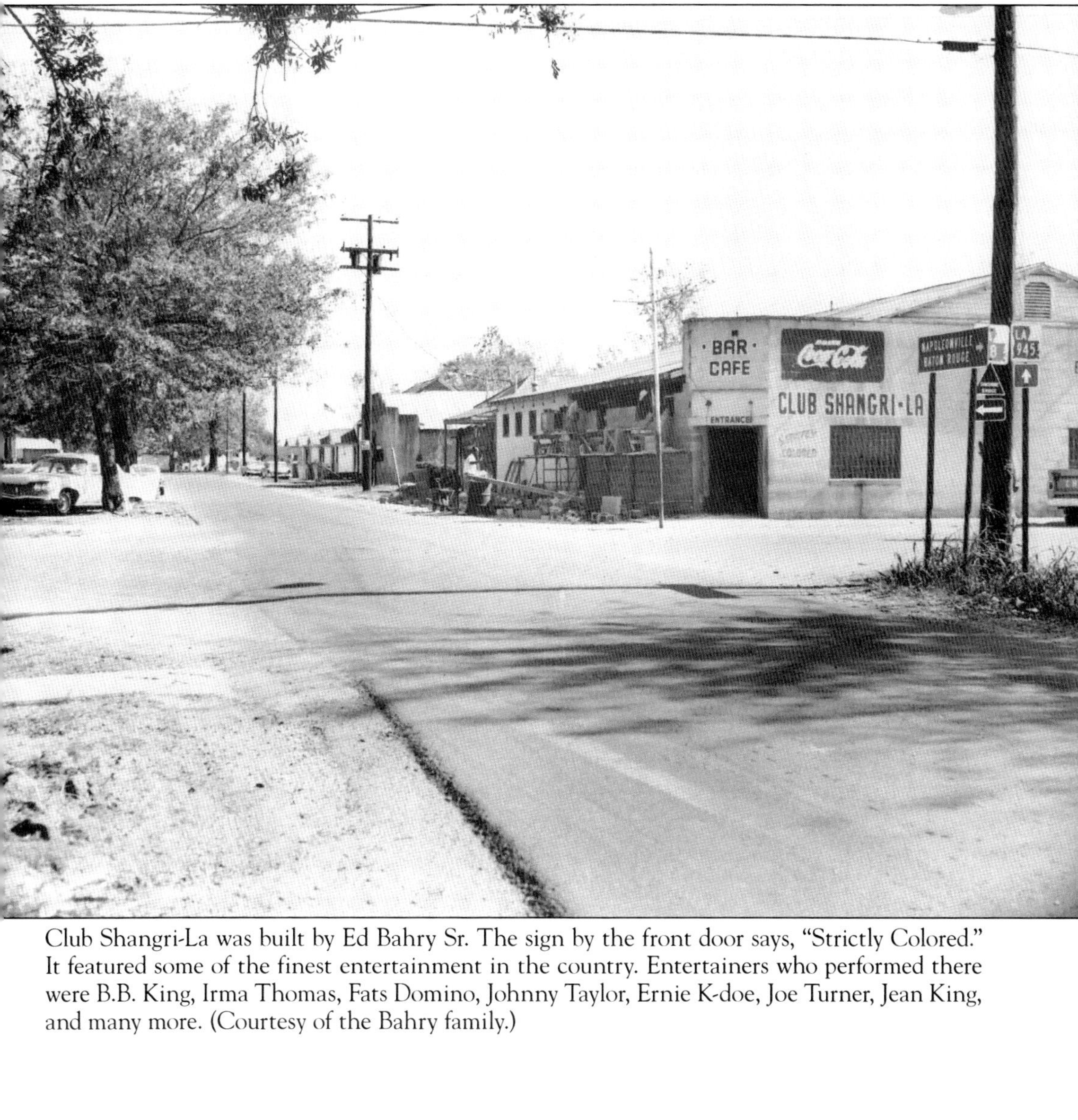

Club Shangri-La was built by Ed Bahry Sr. The sign by the front door says, "Strictly Colored." It featured some of the finest entertainment in the country. Entertainers who performed there were B.B. King, Irma Thomas, Fats Domino, Johnny Taylor, Ernie K-doe, Joe Turner, Jean King, and many more. (Courtesy of the Bahry family.)

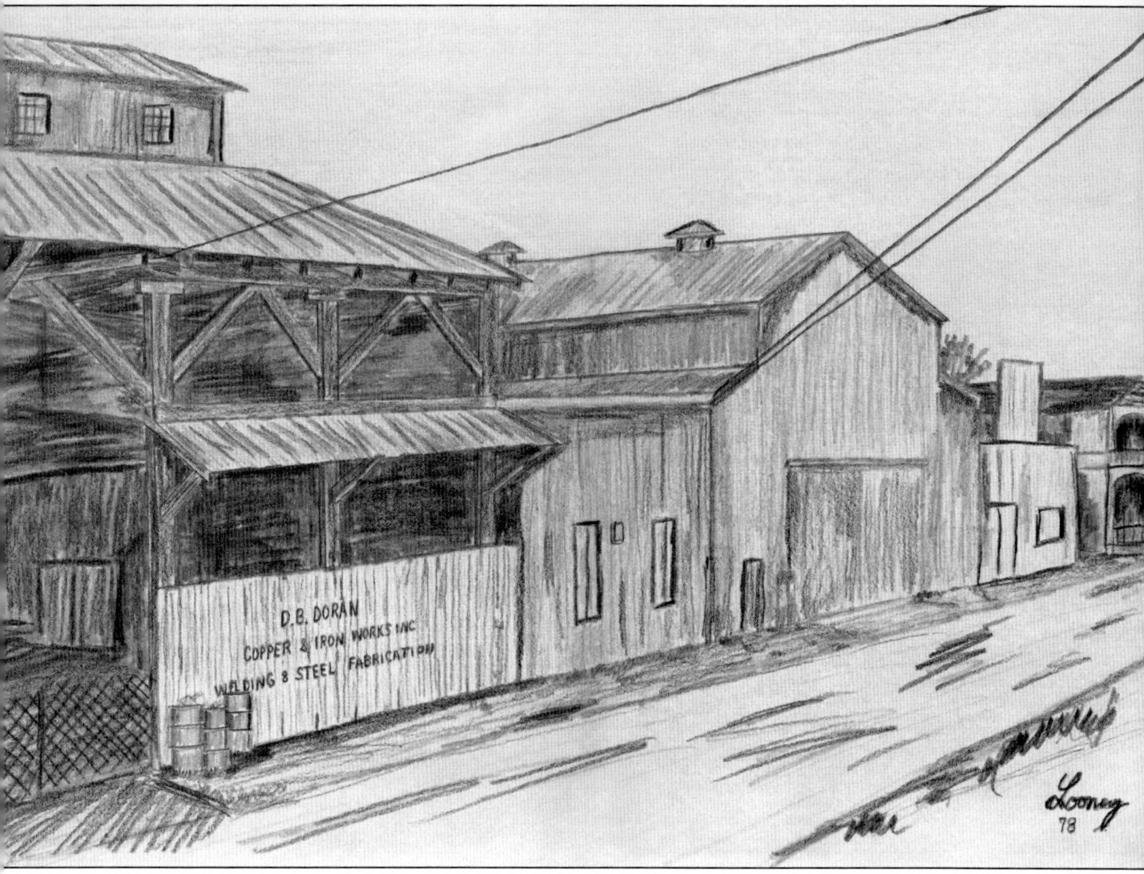

William A. Dill originally established the William A. Dill Copper and Sheet Iron Works business, located at 308–402 Lafourche Street, in the late 1800s. Its primary business was doing copper work for the sugar industry. William Dill brought D.B. Doran to Donaldsonville from New Orleans as an apprentice. Doran eventually bought the business from the Dills' heirs in 1941 and renamed it D.B. Doran Copper and Iron Works. During the late 1940s, company officials added iron and steel fabrication for the petro-chemical industry in the Donaldsonville area. In 1984, the Doran shop was sold but continues to do business under the D.B. Doran Copper and Iron Works name. (Courtesy of the Doran family.)

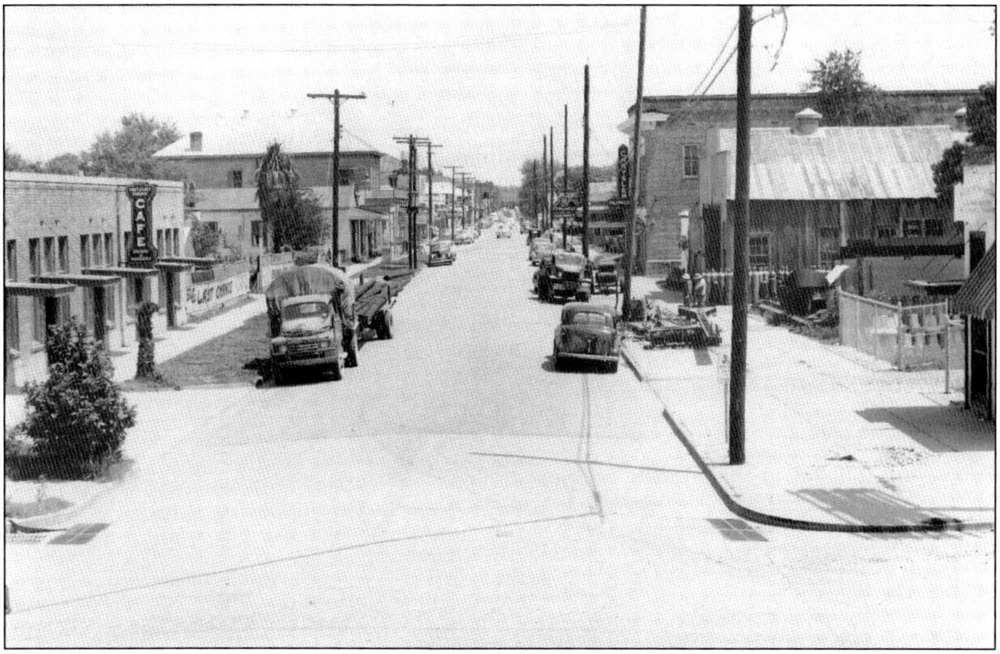

This is Railroad Avenue from the train tracks, looking toward the river. On the left is the First and Last Chance. Farther down about one block is Busy Bee Cleaners. All the way to the right stands the Ascension Lumber and Coal Yard, and the Plymouth dealership is near the end of the block on the right. (Courtesy of the Sotile family.)

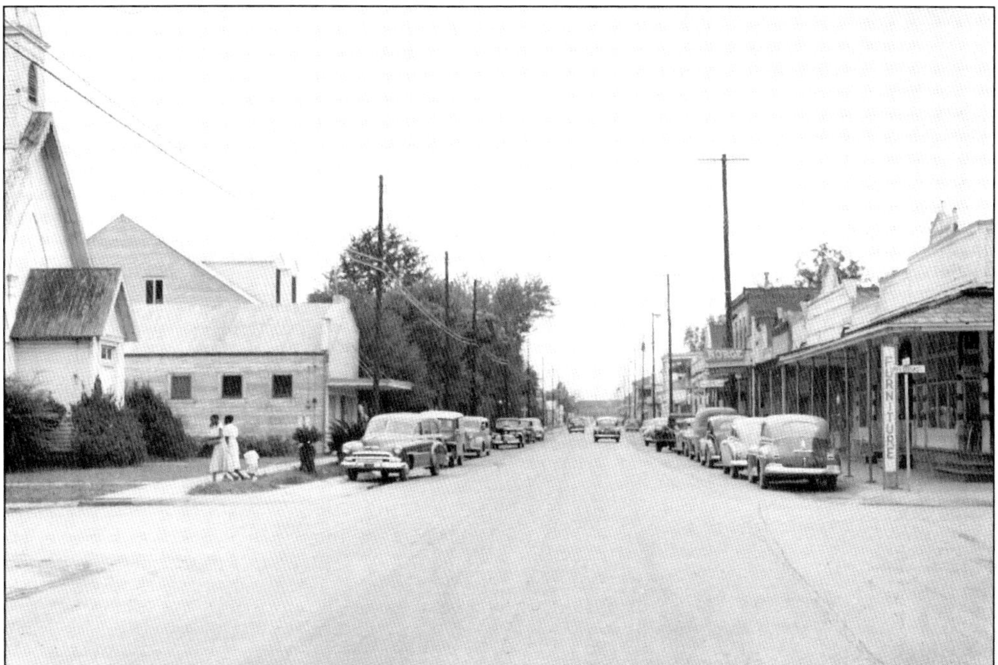

This is Railroad Avenue from in front of Louisiana Square, looking toward the railroad tracks. On the left is the Methodist church, at the end of the road is the train depot, and the business on the right is the J.C. Babin store. (Courtesy of the Sotile family.)

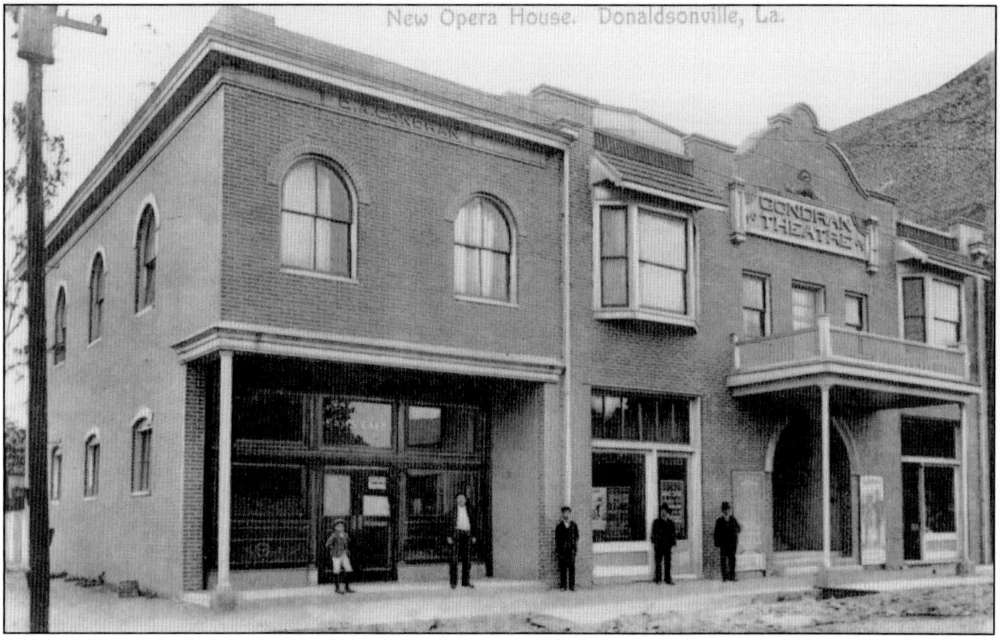

The Donaldsonville Realty Company constructed the new opera house in 1906. It was purchased by local district attorney G.A. Gondran and was named the Gondran Theatre. In 1912, it was sold to Alex Blooensteil, the Donaldsonville commissioner of finance, and the name was changed to the Grand Theatre. (Courtesy of the Landry family.)

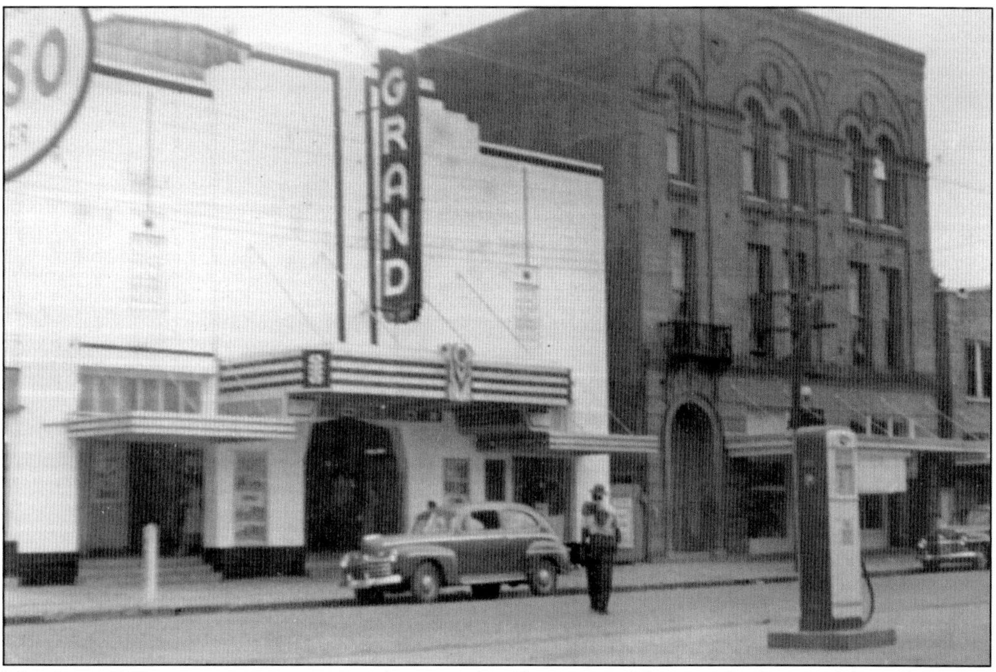

The Grand Theatre was a venue for plays, vaudeville acts, and lectures before its debut of motion pictures in January 1914. In 1929, the talking motion picture arrived at the Grand. Notice the gas pump on the right. There used to be an Esso service station across the street from the Grand. (Courtesy of the Landry family.)

Anyone who ever saw a movie at the Grand Theatre would remember this ticket window. The weekends saw lines of people anxious to get their tickets and sweet popcorn before hurriedly climbing the steps and looking for a good seat. (Courtesy of the Landry family.)

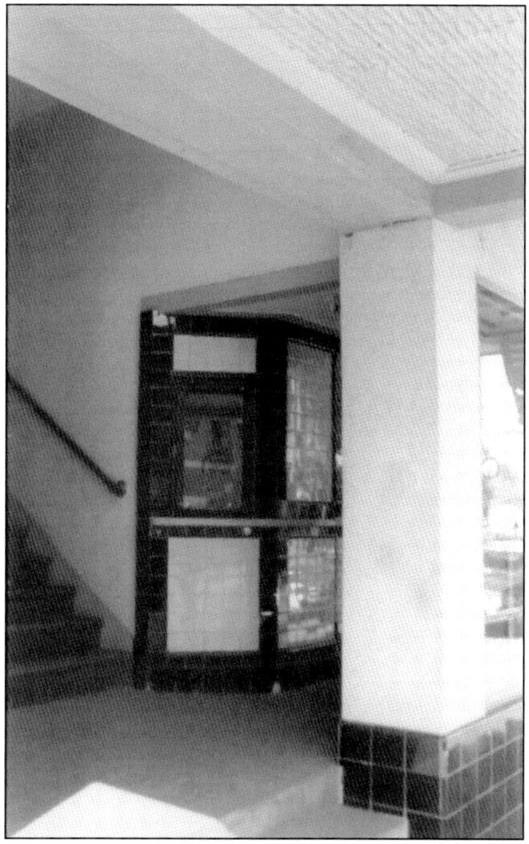

X-Ray Pharmacy, which once housed Montero and Brande's Opera Café, was next door to the Grand Theatre and was demolished with the theater in the mid-1980s. (Courtesy of the Bahry family.)

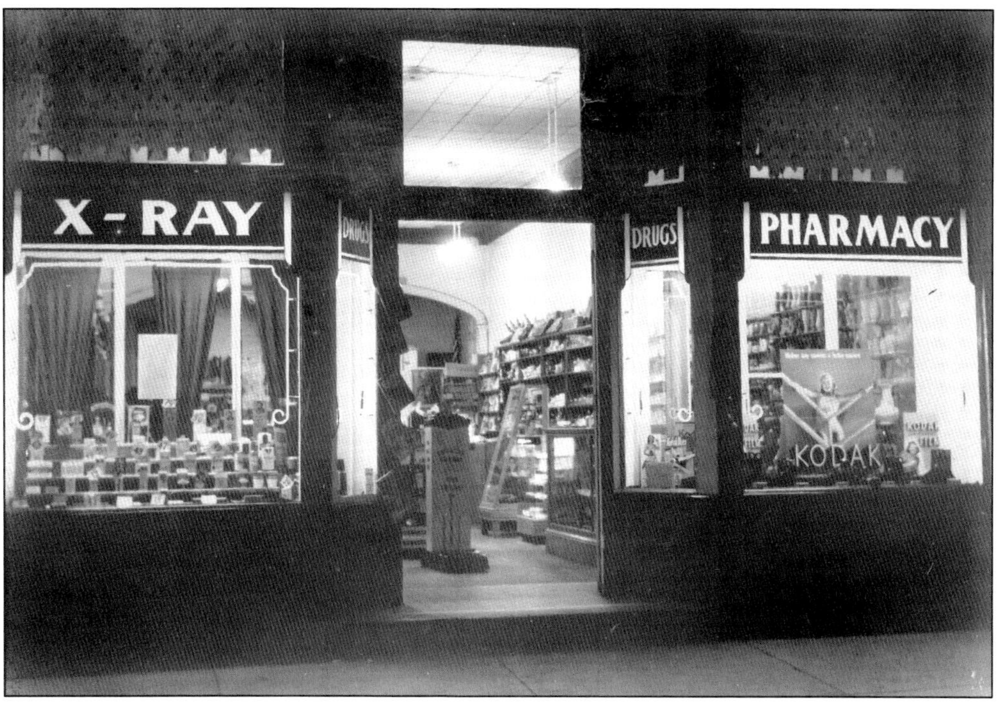

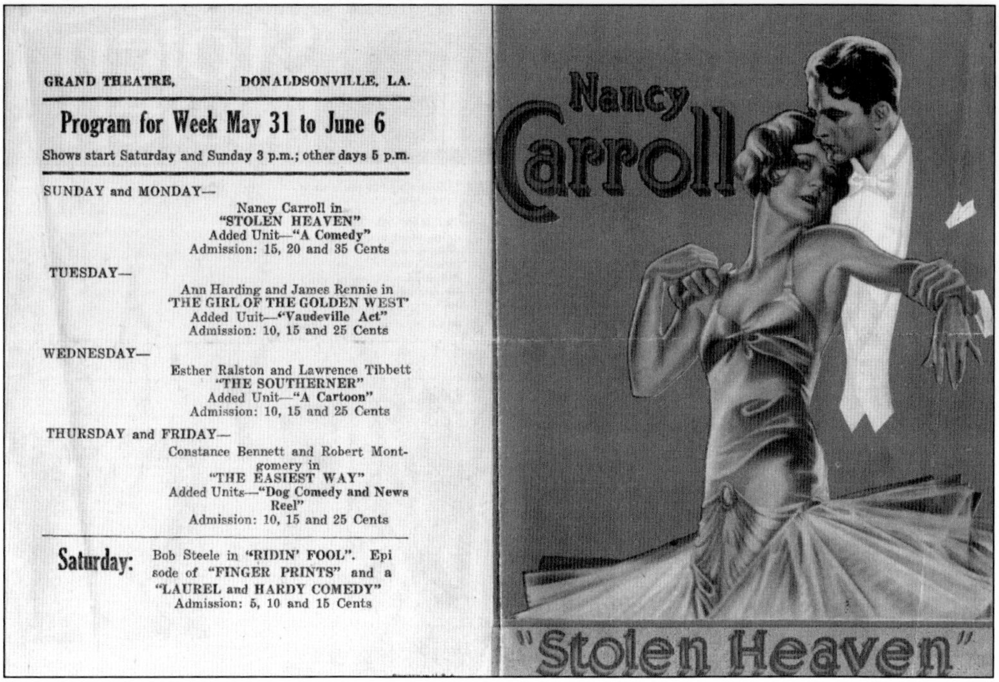

GRAND THEATRE, DONALDSONVILLE, LA.

Program for Week May 31 to June 6

Shows start Saturday and Sunday 3 p.m.; other days 5 p.m.

SUNDAY and MONDAY—
Nancy Carroll in
"STOLEN HEAVEN"
Added Unit—"A Comedy"
Admission: 15, 20 and 35 Cents

TUESDAY—
Ann Harding and James Rennie in
'THE GIRL OF THE GOLDEN WEST'
Added Uuit—"Vaudeville Act"
Admission: 10, 15 and 25 Cents

WEDNESDAY—
Esther Ralston and Lawrence Tibbett
"THE SOUTHERNER"
Added Unit—"A Cartoon"
Admission: 10, 15 and 25 Cents

THURSDAY and FRIDAY—
Constance Bennett and Robert Montgomery in
"THE EASIEST WAY"
Added Units—"Dog Comedy and News Reel"
Admission: 10, 15 and 25 Cents

Saturday: Bob Steele in "RIDIN' FOOL". Episode of "FINGER PRINTS" and a "LAUREL and HARDY COMEDY"
Admission: 5, 10 and 15 Cents

Pictured are the front and back pages of a 1931 advertisement sent out by the Grand Theatre to the residents of Donaldsonville. (Courtesy of the Doran family.)

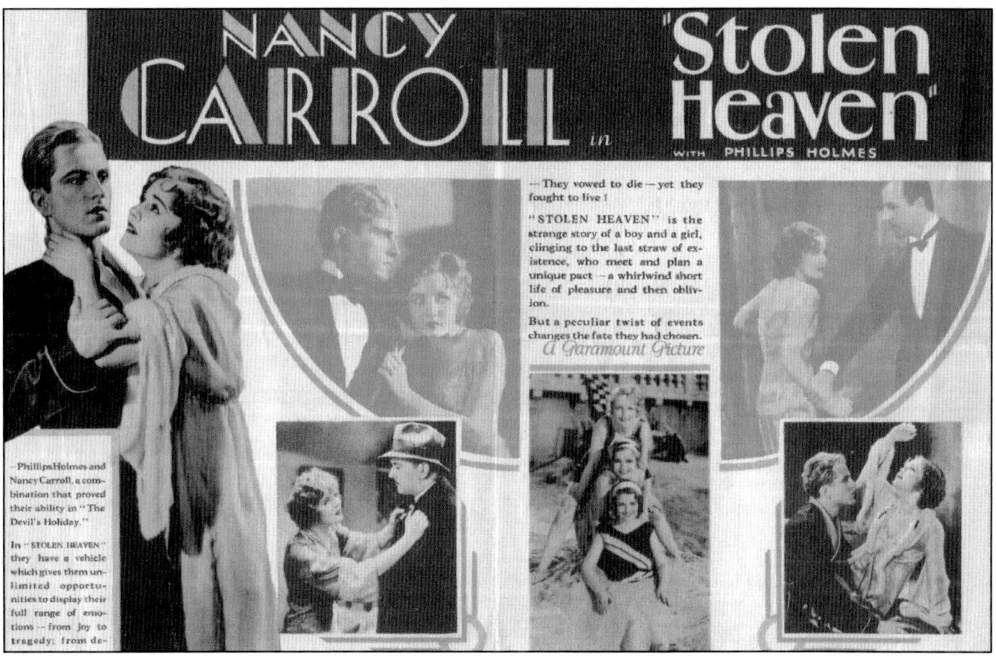

Here are the inside pages of the same 1931 advertisement sent out by the Grand Theatre to the residents of Donaldsonville. (Courtesy of the Doran family.)

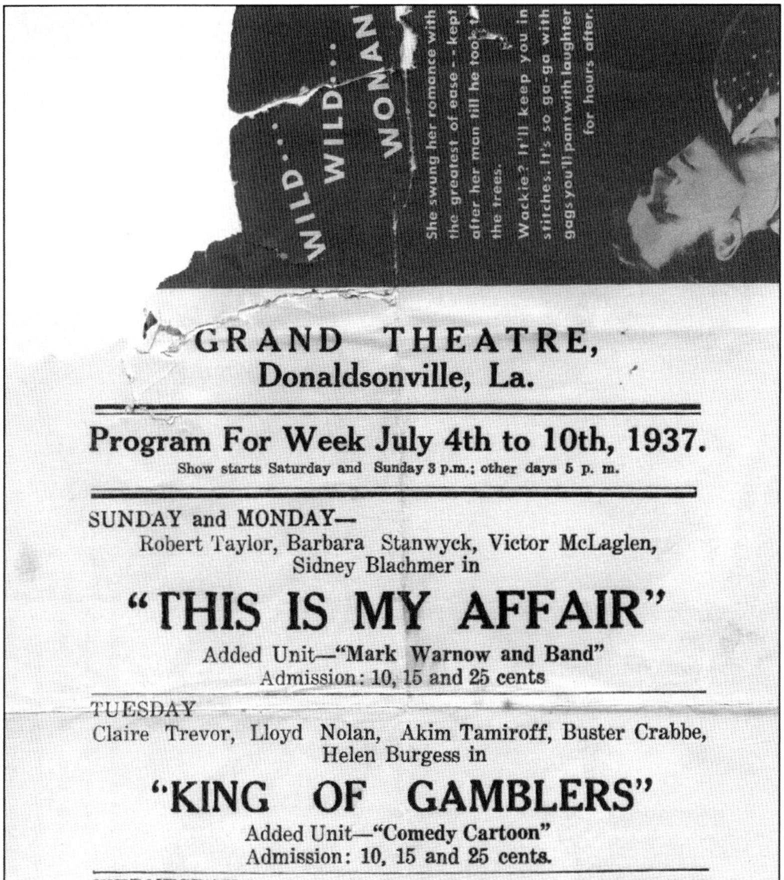

WILD... WILD... WOMAN

She swung her romance with the greatest of ease--kept after her man till he took to the trees. Wackie? It'll keep you in stitches. It's so ga-ga with gags you'll pant with laughter for hours after.

GRAND THEATRE,
Donaldsonville, La.

Program For Week July 4th to 10th, 1937.
Show starts Saturday and Sunday 3 p.m.; other days 5 p. m.

SUNDAY and MONDAY—
Robert Taylor, Barbara Stanwyck, Victor McLaglen, Sidney Blachmer in

"THIS IS MY AFFAIR"

Added Unit—**"Mark Warnow and Band"**
Admission: 10, 15 and 25 cents

TUESDAY
Claire Trevor, Lloyd Nolan, Akim Tamiroff, Buster Crabbe, Helen Burgess in

"KING OF GAMBLERS"

Added Unit—**"Comedy Cartoon"**
Admission: 10, 15 and 25 cents.

WEDNESDAY—
Warner Oland, Pauline Moore, Katherine DeMille, Keye Luke

"CHARLIE CHAN AT THE OLYMPICS"

Added Units—**"Cartoon and Sport Reel"**
Admission: 10, 15 and 25 Cents.

THURSDAY and FRIDAY—
Miriam Hopkins, Joel McCrea, Charles, Winninger, Ella Logan

"WOMAN CHASES MAN"

Added Units—**"An outstanding Musical Revue featuring Dave Apollon, Clark & Halliday, Yvonne Moray and others, also Pathe News"**
Admission: 10, 15 and 25 cents.

SATURDAY—
Buck Jones in

"SMOKE TREE RANGE"

"Joe Palooka Comedy" and episode of "Secret Agent X-9"
Admission: 5, 10 and 15 Cents

This is a Grand Theatre show schedule from July 4–10, 1937. If patrons did not get into the theater when the show started, they could stay through all of the features until the part that they saw came around again. They did not change the house over after every showing. (Courtesy of the Marchand family.)

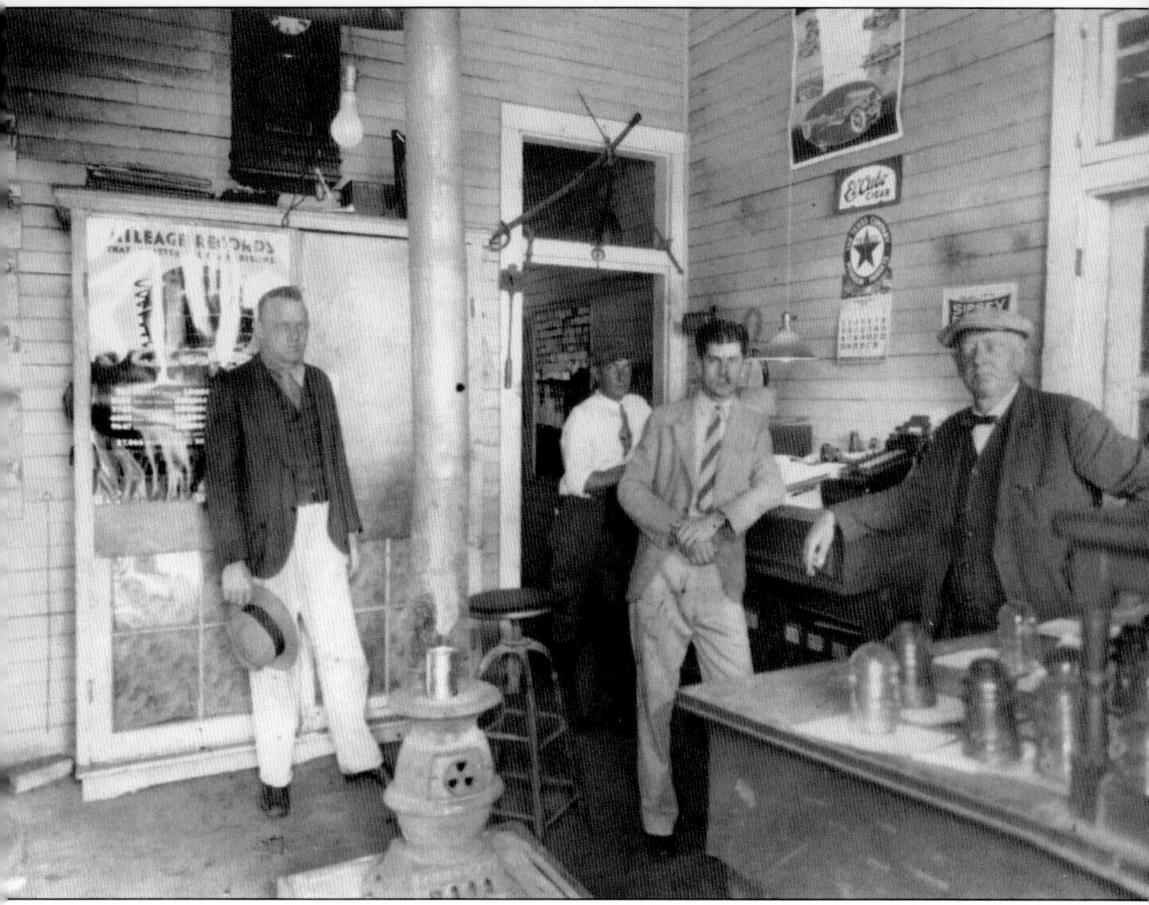

The Kocke family is synonymous with construction in the Donaldsonville area. In 1916, Elray Kocke came to Donaldsonville from New Orleans and formed a scrap iron and metal salvage company. Later that year, his parents joined him. In 1926, coal was sold by the company in 10 varieties and delivered by the ton, by the box, or by the sack. In the 1930s and 1940s, the Kockes became very active in servicing the oilfield industry. Gin pole and trailer trucks were used to load and haul drilling rigs from one location to another. The Kockes sold drilling mud and chemicals to drillers and offered 24-hour service. Warehouses in Gonzales and Donaldsonville were stockpiled with the material to service the huge Darrow Oilfield. At the peak of the oilfield activity, Elray Kocke Service employed 60 people and had 35 trucks in its fleet. This is the first Elray Kocke office building, erected in 1929. Pictured from left to right are Elray Kocke, Henry L. Kocke, Clarence Lorio, and Henry Kocke. (Courtesy of the Kocke family.)

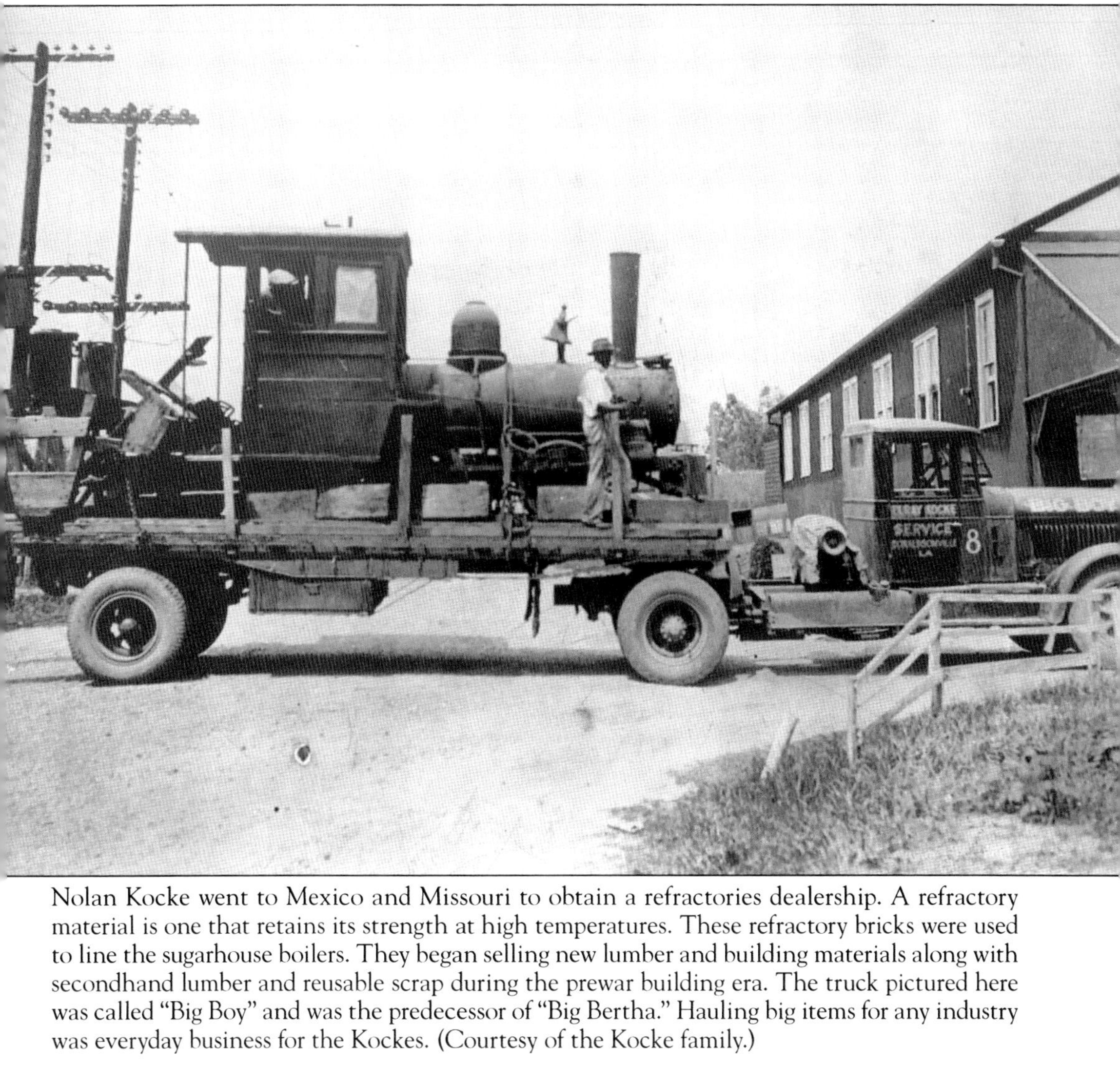

Nolan Kocke went to Mexico and Missouri to obtain a refractories dealership. A refractory material is one that retains its strength at high temperatures. These refractory bricks were used to line the sugarhouse boilers. They began selling new lumber and building materials along with secondhand lumber and reusable scrap during the prewar building era. The truck pictured here was called "Big Boy" and was the predecessor of "Big Bertha." Hauling big items for any industry was everyday business for the Kockes. (Courtesy of the Kocke family.)

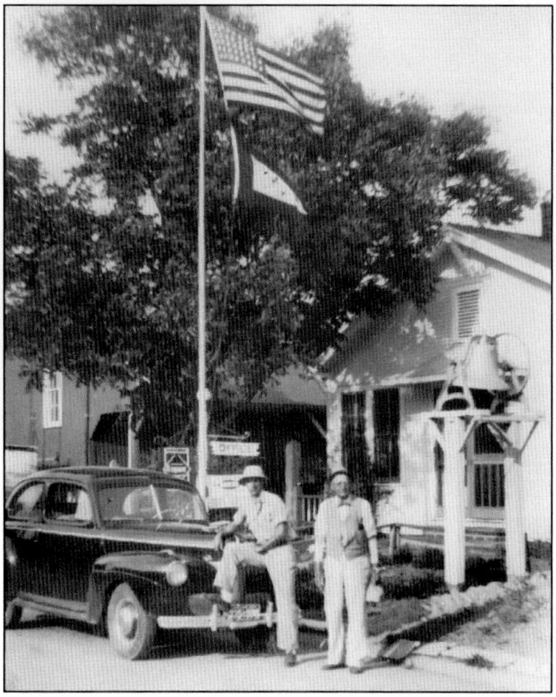

From 1941 to 1945, World War II brought a tremendous demand for scrap metal. The local schools competed to see who could bring in the most scrap metal and iron. In 1942, Elray Kocke Service received national recognition for collecting a record tonnage of scrap. Robert Kocke, the son of Elray Kocke, joined the company and served as president from 1972 until the time of his death in 1991. In this photograph, Nolan (left) and Henry Kocke Sr. are standing in front of the main office on Mississippi Street. (Courtesy of the Kocke family.)

In 1953, Elray Kocke Service opened a ready-mix concrete service along Highway 1 south. Raw materials were unloaded from a private rail spur. (Courtesy of the Kocke family.)

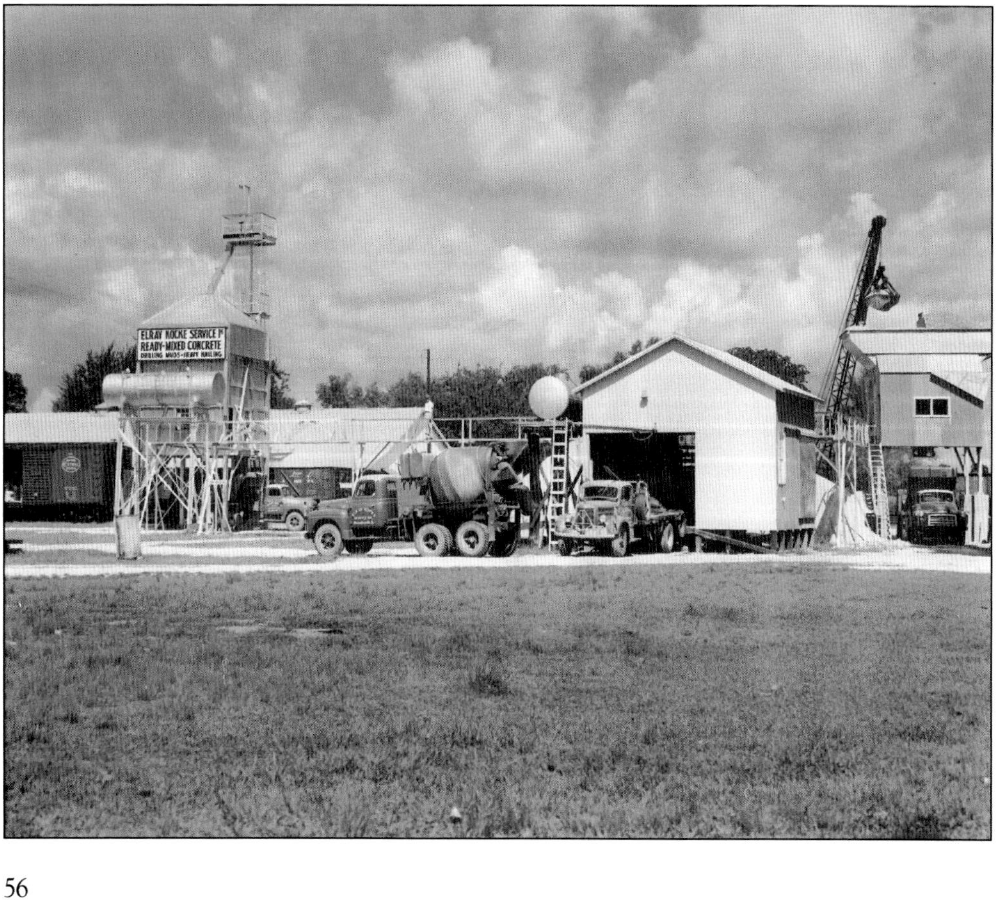

Three

Step Right up, Ladies and Gentlemen

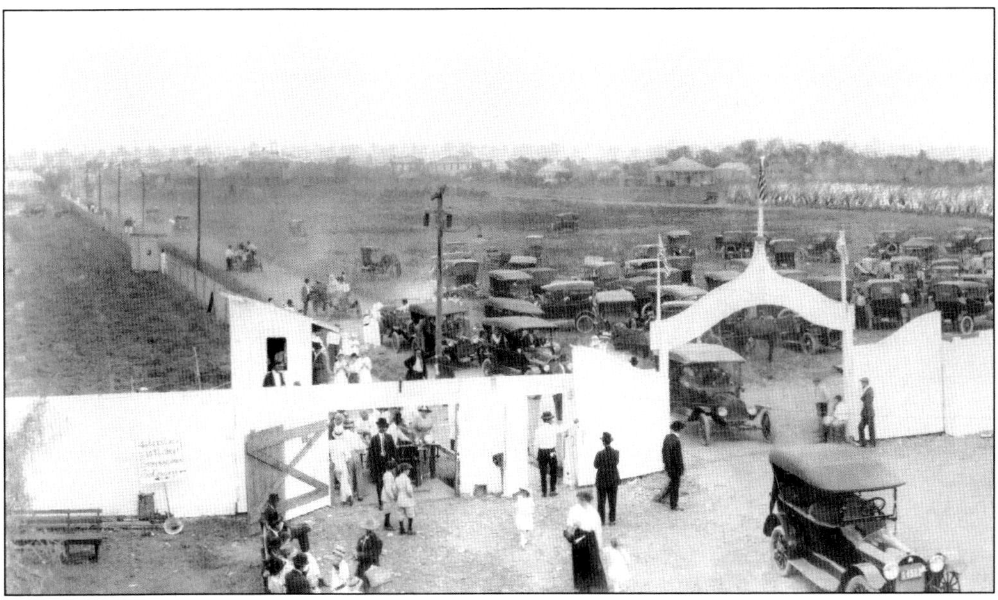

The South Louisiana State Fair was held in Donaldsonville from 1913 to 1964. During its heyday, the fair drew as many as 100,000 people to Donaldsonville over the course of a weekend. This is the entrance on Church Street. The trees in the background line the Mississippi River. (Courtesy of the Landry family.)

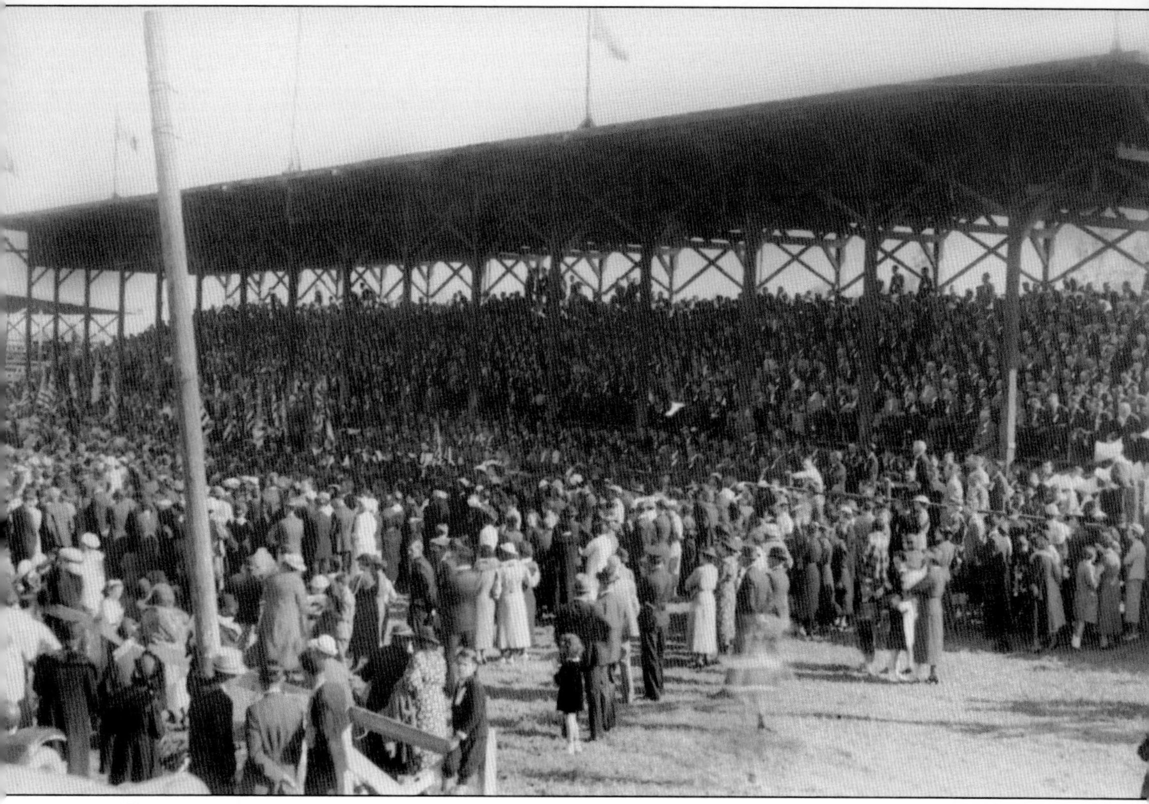

Billboard magazine wrote the following article about the South Louisiana State Fair in Donaldsonville on October 6, 1951:

> Donaldsonville ups attractions for four day run Donaldsonville, La. – Sept. 29 – South Louisiana State Fair will open its four-day run here Thursday (4), with one of the most ambitious attraction programs the annual has presented. In addition to Buff Hotel Shows as the midway attraction for its fourth consecutive year, the annual's nigh grandstand show will be one of its largest. Booked thru the Ruth Tiblier Theatrical Agency, New Orleans, acts will include Sky-High Alcidos, high act; Smetona perch; Emil and Evelyn, teeterboard; Alfredo Landon's Midgets, Gene Schaefer at the organ and Emile Parra, emcee. Paramount Fireworks Company will wind up each nights show with pyrotechnics. The annual, which operates with a free front gate, will be opened by Gov. Earl K. Long. The grand stands at the South Louisiana State Fair for the opening events.

(Courtesy of the Marchand family.)

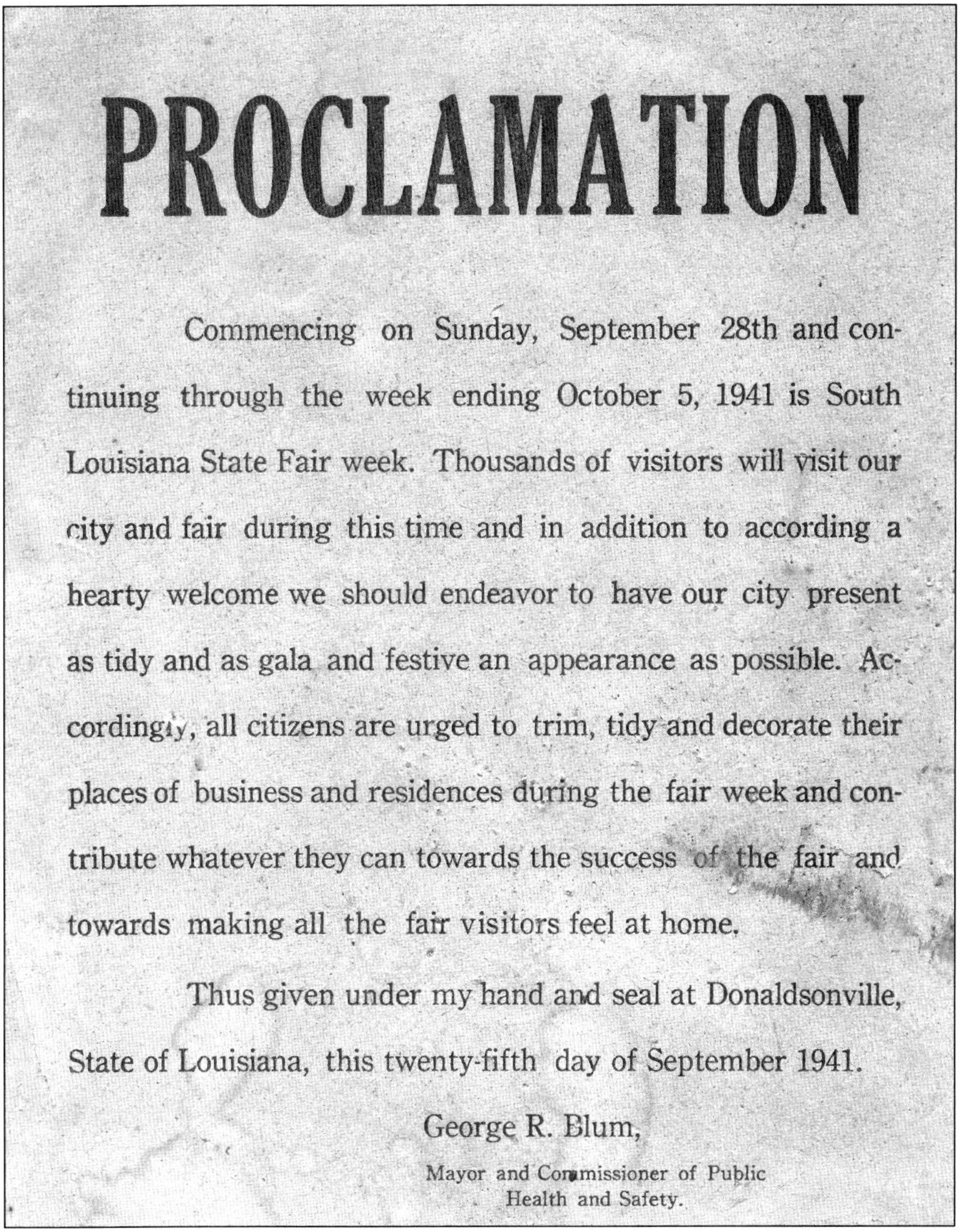

PROCLAMATION

Commencing on Sunday, September 28th and continuing through the week ending October 5, 1941 is South Louisiana State Fair week. Thousands of visitors will visit our city and fair during this time and in addition to according a hearty welcome we should endeavor to have our city present as tidy and as gala and festive an appearance as possible. Accordingly, all citizens are urged to trim, tidy and decorate their places of business and residences during the fair week and contribute whatever they can towards the success of the fair and towards making all the fair visitors feel at home.

Thus given under my hand and seal at Donaldsonville, State of Louisiana, this twenty-fifth day of September 1941.

George R. Blum,

Mayor and Commissioner of Public
Health and Safety.

Here is a proclamation from Mayor George M. Blum for the 1941 state fair. (Courtesy of the Lemann family.)

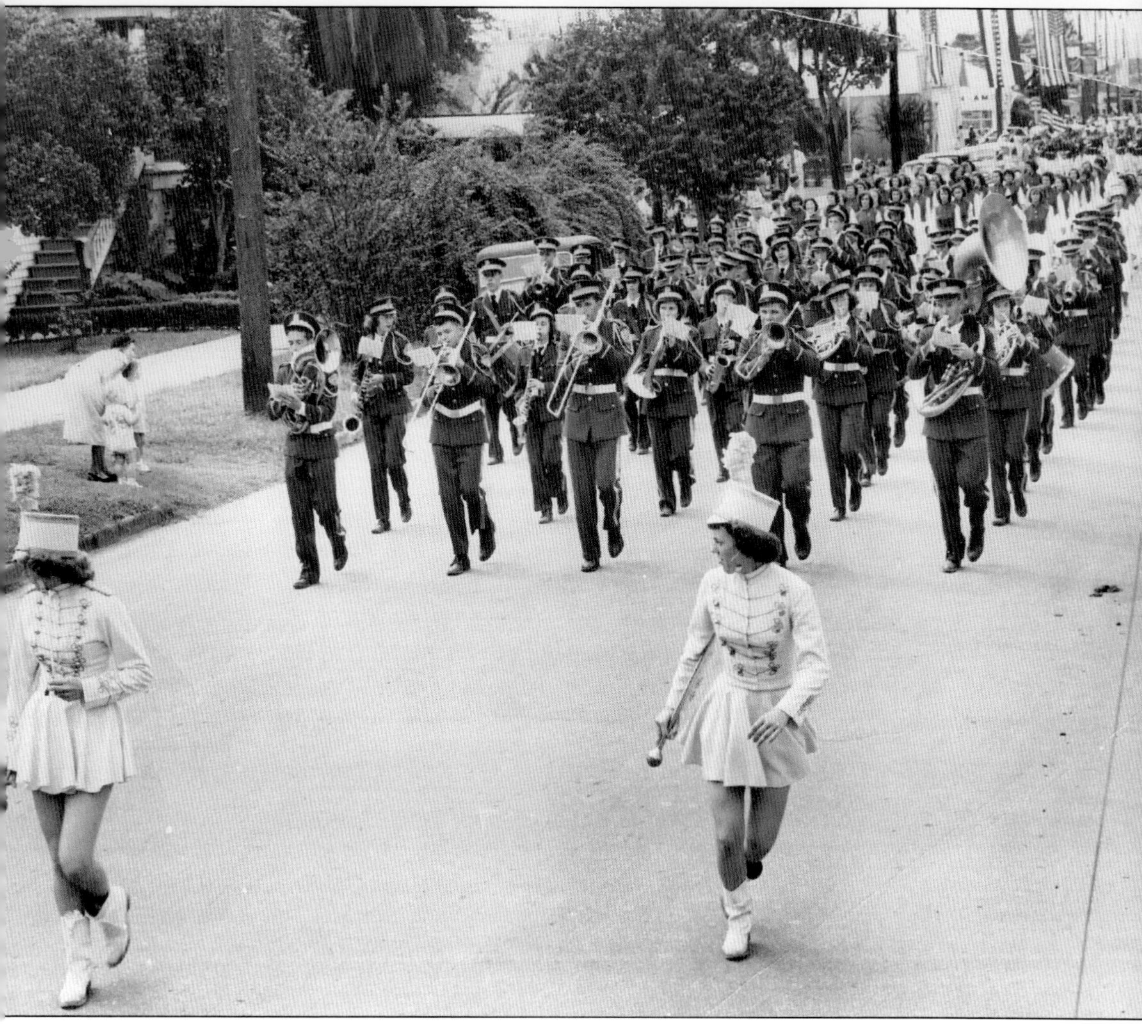

The following is from the 1924 South Louisiana State Fair program:

> The South Louisiana Fair is primarily an educational institution organized and operated solely in the interests of the farms, schools, homes and general industrial development of South Louisiana. The plant consists of 25 acres of land, 10 exhibit buildings, 2 grandstands, a dance pavilion, racing stables, a half mile track, a baseball diamond, city water supply and day and night alternating current. The Fair can be reached by the Texas and Pacific Railway, east and west main line, the Lafourche branch, or by the Yazoo and Mississippi Valley Railroad north and south main lines. Livestock exhibits can be unloaded directly onto the grounds through a cattle chute on a spur from the mail line of the Texas and Pacific Railroad. Water transportation in three directions is furnished by the Mississippi River and Bayou Lafourche. School bands would parade down Railroad Avenue in route to the State Fair grounds. (Courtesy of the Sotile family.)

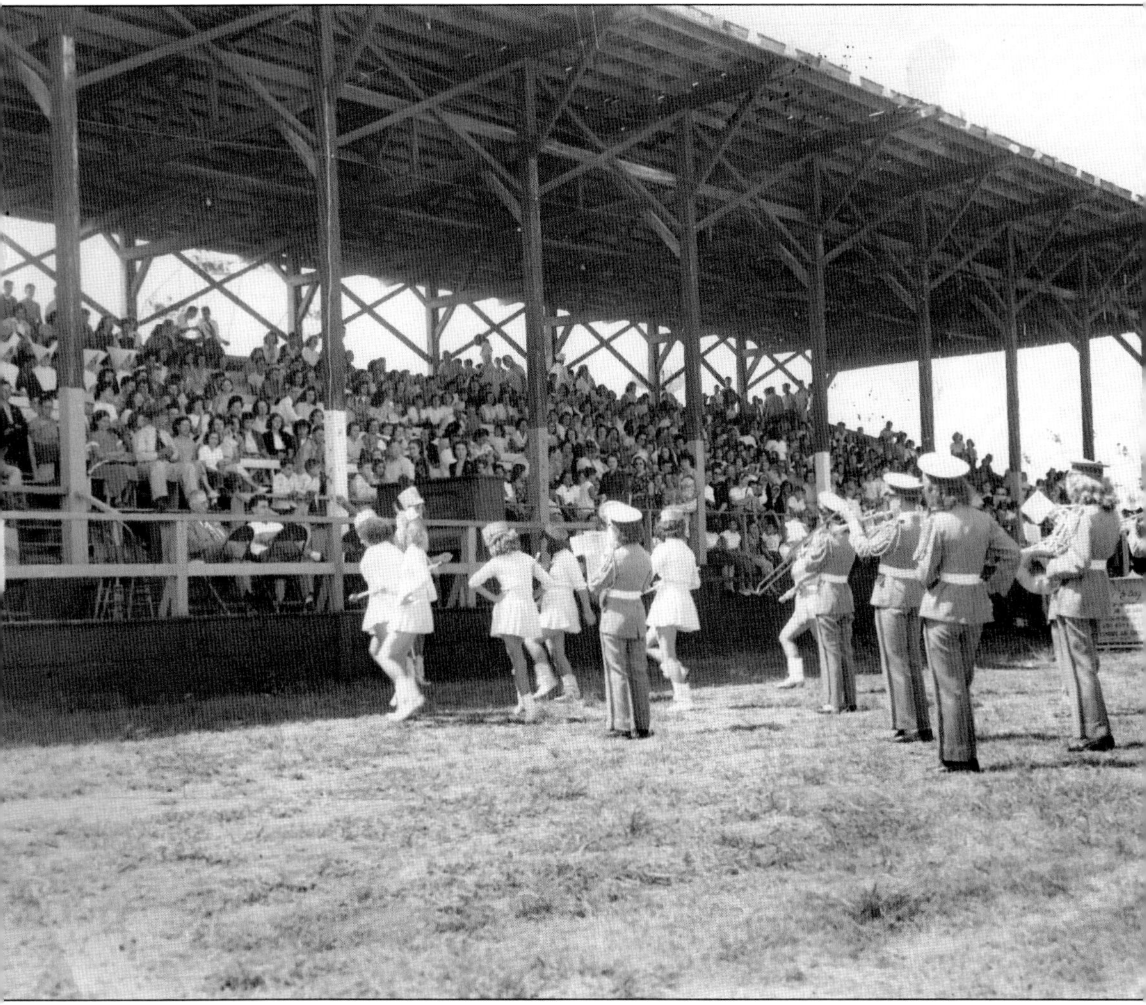

Six hard-surfaced roads radiate from Donaldsonville to connect the South Louisiana State Fair with all the cities, towns, and villages in the 14 parishes, which officially compose the fair association. Within this 60-mile radius is concentrated a population of three-quarters of a million people, more than one-third the total population of the entire state. Rich soil is found in the fertile alluvium, which forms the famous valleys of the Mississippi River and Bayou Lafourche, where sugarcane, rice, cotton, corn, tobacco, citrus fruits, and every variety of trees both grow and flourish, verily a good country to live in. Here is a school band performance at the main grandstand of the South Louisiana State Fair. (Courtesy of the Sotile family.)

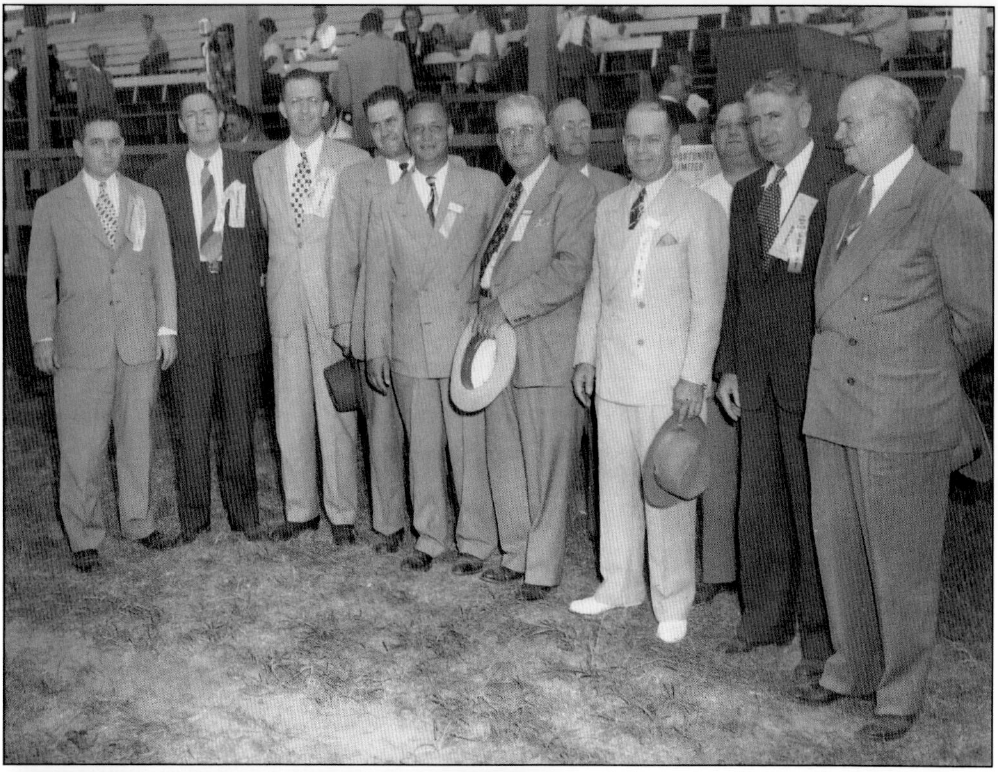

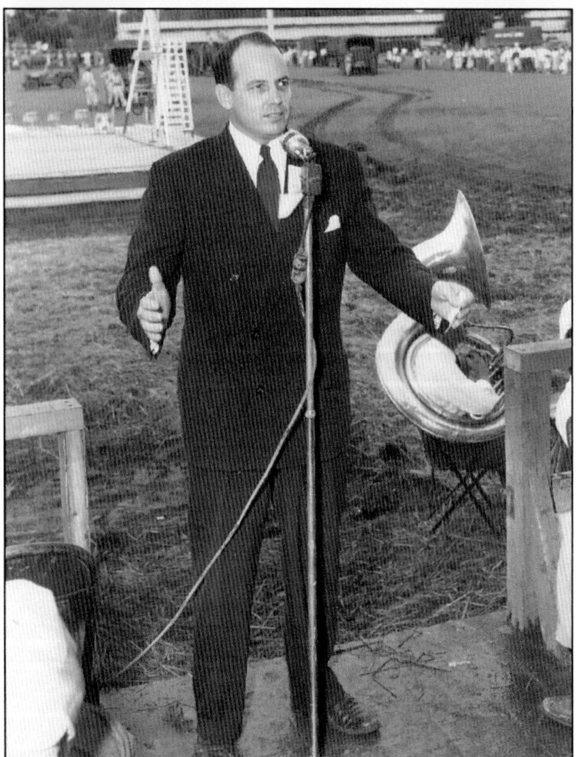

Politicians often made appearances at the South Louisiana State Fair due to the large number of people there and the festive atmosphere. (Courtesy of the Lemman family.)

The South Louisiana Fair Association drew from St. Francisville, New Roads, Vacherie, Hahnville, Thibodaux, Houma, Lockport, Destrahan, Kenner, Gretna, and New Orleans. (Courtesy of the Lemman family.)

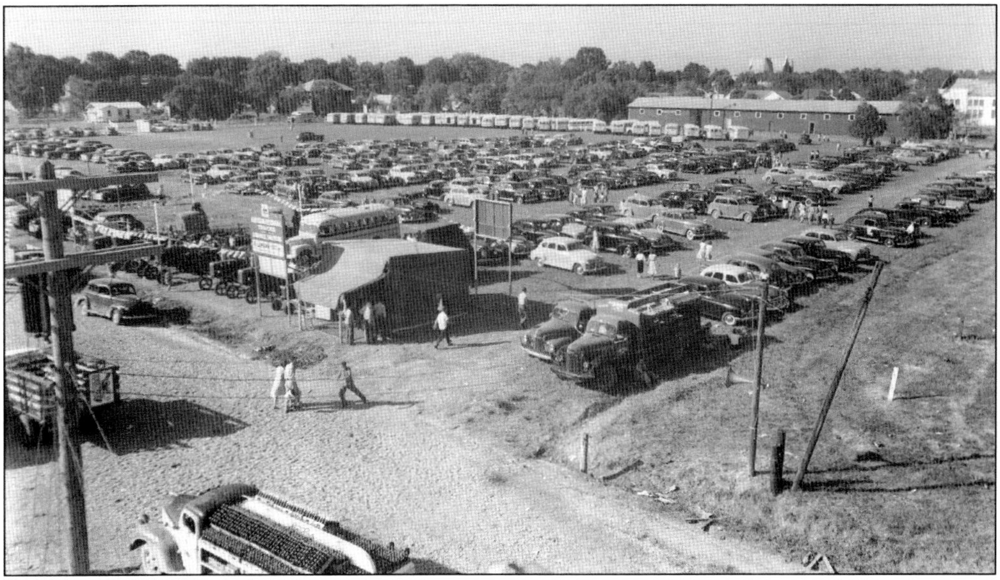

Schools and vendors would arrive early to prepare for their big weekend at the South Louisiana State Fair. The truck in the bottom of the picture is loaded with soda bottles. School buses line the back end of the parking lot. (Courtesy of the Sotile family.)

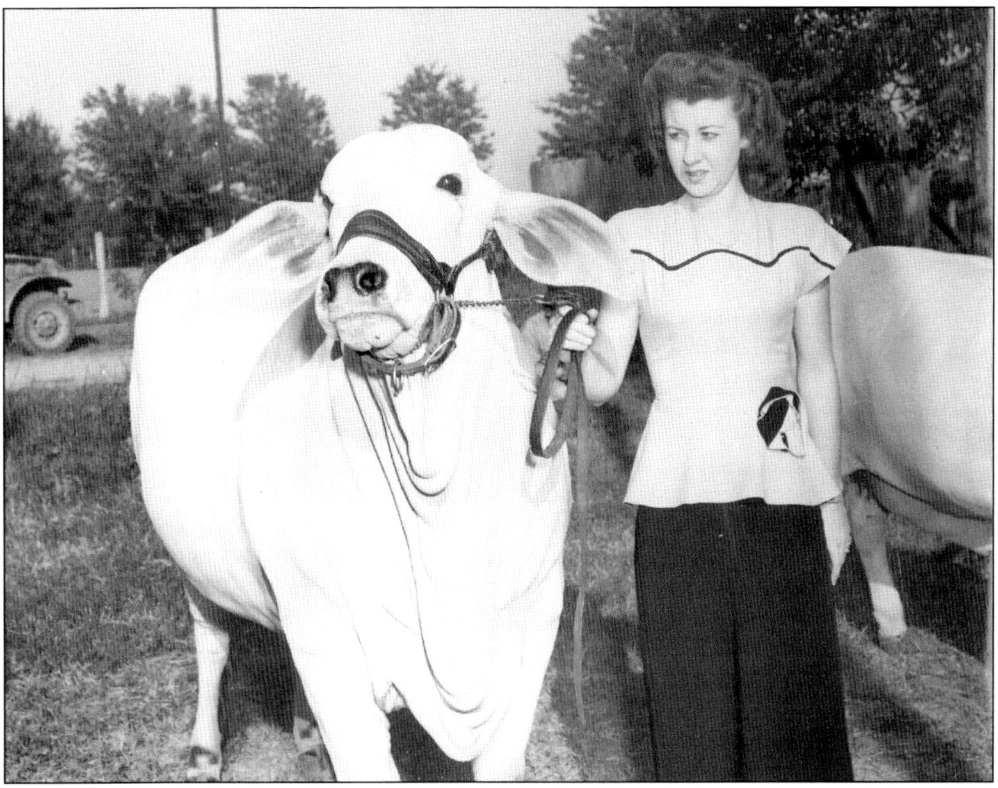

Livestock, farming exhibitions, and cooking contests were well attended and very competitive at the fair. Special ribbons and medals were given and coveted by the winners. (Courtesy of the LeBlanc family.)

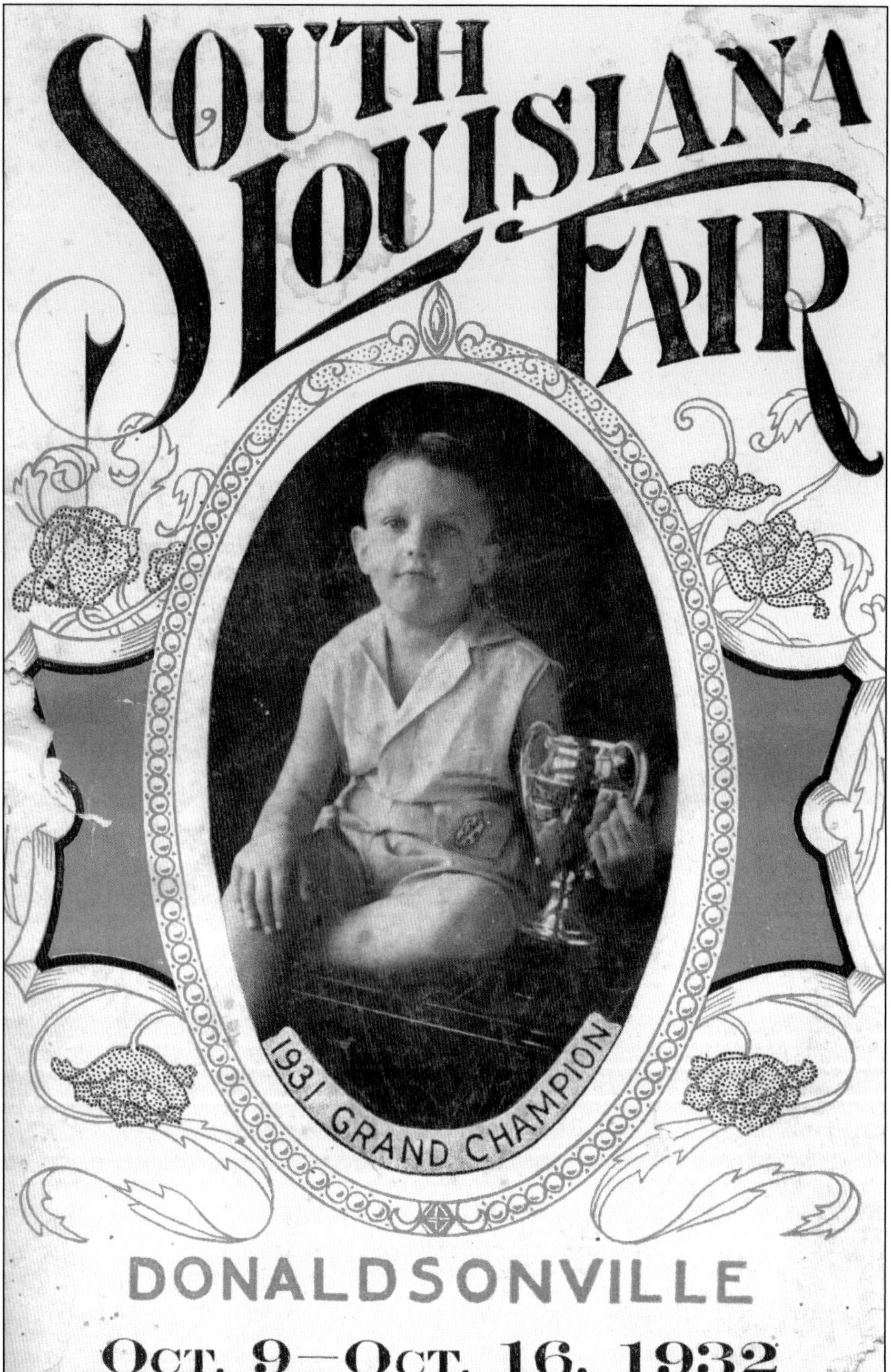

Albert Reynaud was the grand champion baby winner at the 1931 South Louisiana State Fair. His photograph graced the cover of the next year's program. Albert later became the owner of Reynaud Dairy Farm just down the bayou from Donaldsonville. (Courtesy of the Reynaud family.)

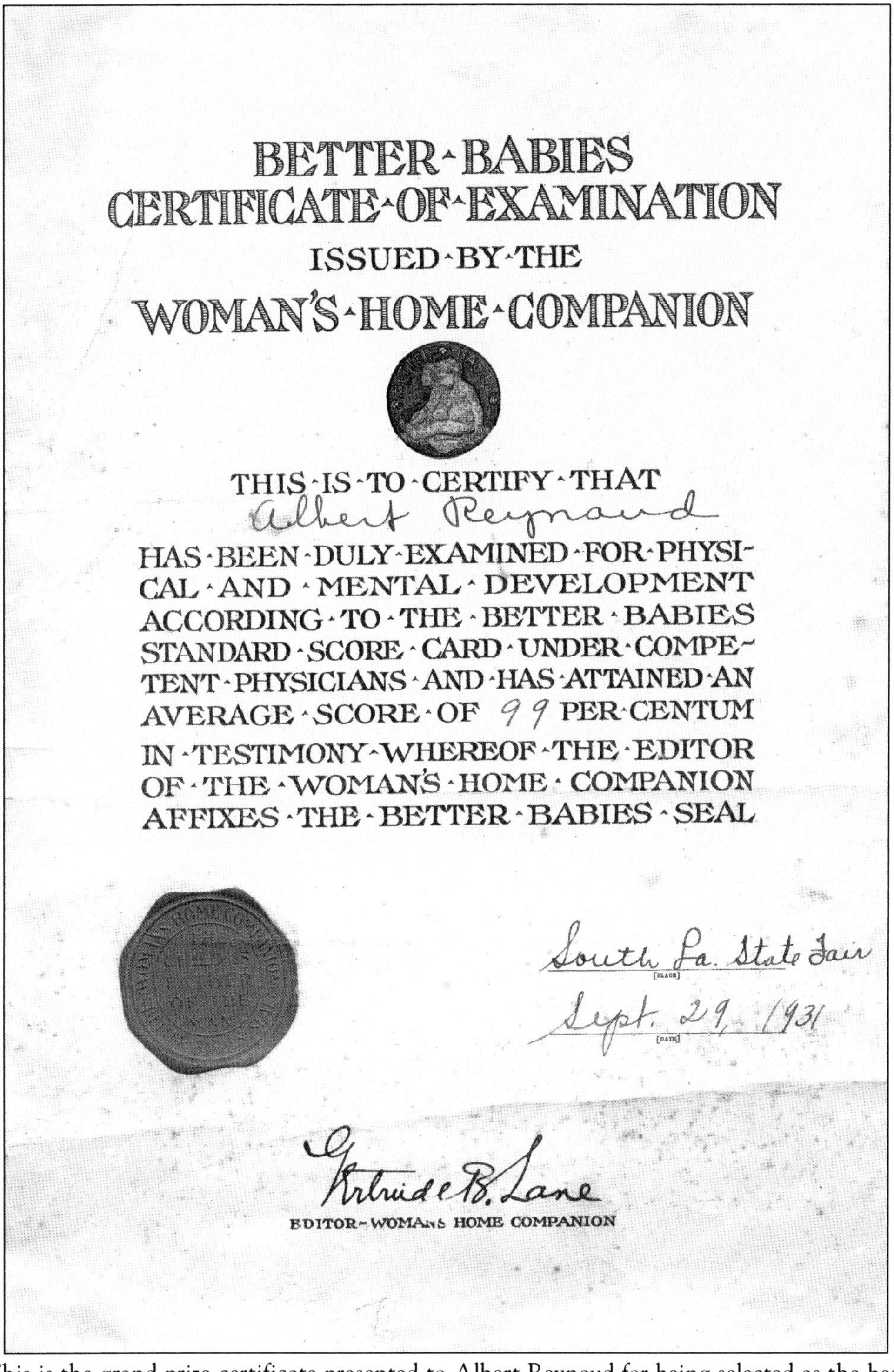
BETTER·BABIES
CERTIFICATE·OF·EXAMINATION
ISSUED·BY·THE
WOMAN'S·HOME·COMPANION

THIS·IS·TO·CERTIFY·THAT
Albert Reynaud
HAS·BEEN·DULY·EXAMINED·FOR·PHYSICAL·AND·MENTAL·DEVELOPMENT ACCORDING·TO·THE·BETTER·BABIES STANDARD·SCORE·CARD·UNDER·COMPETENT·PHYSICIANS·AND·HAS·ATTAINED·AN AVERAGE·SCORE·OF 99 PER·CENTUM
IN·TESTIMONY·WHEREOF·THE·EDITOR OF·THE·WOMAN'S·HOME·COMPANION AFFIXES·THE·BETTER·BABIES·SEAL

South La. State Fair
[PLACE]
Sept. 29, 1931
[DATE]

Gertrude B. Lane
EDITOR–WOMAN'S HOME COMPANION

This is the grand prize certificate presented to Albert Reynaud for being selected as the best baby in 1931. Notice his score is "99 per centum." There is no indication as to what demerit he received during this examination. (Courtesy of the Reynaud family.)

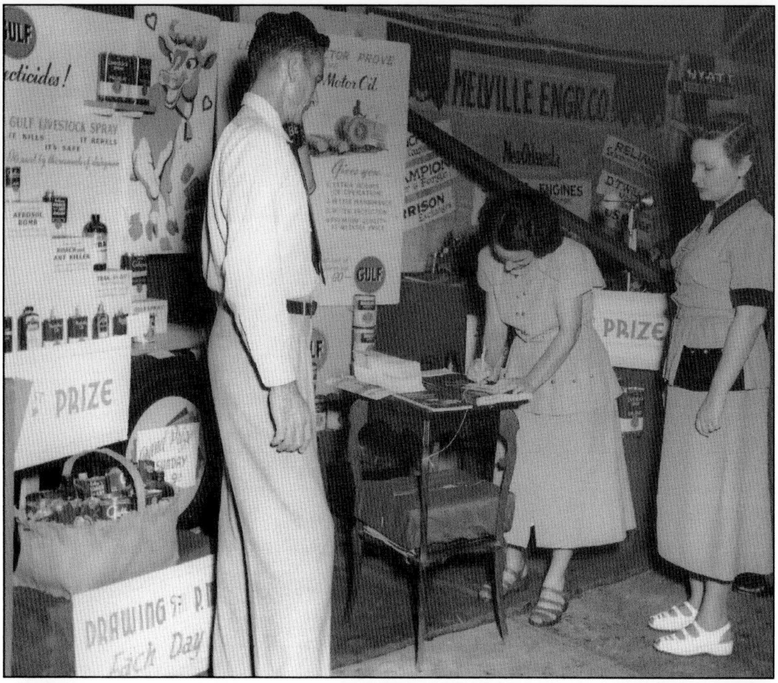

Wherever large groups of people would be, commercial vendors were sure to follow. Tens of thousands of people flocked to the state fair and were met by salesmen with a solution for whatever ailed them. (Courtesy of the Lemman family.)

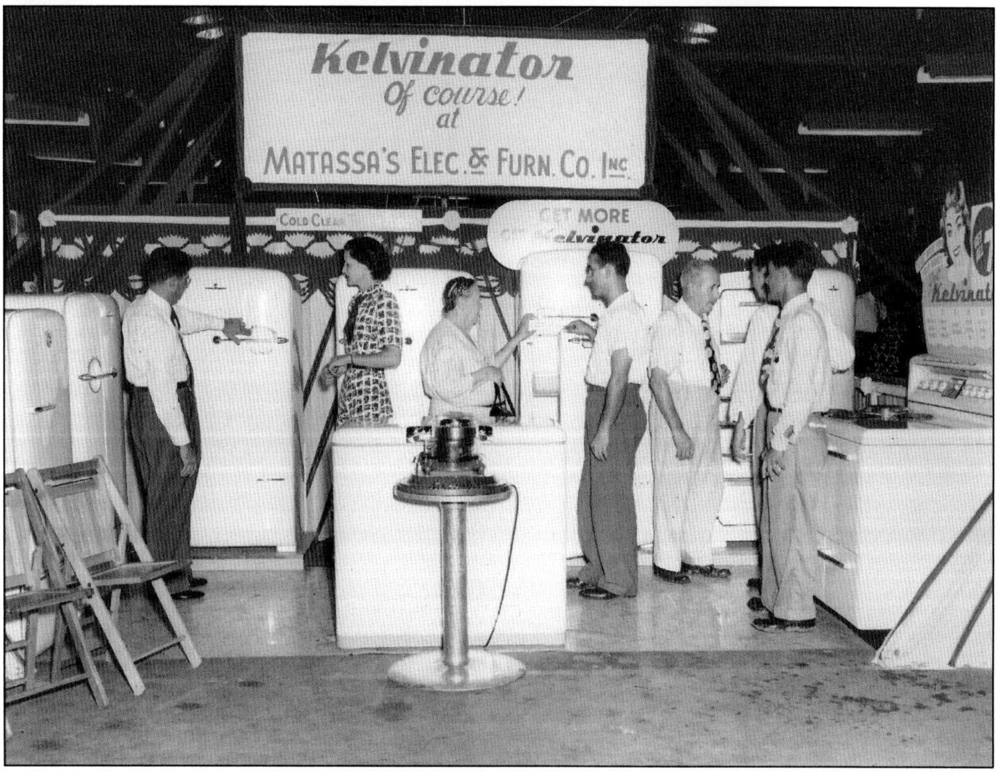

All of the latest appliances and conveniences available were on display at the state fair. Who would want a kitchen without the latest refrigerator and stove from Matassa's Electric and Furniture Company? (Courtesy of the Lemman family.)

Shown is the opening ceremony at the South Louisiana State Fair. Bands from all over South Louisiana would march and take part in the celebration. (Courtesy of the Lemman family.)

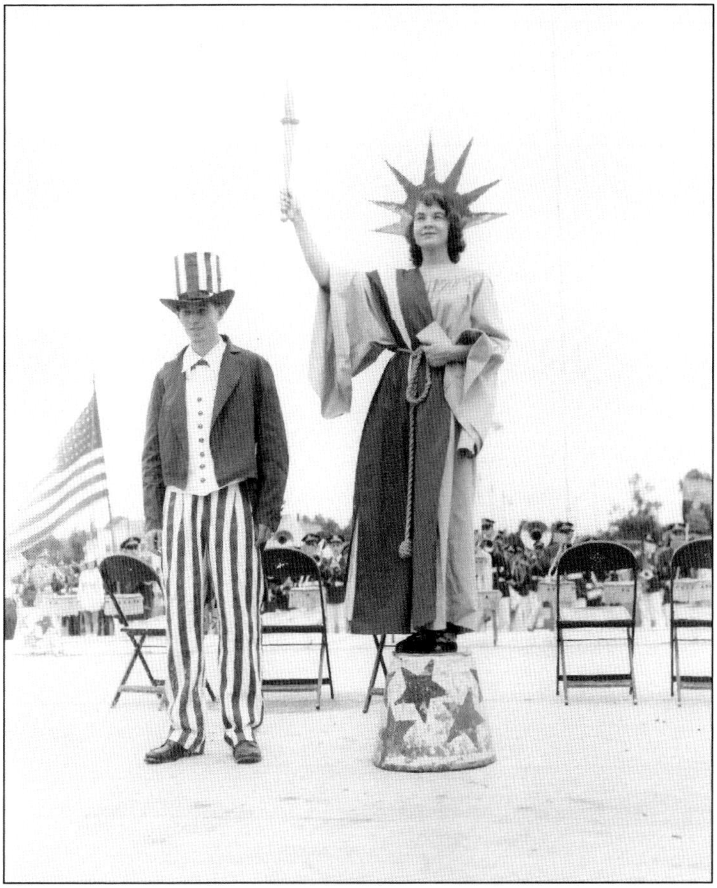

Entertainment was a big part of the South Louisiana State Fair activities. High-wire acts were among the showstoppers. (Courtesy of the Lemman family.)

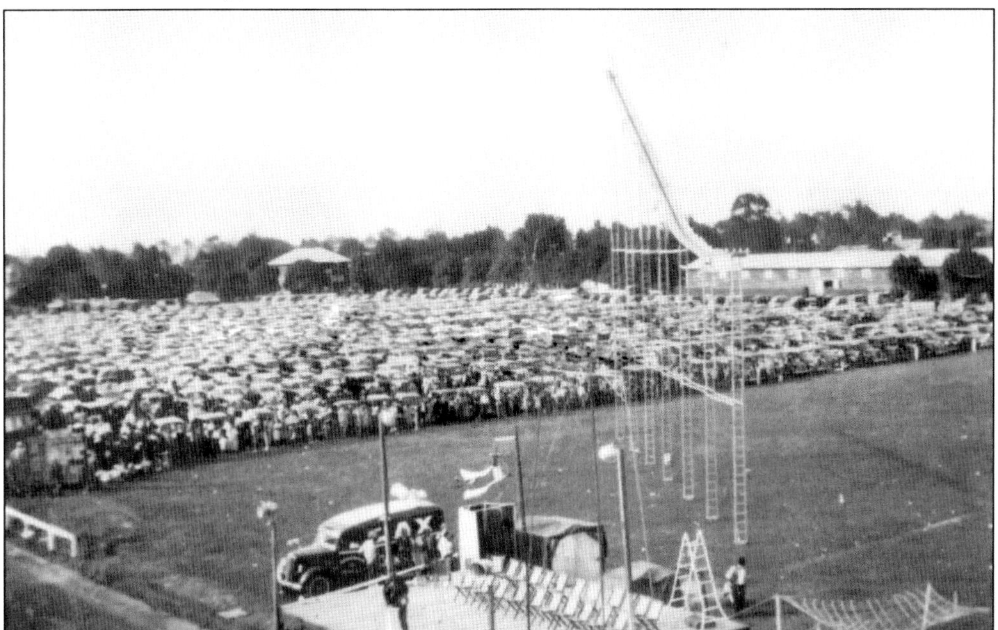

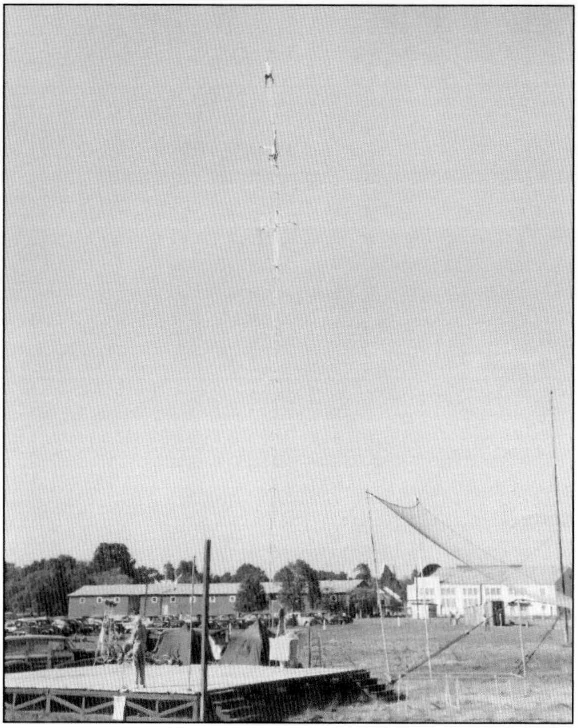

Entertainers prepare and rehearse prior to the big show that evening. Notice the acrobat at the very top and another a few feet below him. The performers were of the highest quality and would even be written about in *Billboard*, an entertainment magazine. (Courtesy of the Lemman family.)

High school bands gather around the main stage in preparation for the day's events. Some schools would spend a whole day riding in a bus just to get to Donaldsonville. (Courtesy of the Lemman family.)

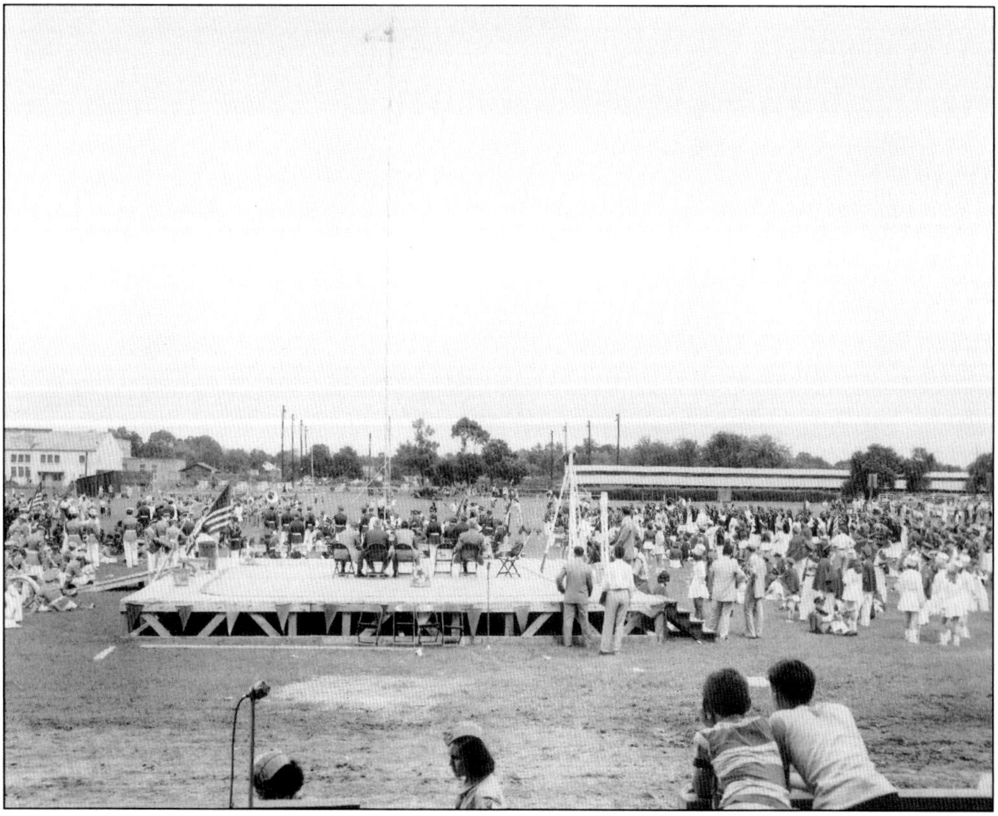

Four

IN NOMINE PATRIS ET FILII ET SPIRITUS SANCTI AMEN

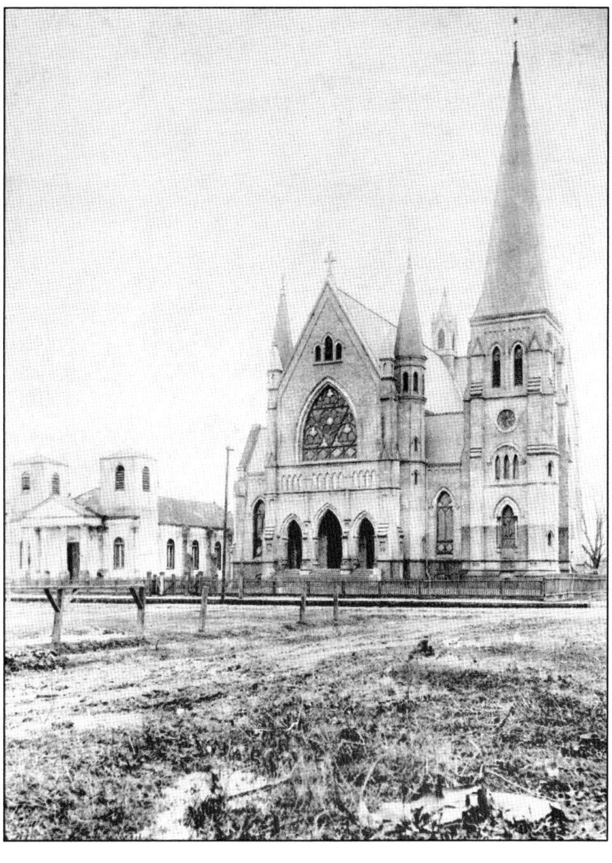

A drive for funds to construct a new Catholic church, pictured here on the right, ignited the spark that began a church war lasting from 1874 to 1891. On the left is the old church, built in 1840 and demolished in 1911. The wood post and rails in front of the church were for tying up horses during services. (Courtesy of the Sotile family.)

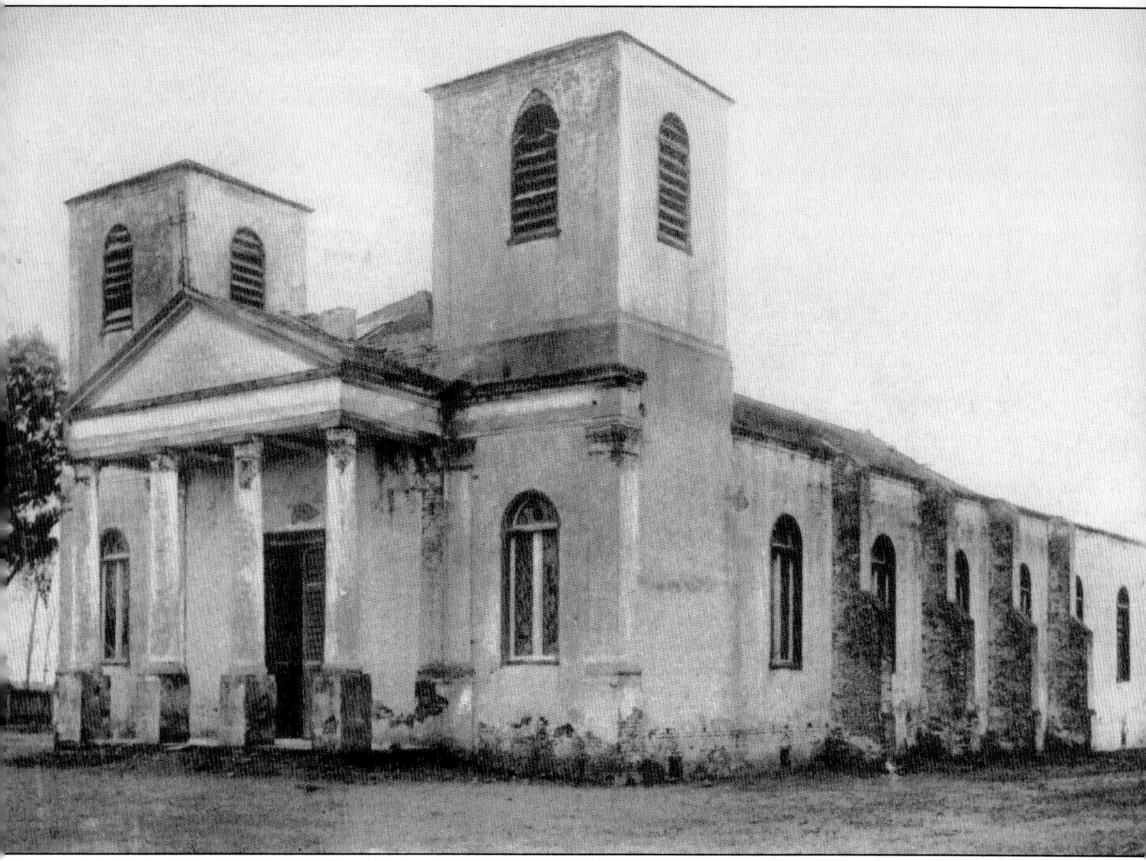

Ascension Catholic Church parish was established on August 15, 1772, by order of King Charles of Spain. Fr. Angelos Reuillogados was named the first pastor of the little parish at the juncture of Bayou Lafourche and the Mississippi River. The original flock was largely made up of Acadian exiles. Completed in 1843, the Ascension Catholic Church, shown here, was actually the third Catholic church in Donaldsonville. The late Sidney Marchand says in *Acadian Exiles in the Golden Coast of Louisiana* that it is doubtful that the church was a new structure throughout but possibly a renovation of the church of 1819. (Courtesy of the Landry family.)

The history of the Ascension Catholic Church was stained with a 2.5-year closure between rival groups. On Easter Sunday, March 25, 1883, after Easter Mass, the church was closed and locked. The Blessed Sacrament was removed from the tabernacle and taken to St. Vincent Covent. A petition to form a corporation to manage the temporal affairs of the church was circulated and signed by the Catholics of Donaldsonville. (Courtesy of the Rodrigue family.)

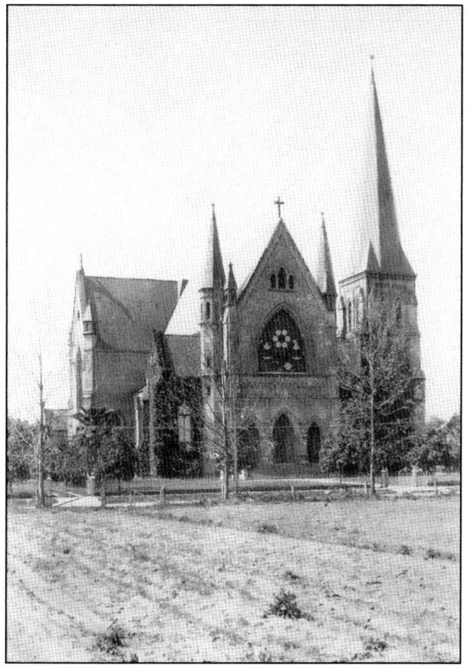

Not all parishioners accepted the new corporation and a battle ensued. On June 27, 1885, the *Donaldsonville Chief* reported that it had it on good authority that the archbishop would send another priest. Mass was resumed on July 5, 1885. (Courtesy of the Sotile family.)

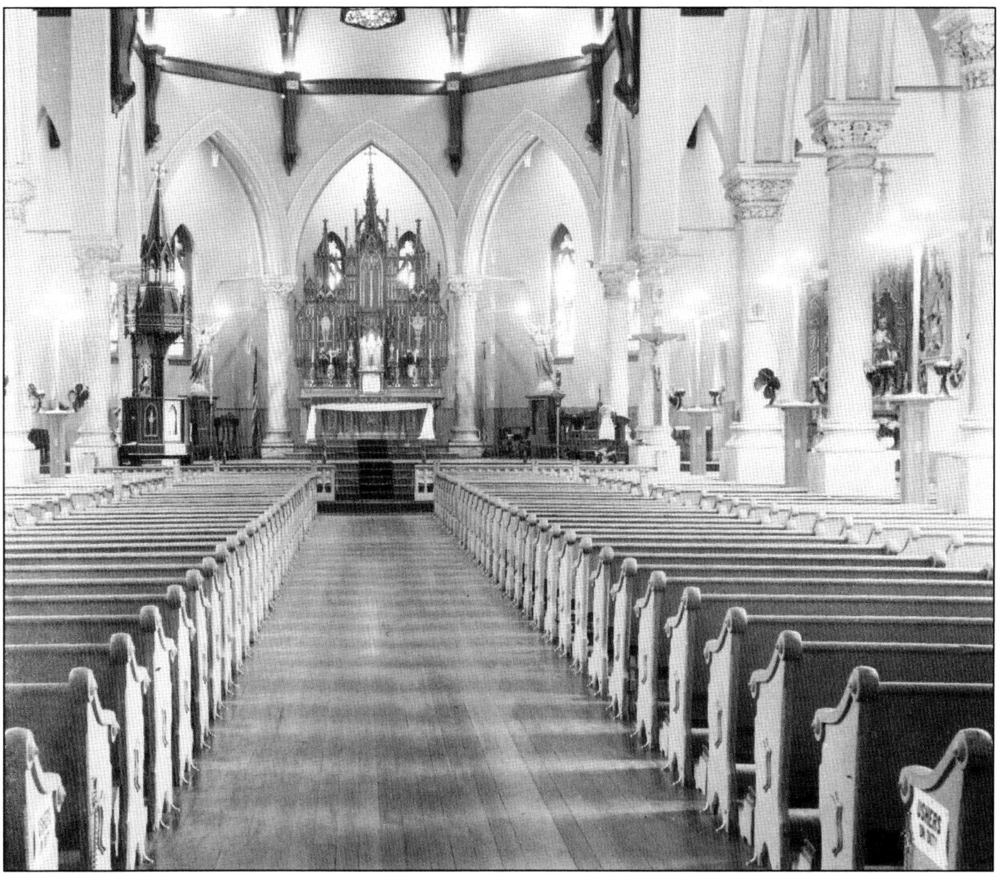

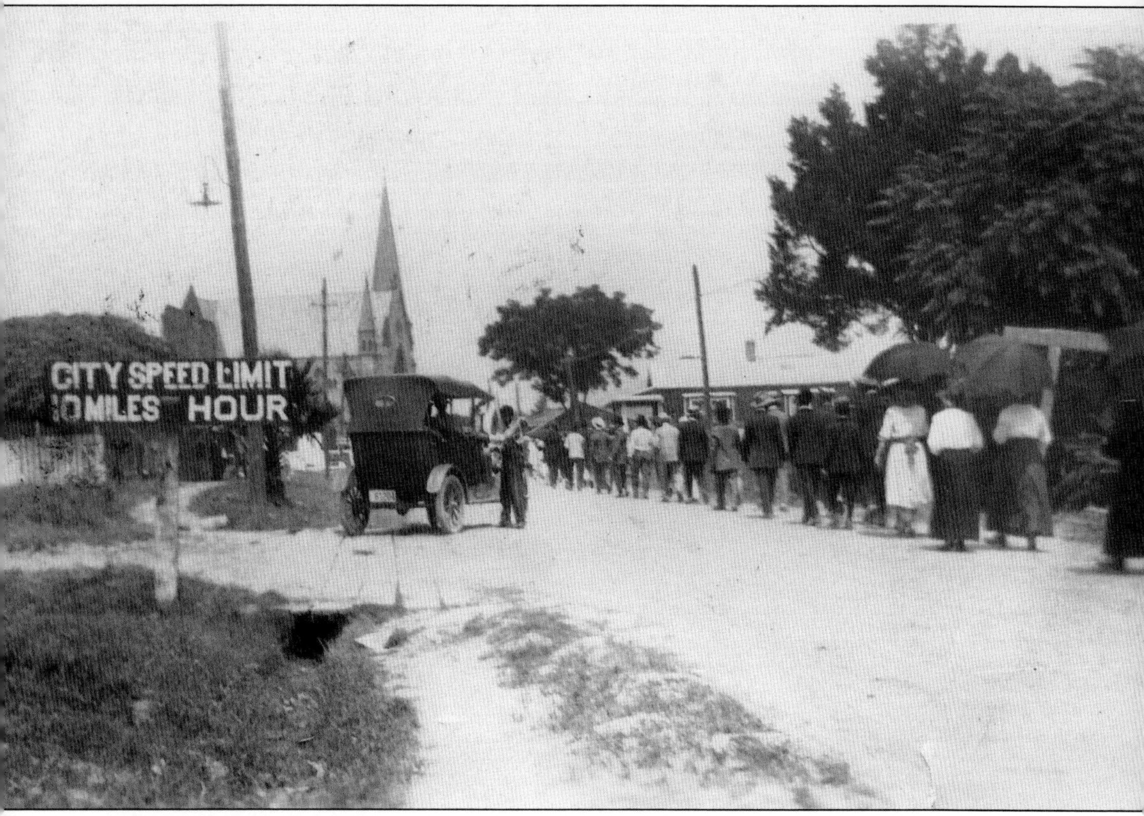

As the story of St. Amico is told, in 1912, Anthony Musco and his wife, Maria Micolina DiTella, were praying for their ill son. St. Amico appeared to them and Anthony promised that if their son was spared, they would build a chapel in honor of St. Amico and give thanks until their death. The boy survived and the Muscos kept their promise. (Courtesy of the Poirrier family.)

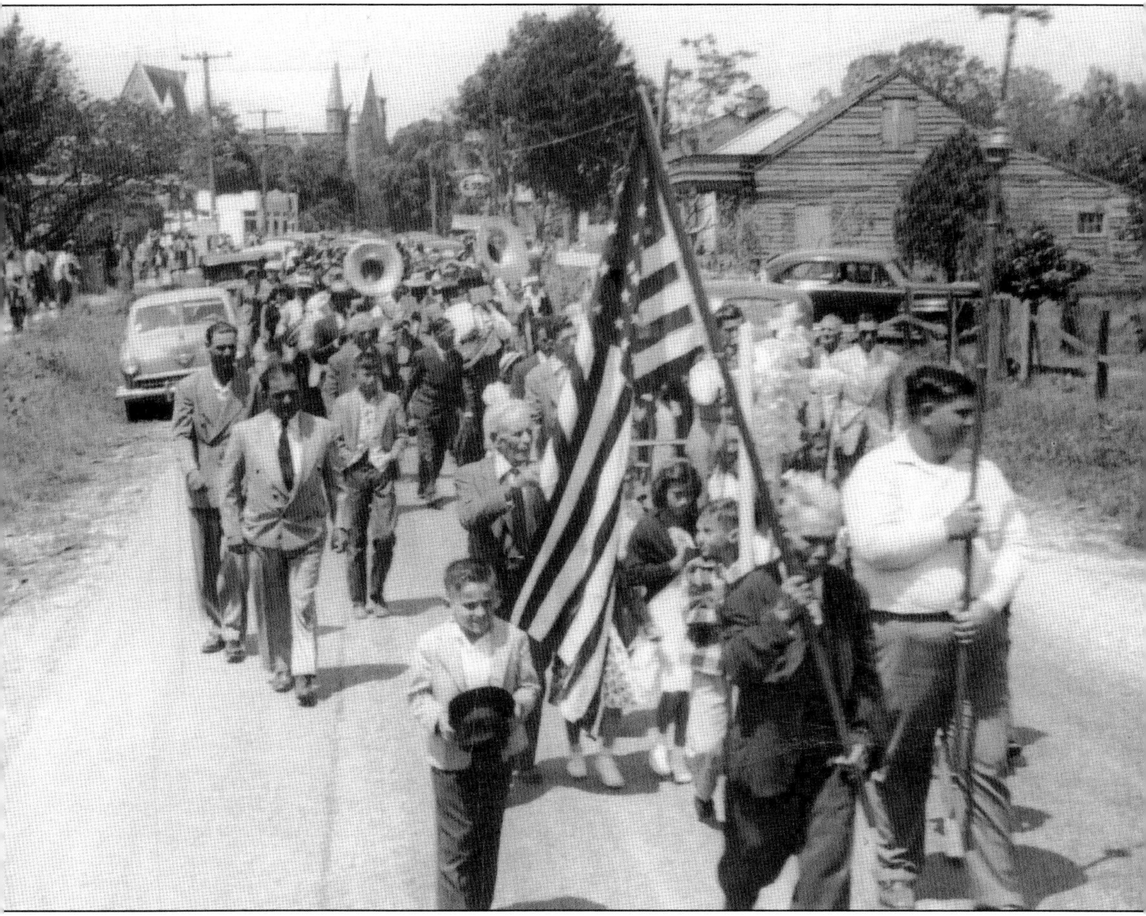

The Musco family, their friends and neighbors, many barefoot, would make the 2.5 mile journey every year to the Ascension Catholic Church for the blessing by the priest. It took eight people to carry the statue of St. Amico. This tradition was carried on and grew through the 1960s. Hundreds of people would watch or join the procession every year until the church decided to quit participating in the blessing in 2001. (Courtesy of the Poirrier family.)

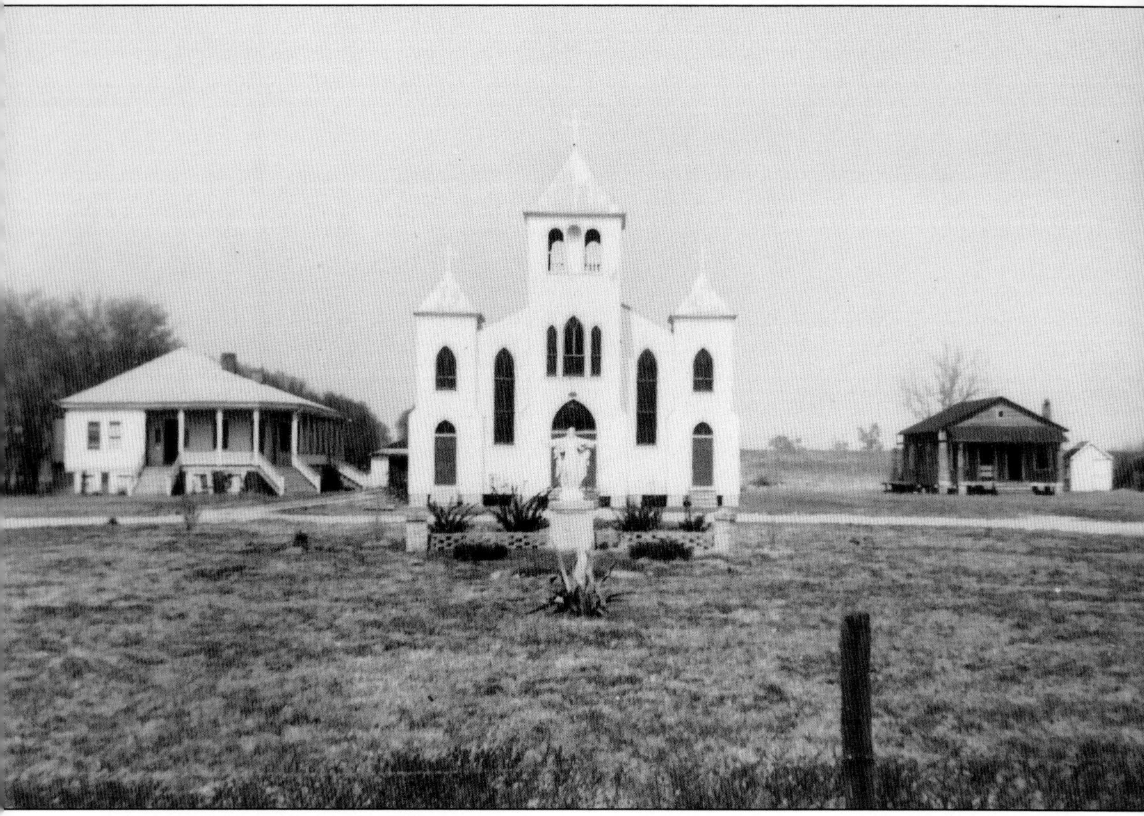

The residents of the small community organized St. Francis of Assisi in Smoke Bend after Father Ceuppens left Ascension Catholic Church over a disagreement with the churchwardens. Smoke Bend parish has its own parish hall and cemetery and served as the headquarters for the Smoke Bend School at one time. (Courtesy of the Marchand family.)

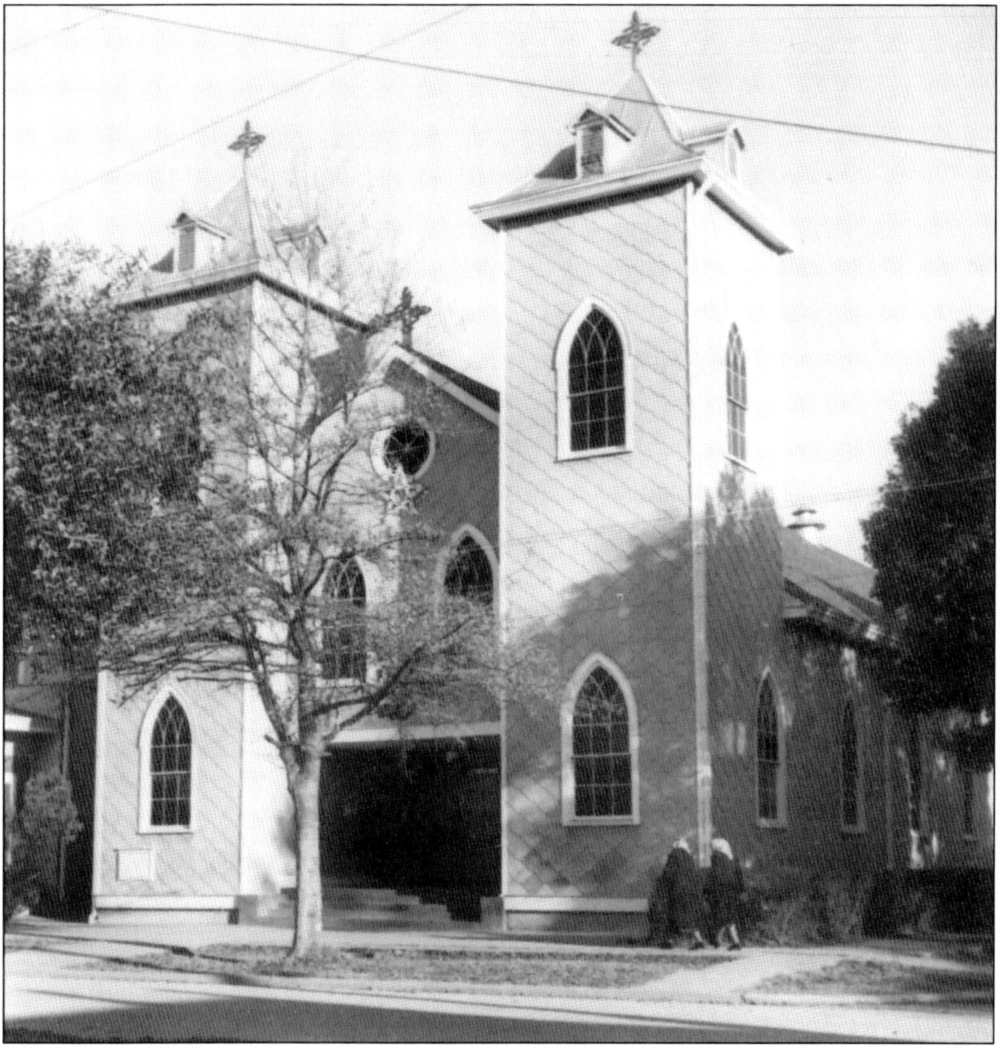

Catherine of Siena was born in Italy. As a child, she could see guardian angels and became a Dominican tertiary at the age of 16. Her visions of Christ, Mary, and many of the saints and her theological knowledge astounded the church, especially considering her lack of formal education. St. Catherine lived only to 33, and when her body was exhumed in 1430, people were astounded to find it to be incorrupt. April 29 was declared as a feast day in her honor. On January 24, 1926, St. Catherine of Siena Church was dedicated. (Courtesy of the Marchand family.)

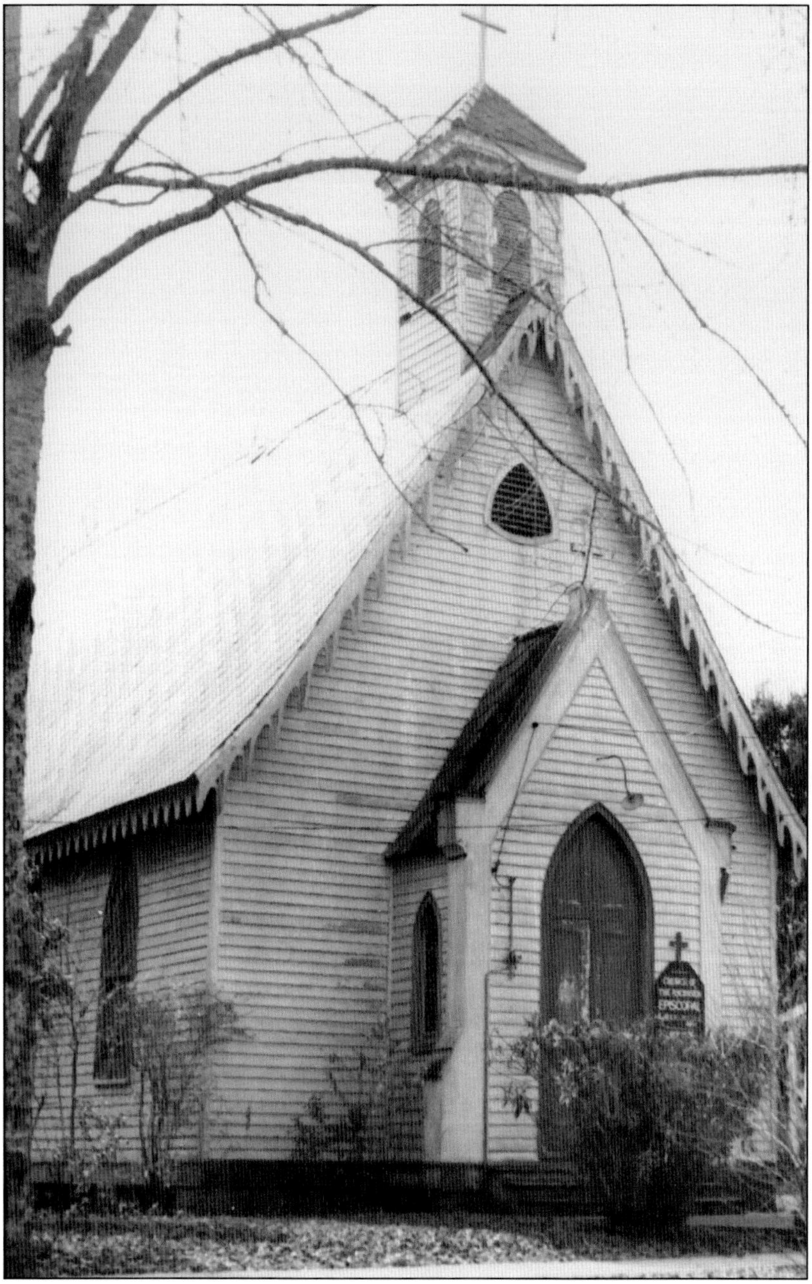

The Episcopal Church of Ascension was organized in 1842, and services were conducted intermittently by visiting clergymen from established parishes in the diocese. During the Civil War, services were suspended from 1861 to 1870. Reverend Dillon-Lee of Bayou Goula then reorganized the parish. Former Louisiana governor Henry Johnson donated a valuable piece of property to the congregation when the church was chartered in 1852. Standing on the site was the Johnson Female Academy, founded in 1838, and the deed stipulated that the "large two-story building and school standing on it should be used as a rectory and Episcopal Institute." The academy later became the Johnson Institute, which was torn down in 1873 to make room for the Episcopal Church of Ascension. The church still stands today. (Courtesy of the Marchand family.)

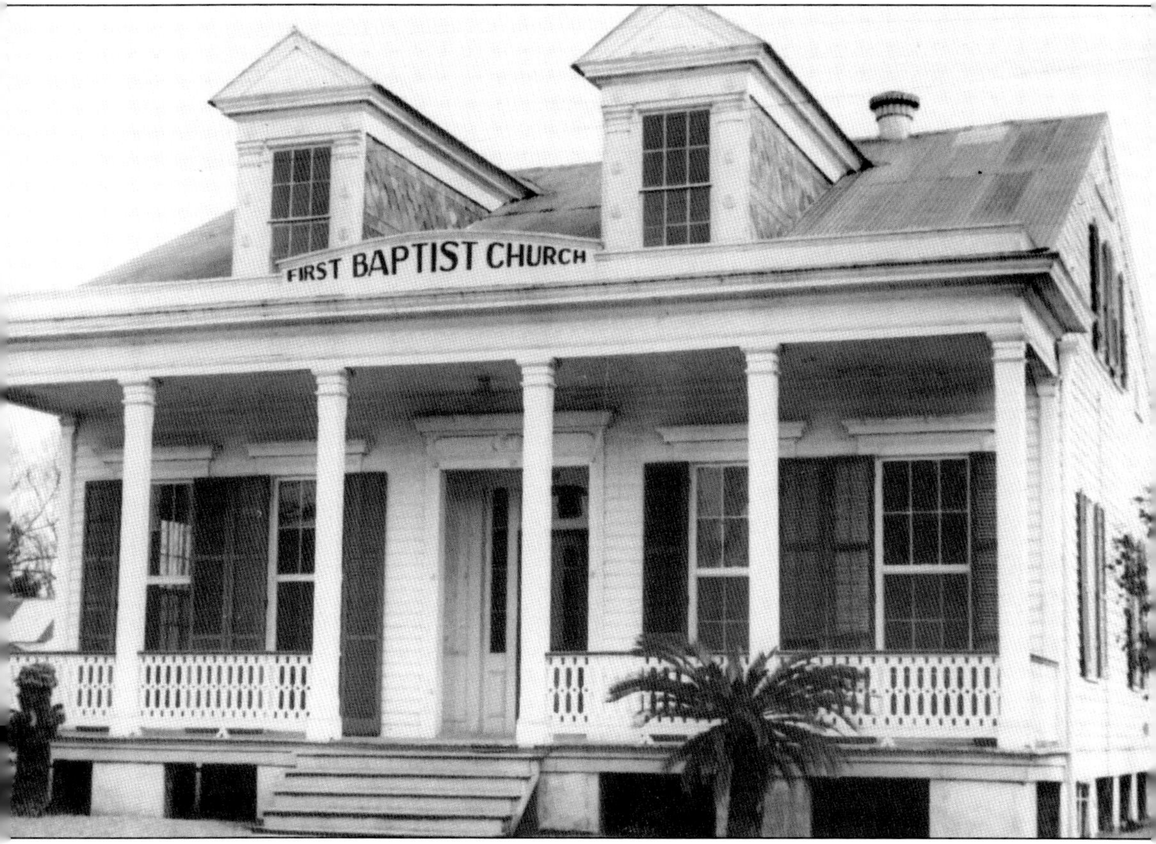

The First Baptist Church of Donaldsonville was established in 1939 with a membership of only 17. The church property at the corner of Iberville and Chetimaches Streets was acquired a few years later. For several years, the old residence at the corner, formerly owned by Henry Goette, served the Baptist congregation as a church. A modern brick edifice, erected adjacent to the old house, now provides a setting for services for the greatly enlarged congregation. (Courtesy of the Marchand family.)

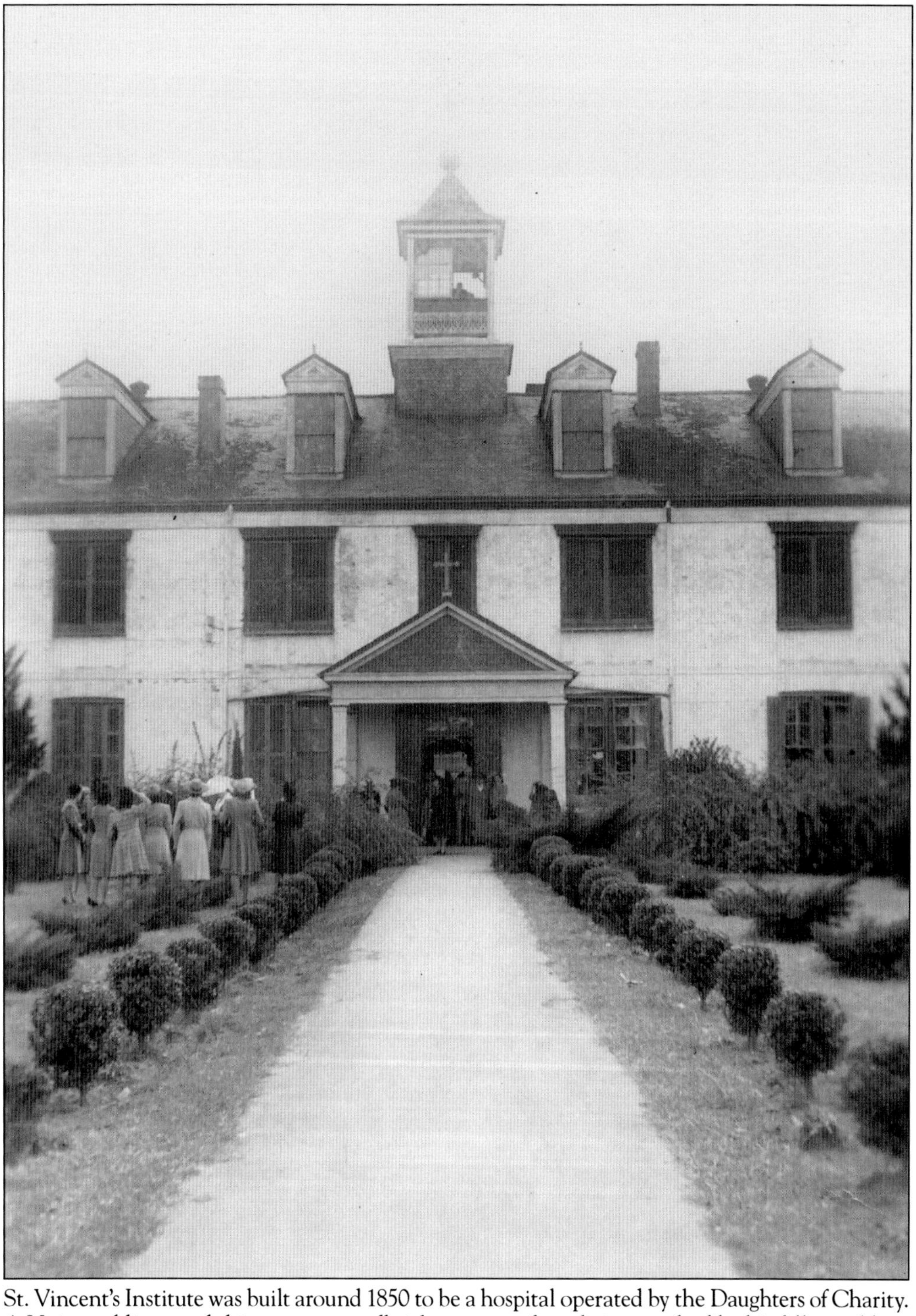

St. Vincent's Institute was built around 1850 to be a hospital operated by the Daughters of Charity. A Union soldier saved this two-story redbrick structure from being torched by his fellow soldiers during the Civil War. The hospital was closed in 1861 because of lack of state funding. It was then used as an orphanage, convent, and boarding school. It continues to serve the Catholic school system today. (Courtesy of the Landry family.)

The Daughters of Charity were well known for their "flying nuns" apparel and the tremendous work they performed in the community. They aided in offering medical services, teaching, and even taking in orphans during their service in Donaldsonville. The Daughters of Charity withdrew from Donaldsonville in 1987 after 142 years of service here. (Courtesy of the Lemman family.)

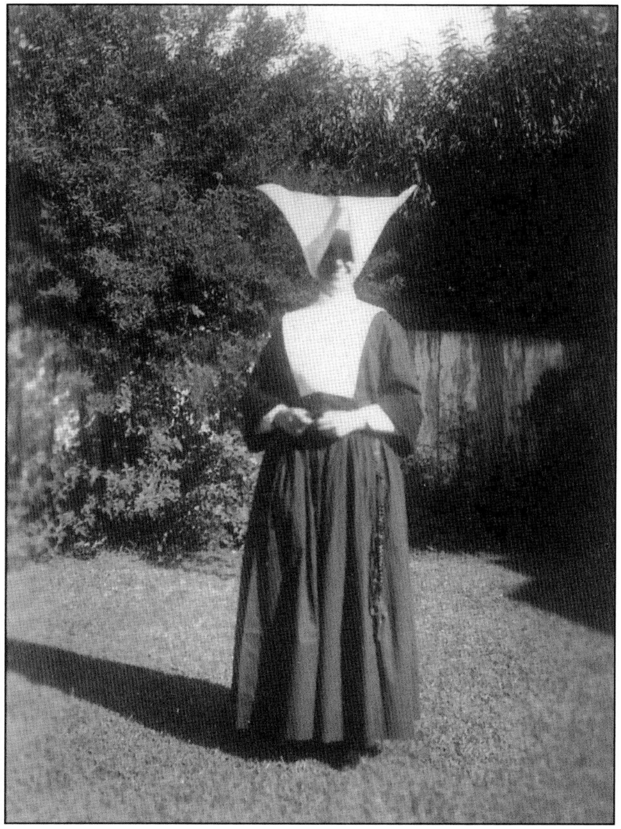

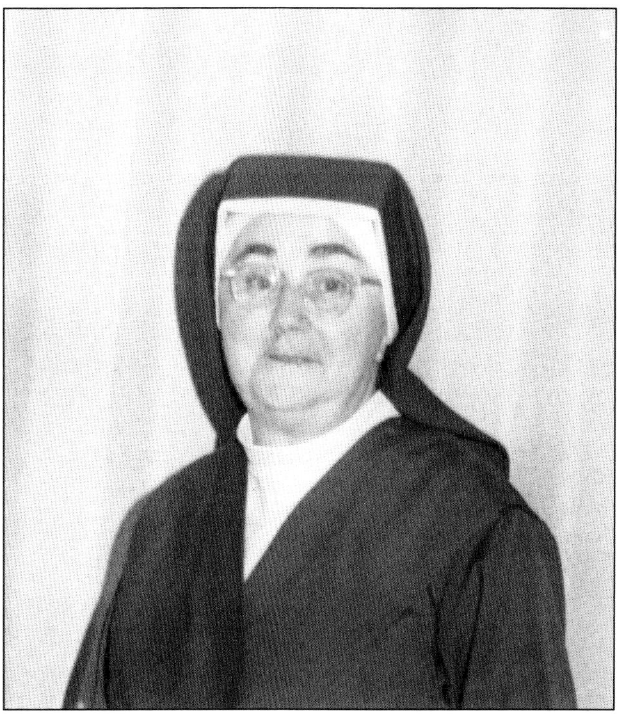

Sr. Marie Fogerty was assigned to St. Vincent's Institute in 1931. She was known for collecting food and clothes for the poor. While she had a compassionate heart, she could be as tough as any Marine Corps drill sergeant. Many misbehaved kids spent their cooling-off period behind her famous piano. Sister Marie died in 1981. (Courtesy of the Marchand family.)

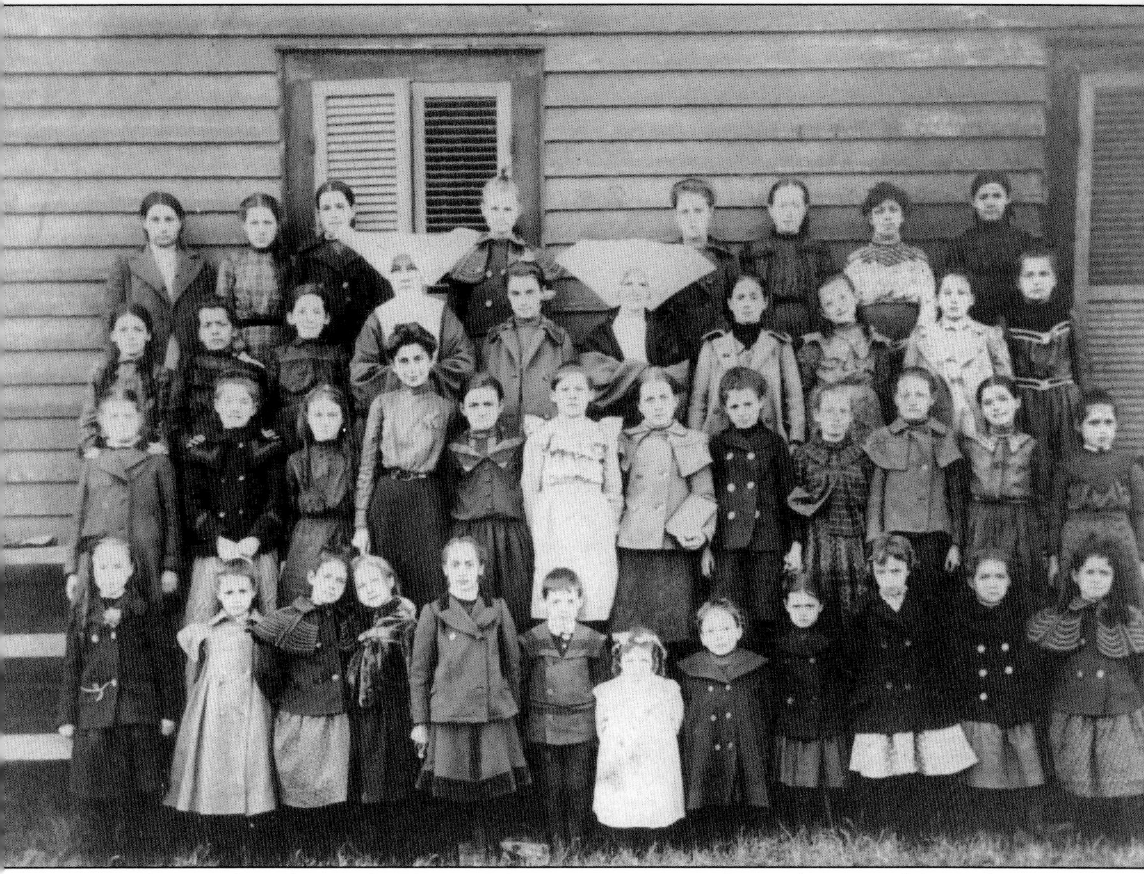

Students and teachers at St. Vincent's Institute are pictured near the turn of the 20th century. The Daughters of Charity received criticism for teaching in English instead of French but soon redeemed themselves with their quality education. (Courtesy of the Lemman family.)

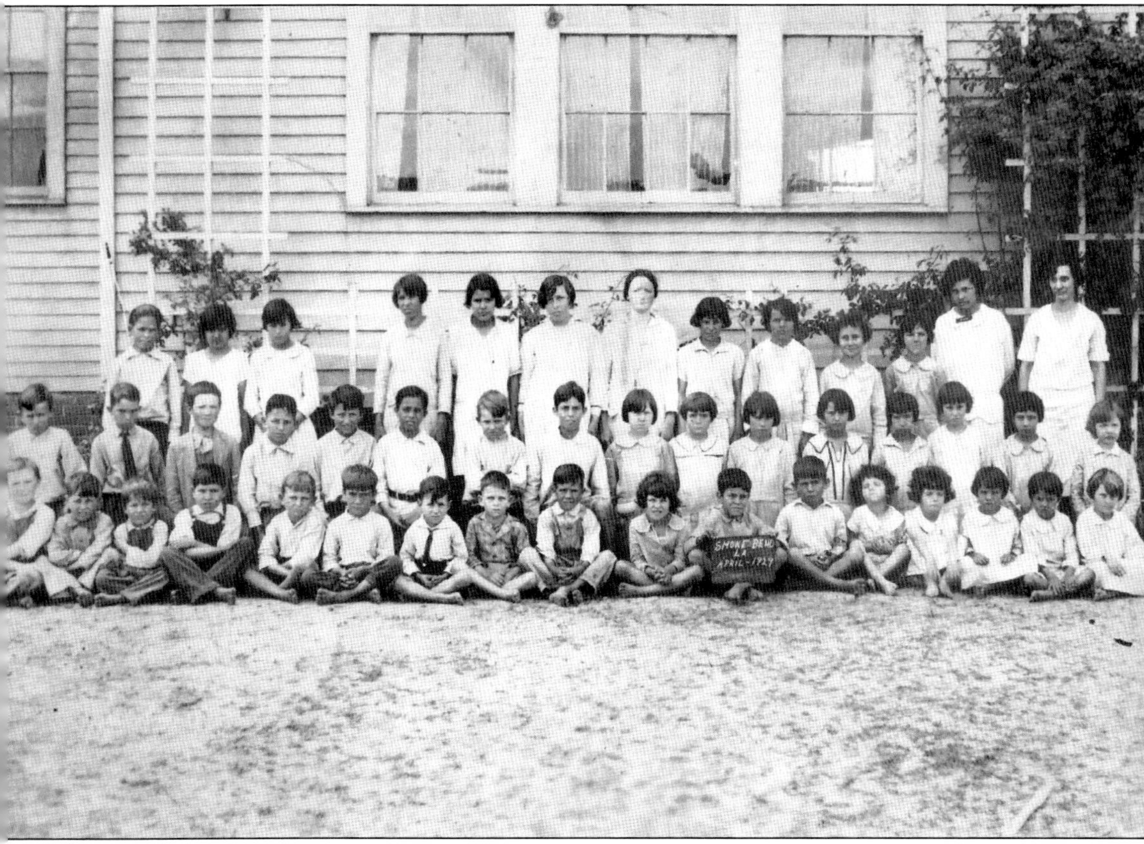

This is Smoke Bend School around 1929. Pictured from left to right are (first row) Nat Gridewell, Earl Alonzo, Dyer Veron, Clarence Alonzo, Schuyler Veron, Delmayne Veron, Uyless Rome, Carlton Rome, Earl Lanoix, Rose Mary Alonzo and Earl Veron, Oneil Veron, LeBlanc twins, Una Lanoix, Gertie Rodrigue, and Catherine Brasset; (second row) Milton Veron, Penrose Alonzo, Francis Bridewell, Wesley Rome, Wesley Veron, George Veron, Oscar Lanoix, Belmont Veron, Majorie Dill, Alibi Alonzo, Rita Brasset, Mildred Dill, Roberta Rodrigue, Una May Veron, Beryl Dugas, and Margie Richard; (third row) Anna Giambrone, Eunice Rodrigue, Rena Guedry, Percy Falcon (He ducked just as the picture was taken.), Mabel Falcon, May Dugas, Ellen Bridewell, Nita Brasset, Florence Lanoix, Rose Mary Dugas, Laura Dill, Mrs. Beulah Rome, and Mrs. Henry Dugas. (Courtesy of the Regira family.)

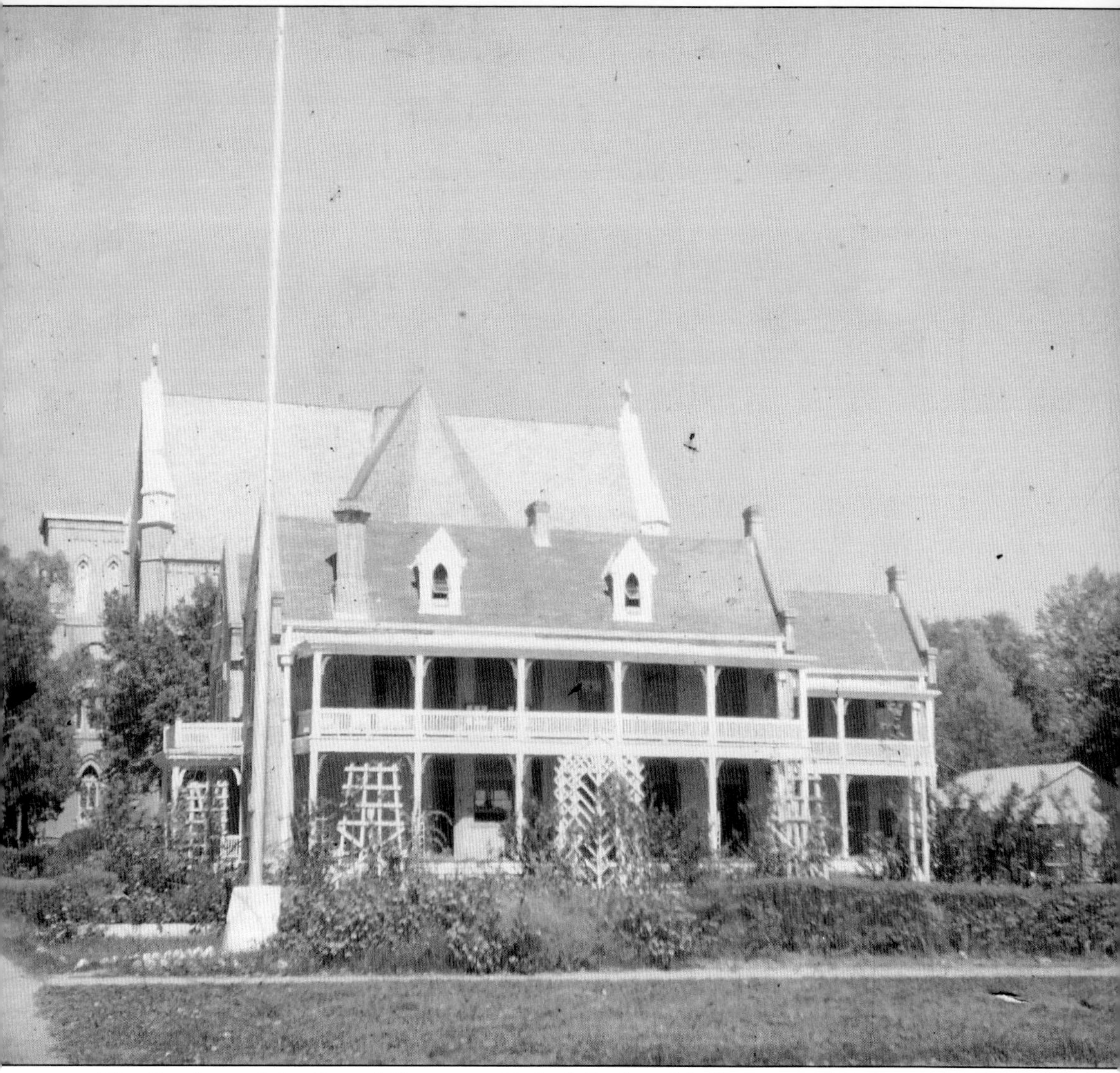

The Brothers of the Sacred Heart established St. Joseph's Commercial Institute, a school for boys, in 1885. In 1916, the school moved to the Presbytery, also known as the Brother's School. In 1933, the name was changed to Catholic High School, then in 1955 to Ascension Catholic High School. (Courtesy of the Marchand family.)

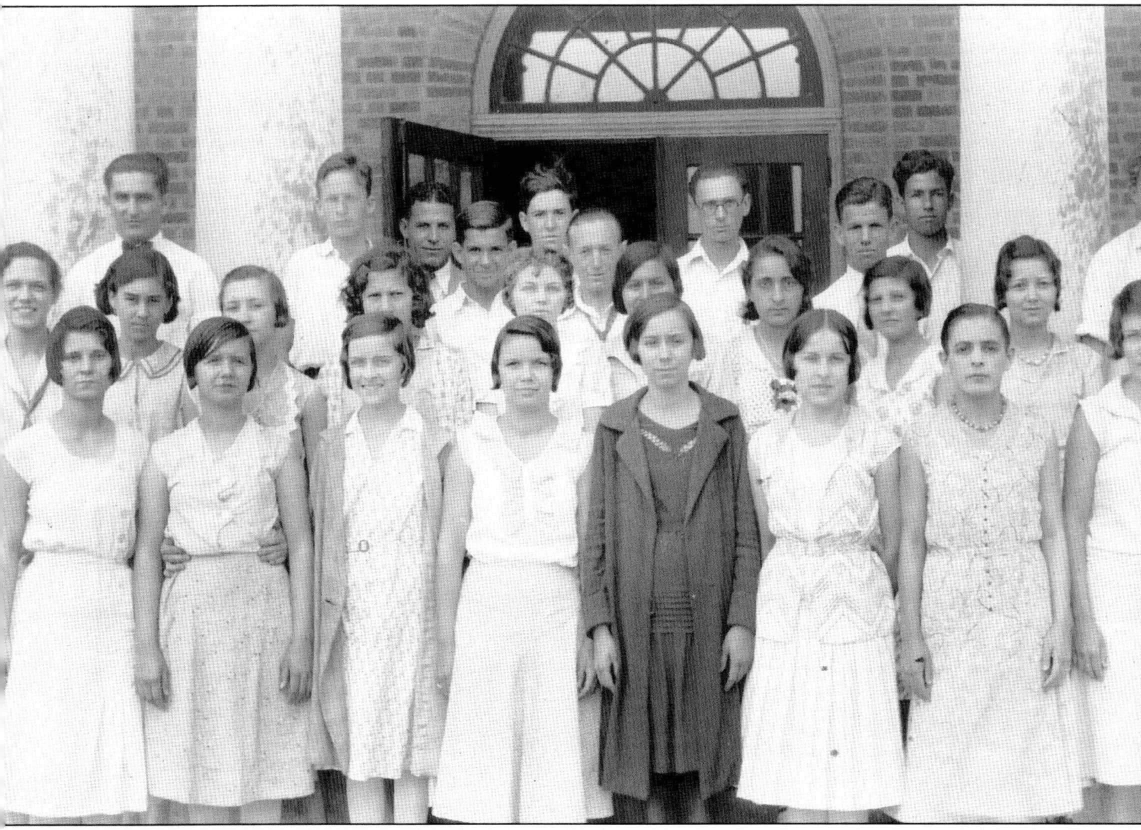

This is the Donaldsonville High School 10th-grade class of 1930–1931. Pictured are, from left to right, (first row) Pearl Denoux, Daisy Acosta, Lillian Haffman, Hazel Guedry, Leona Gaudin, Frances Bonnecane, Josephine Giofne, and Octavia Babin; (second row) Elaise Docladie, Gladys Simoneaux, Ruth Retit, Sylvia Comeaux, Ruby Aucoin, Rosa Sanchez, Marie Frorenza, Annette Bacala, Rena Laland, and Ethel Acosta; (third row) Paul Giofne, Neal Blanchard, Professor LeBlanc, Joe Rivet, Maurice LeBlanc, George Zeringue, Waldron Oubre, Lynden Bejou, and Ray Hebert. (Courtesy of the Marchand family.)

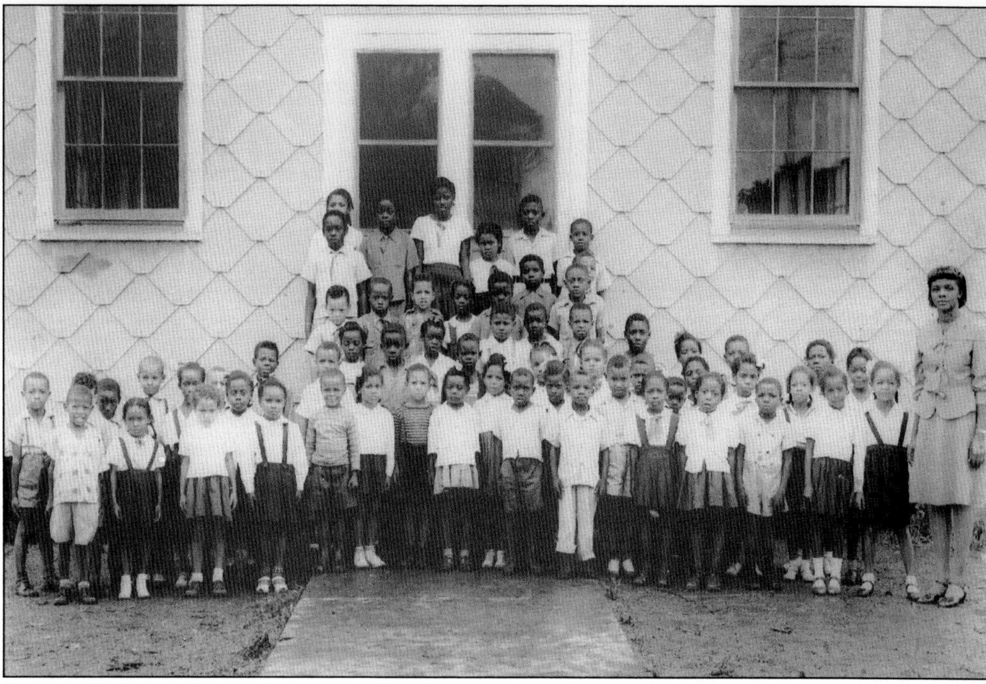

In 1924, Father Dubernard, pastor of the Church of the Ascension of our Lord, brought the Sisters of the Holy Family from New Orleans to establish a Catholic school for black children. It was called the St. Catherine's School. Mary James was a teacher. (Courtesy of Kathie Hambrick.)

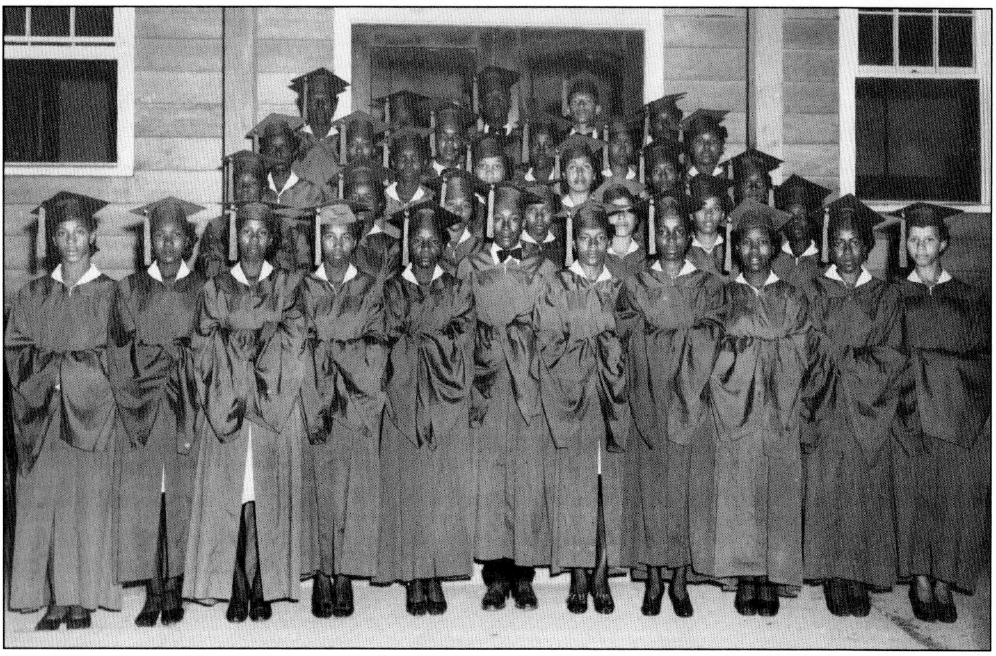

The Donaldsonville Academy was the first Donaldsonville public school for the education of African American children in the late 1800s. Lowery High School was constructed after World War II. It was merged with Donaldsonville High School in 1970. This is the Lowery High School graduation class around 1945. (Courtesy of Kathie Hambrick.)

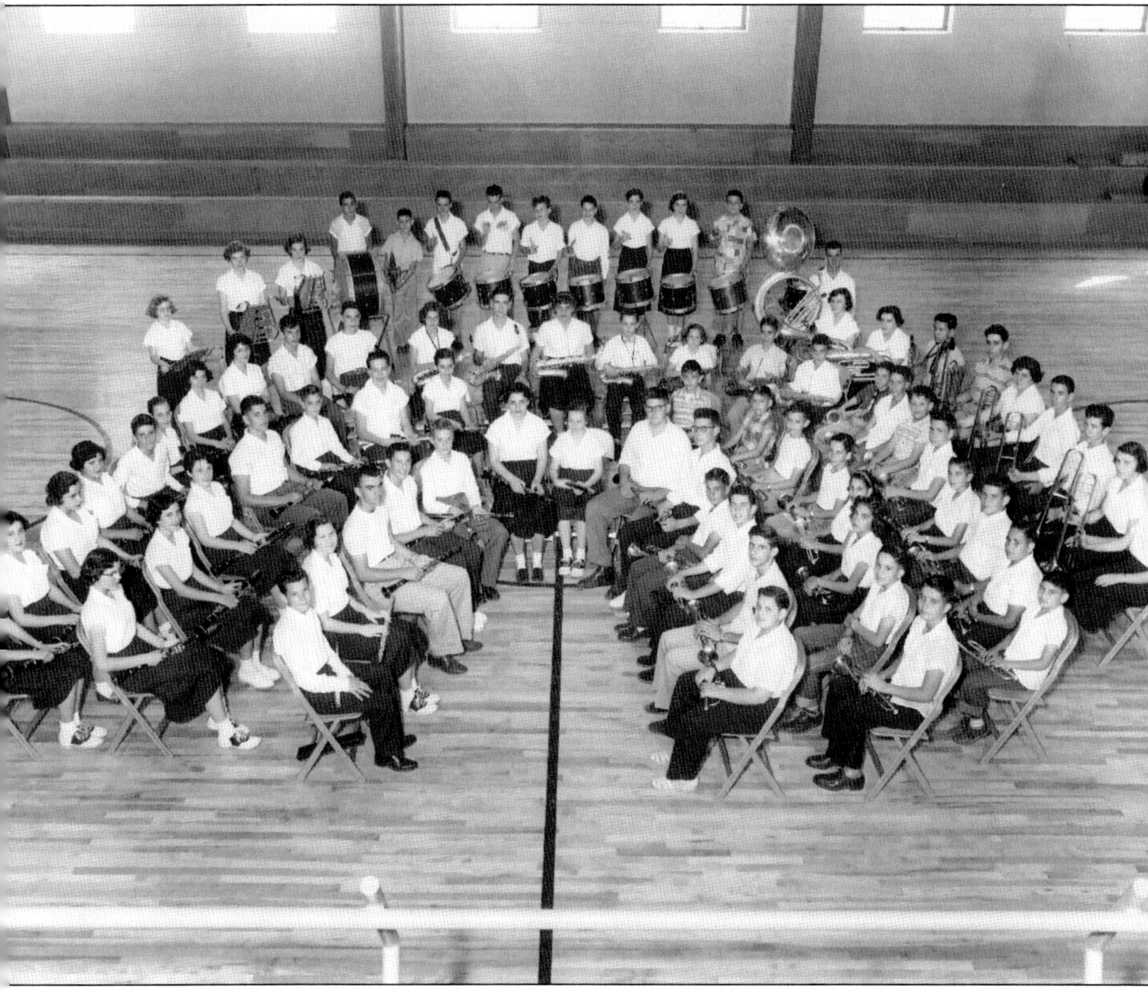

Tom Jack Nizzo was an employee of Ascension Parish Public School District as band teacher at Galvez Middle School. He would teach all day and then drive back across the river to Ascension Catholic High School to teach band in the evening and on Saturdays for free. The band could not afford new marching uniforms, but Nizzo managed to get Louisiana State University to donate their used uniforms to the school. It helped that LSU and ACHS had the same team colors, purple and gold. Nizzo is well remembered for his glasses that were always resting at the end of his nose. Often, when he wanted to make a point, he would tilt his head down and look over them at people. He instilled discipline and a deep sense of camaraderie in the band. Every member of his band was important. This is the 1955 ACHS band. (Courtesy of the Mistretta family.)

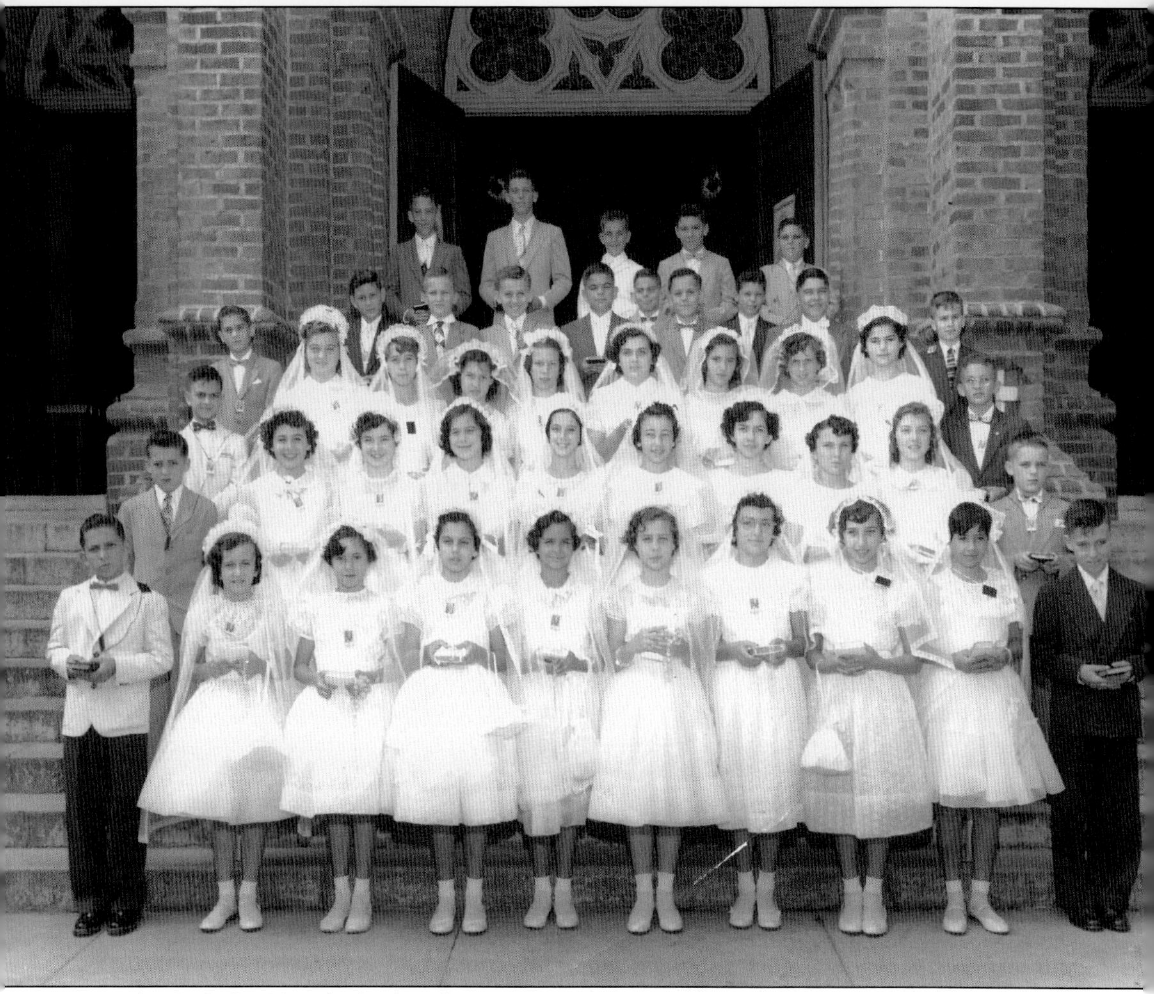

In the Catholic Church, the first three sacraments were Baptism, Confirmation, and Communion. The sacrament of Confirmation was to more perfectly bind the baptized to the Church and enrich the strength of the Holy Spirit in the soul. Pictured here on the steps of the Ascension Catholic Church is the 1955 confirmation class. (Courtesy of the Mistretta family.)

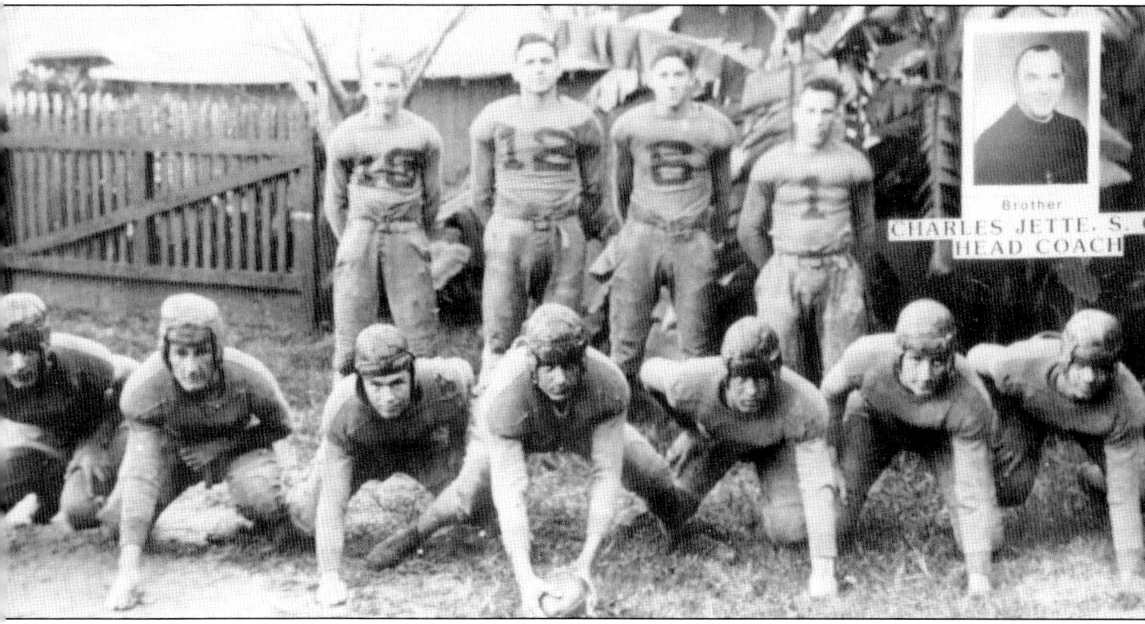

This is the 1930 Catholic High School football team. From left to right are (first row) John Blanchard, right end; Ernest Veron, right tackle; Andre Waguespack, right guard; Brennan Gisclard, center; Harry Guillot, left guard; Nicholas Costanza, left tackle; and Joe Graffeo, left end; (second row) Claude Hymel, quarterback; Evans Casso, fullback; Raymond Landry, left halfback; Jack Gremillion, right halfback; and coach Brother Charles Jette, S.C. (Courtesy of the Capone family.)

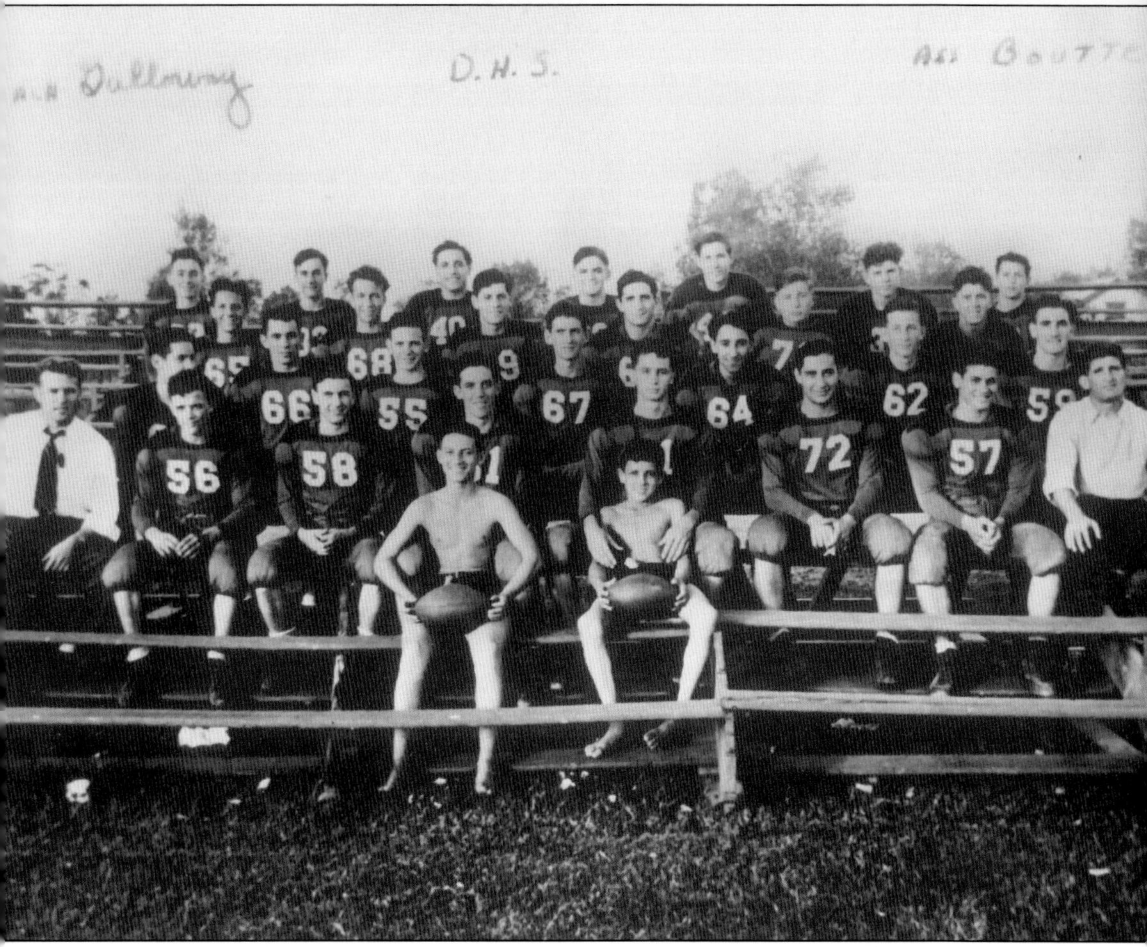

Galloway launched his football-coaching career at Donaldsonville High in 1939 after turning down an offer from Mount Hermon High. He later went on to coach at Southeastern University. Speaking of his success at Southeastern, Galloway said, "I believe sincerity, hard work and preparation are the keys." The highlight of his college coaching career came when quarterback Ray "Coon" Porta led the 1954 Lions to a perfect 9-0 season, which included a 13-7 victory over Southern Mississippi. With Southern Mississippi defeating Alabama and Alabama beating LSU, Southeastern used comparative scores to claim the unofficial "state championship" that year. Floyd Boutte became head coach after Stan Galloway left and won the state championship in 1954. The 1939 DHS football team is pictured with Coach Stan Galloway (left) and assistant coach Floyd Boutte (right). (Courtesy of the LeBlanc family.)

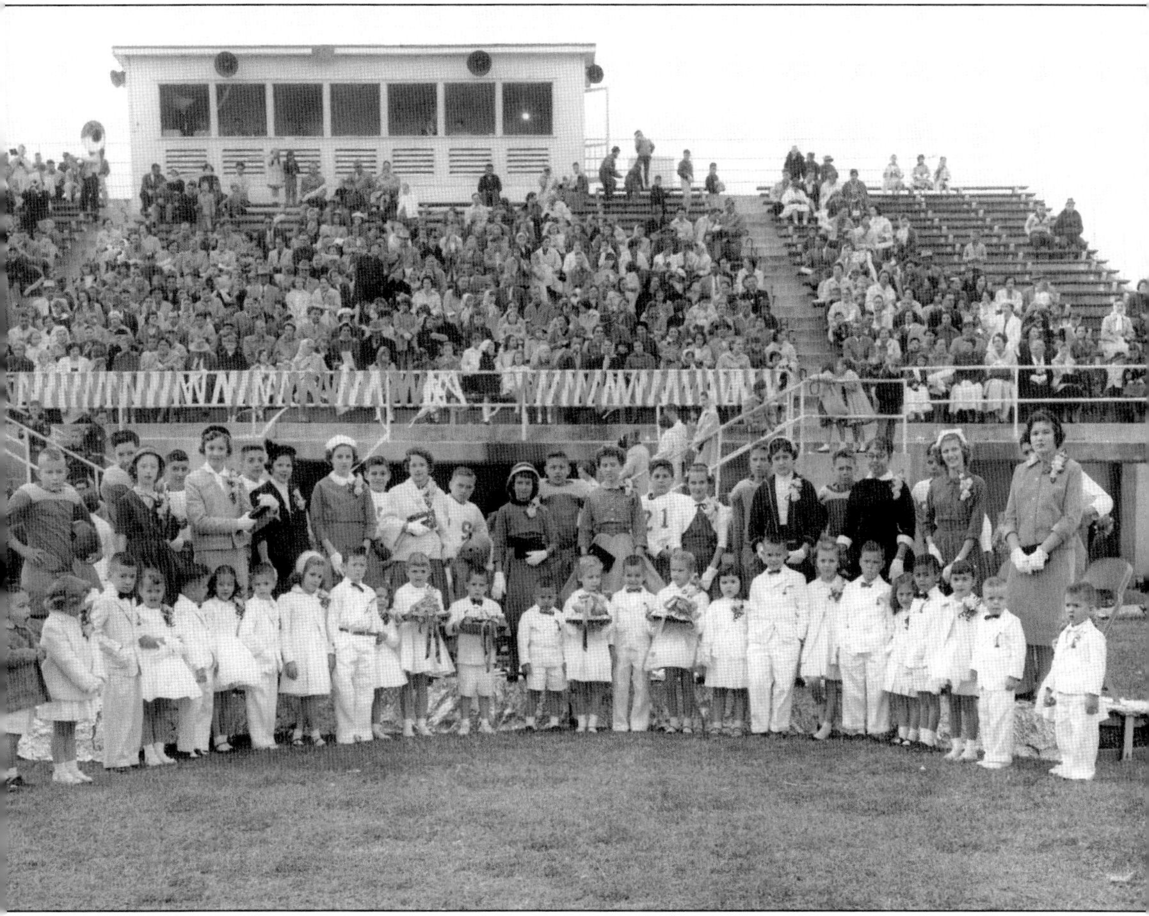

Pictured around 1957 are some football players from Donaldsonville's Tiny and Mites Leagues. In the second row are the girls in the court, from left to right, Mary Joel Vetter, Sarah Tortorich, Janie Graffeo, Mary Aucoin, Sandra Schexnayder, Linda Burns, Sheryl Burns, Susan Inness, Virginia Denino, Skipper Milano, Paula Zeringue, and Rosemary Simms. (Courtesy of the Mistretta family.)

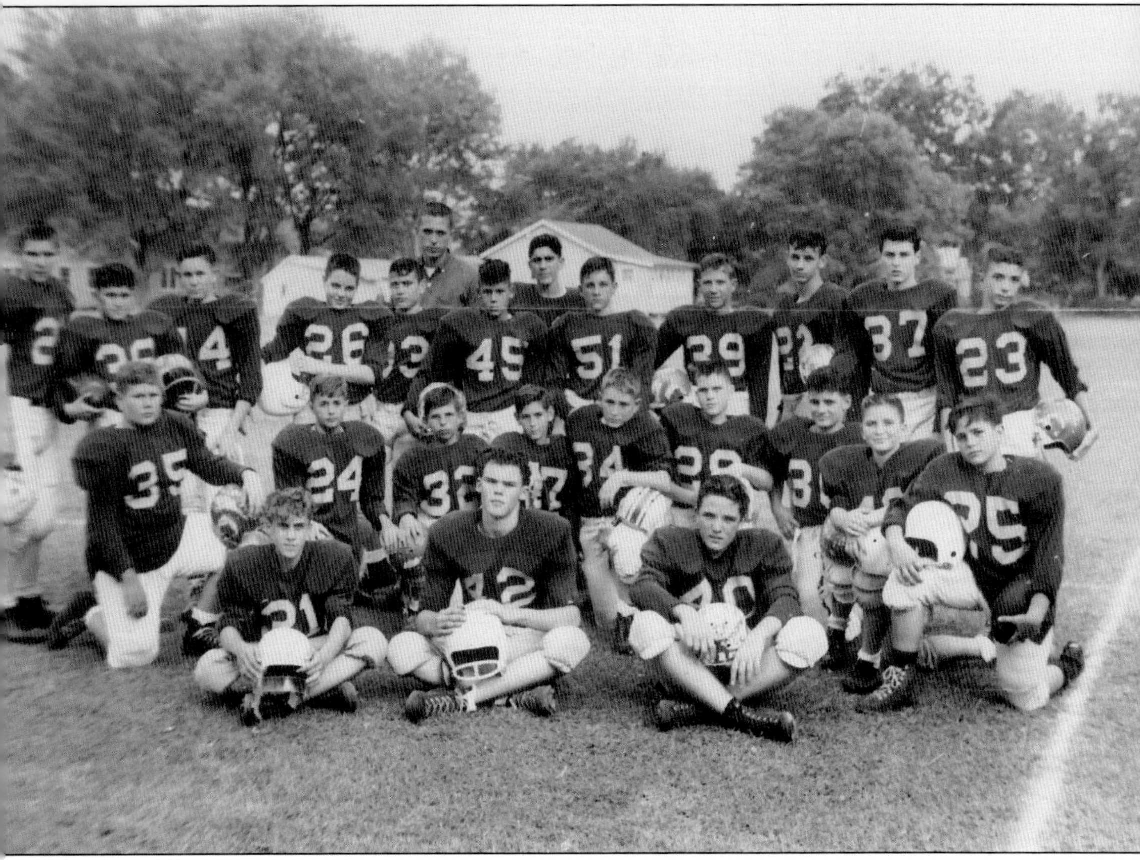

This is the 1958 ACHS junior varsity football team. Pictured from left to right are (sitting) Johnny Latino, Chester James Carville, and Bill Gibson; (kneeling) Mark Haik, Calvin Bessonett, Don Ramirez, Kenneth Landry, Bill LeBlanc, Allen Hebert, Rodney Murry Byron Milliet, and Jerry Ramiez; (standing) Bernard Becnel, David Daigle, Duncan Crawford, Jerome Acosta, Coach Jerry McKernan, Black LeBlanc, Joe Melancon, Richard Castingnos, Steve Diron, N.J. Tripode, Andrew Capone, and Roy Katz. (Courtesy of the Capone family.)

These are the members of the 1945 DHS girls' basketball team. (Courtesy of the Lassere family.)

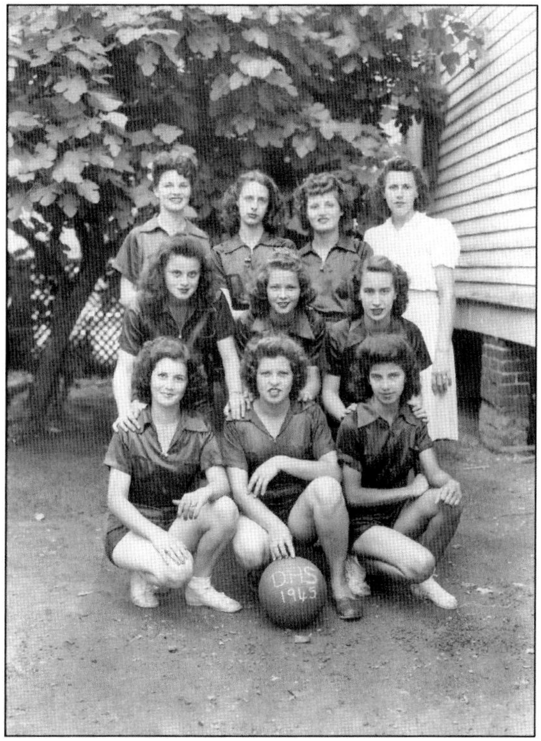

This image shows the 1948 B.B. Back Club. From left to right are Maxine Cointment, Claudette Bloch, Anna Claire Kocke, Grace Reynaud (hidden), Barbara Redmond, Katherine Daigle, Joycelyn Daigle, and Gayle Schexnayder. (Courtesy of the Reynaud family.)

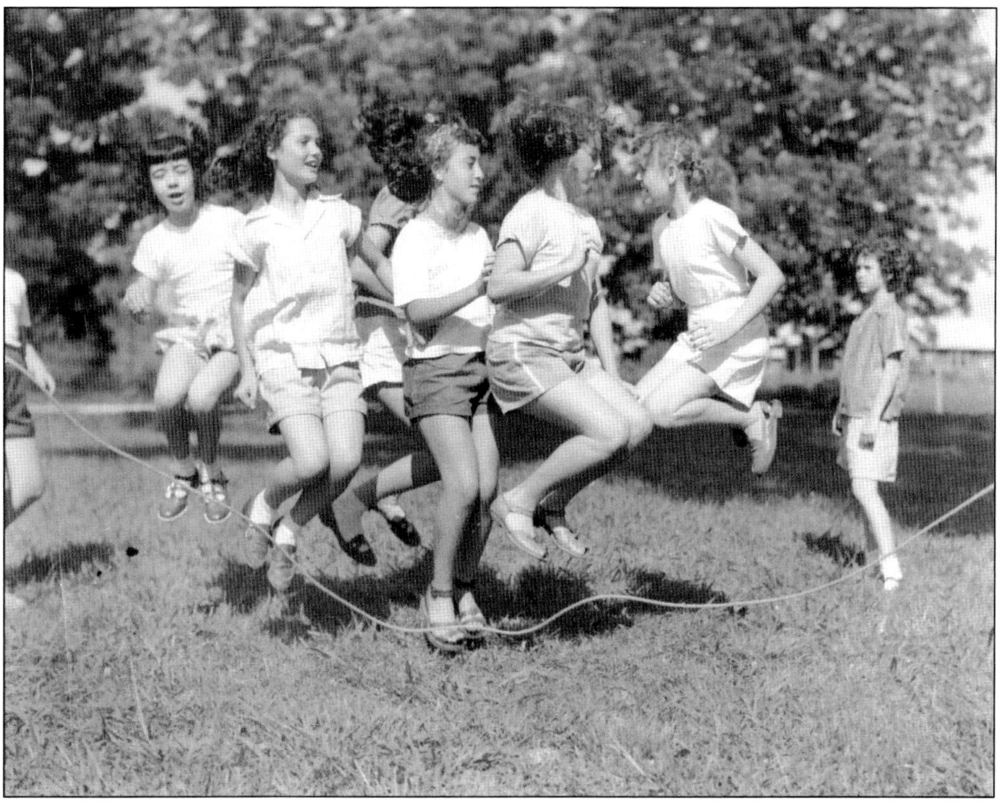

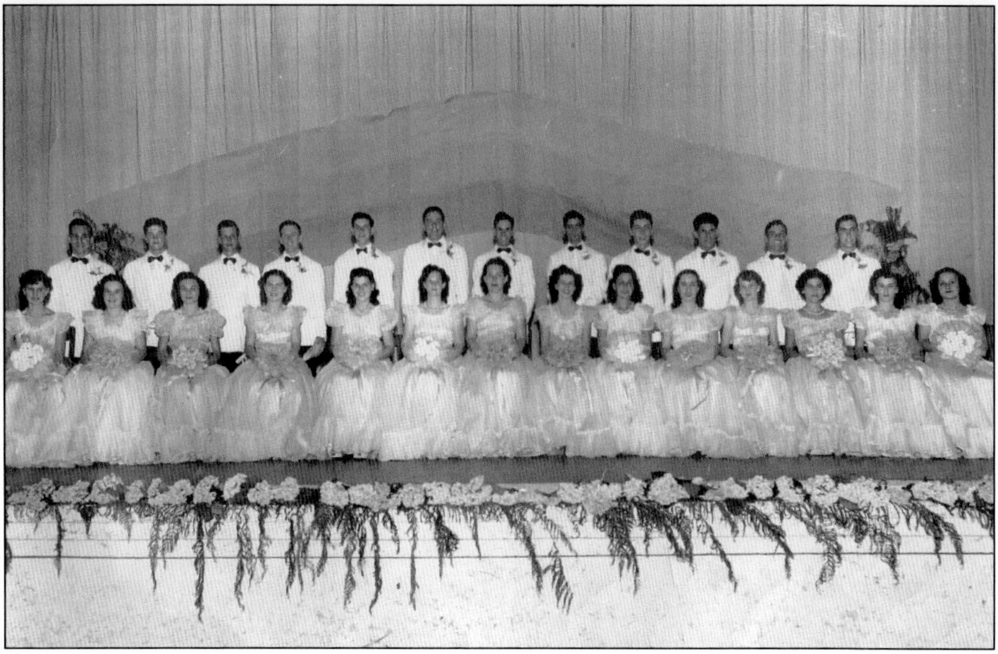

It was not uncommon for high schools to only go to 11th grade; in fact, until the late 1940s, it was the norm. Most people were dependant on agriculture for a living and needed the help of all able-bodied children. Above is the last 11th-grade graduation class at DHS in 1948. (Courtesy of the Poirrier family.)

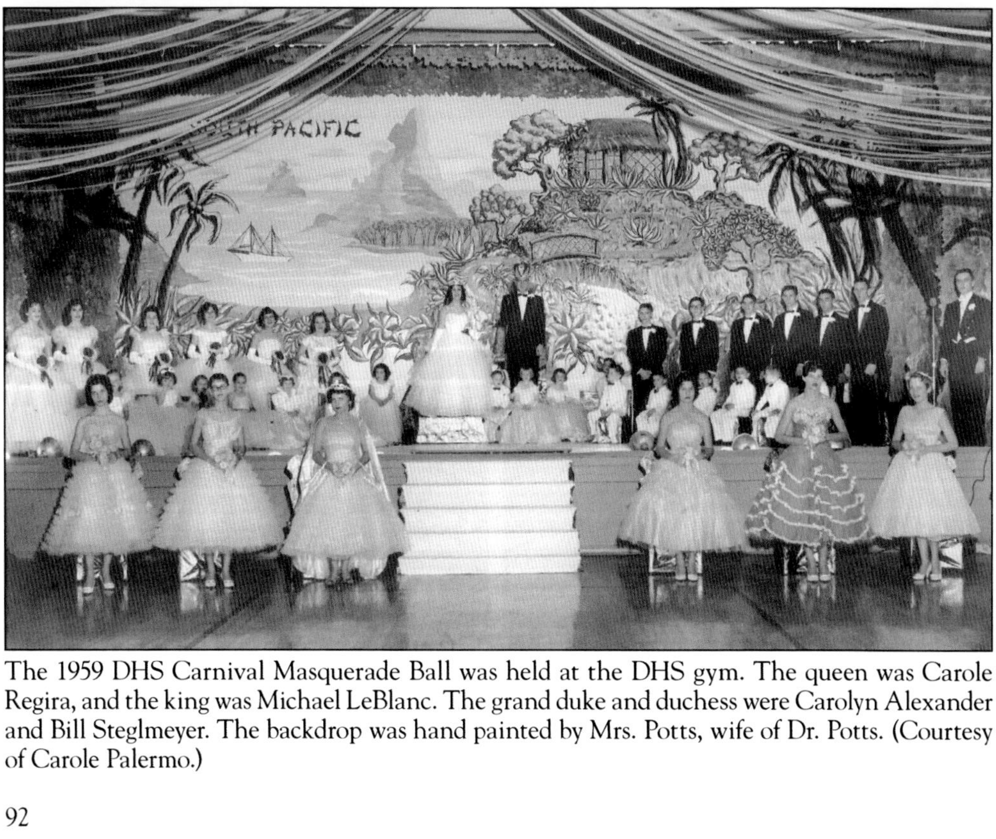

The 1959 DHS Carnival Masquerade Ball was held at the DHS gym. The queen was Carole Regira, and the king was Michael LeBlanc. The grand duke and duchess were Carolyn Alexander and Bill Steglmeyer. The backdrop was hand painted by Mrs. Potts, wife of Dr. Potts. (Courtesy of Carole Palermo.)

Five

At the Fork in the River

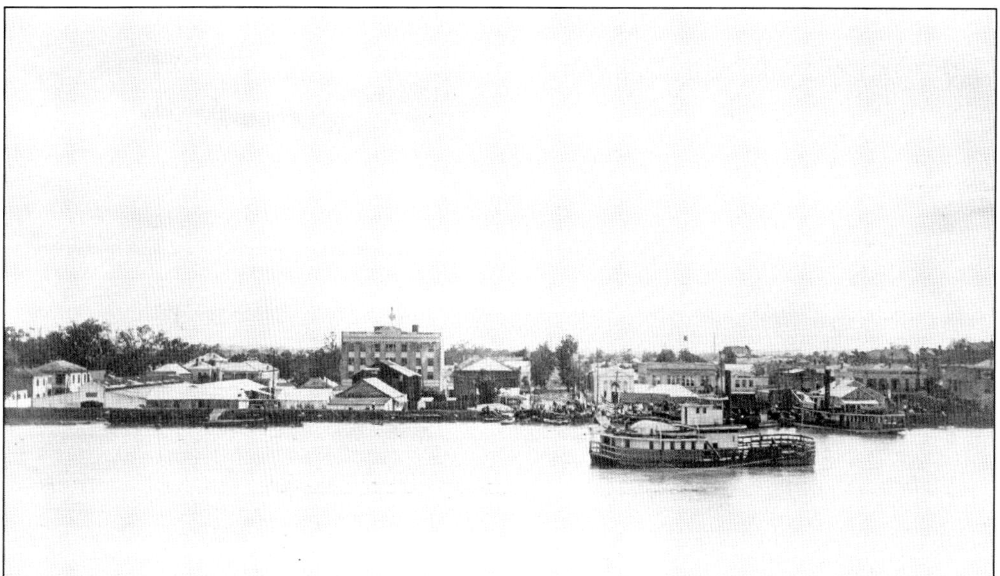

This is a riverfront view of Donaldsonville in the early 1900s as taken from the Mississippi River. The large structure near the middle left is the Hotel Donaldson, built in 1912. All the way to the right are the first three letters of the Cheap Tony's sign. The river was a main thoroughfare and played an important part in the city's economy. (Courtesy of the Landry family.)

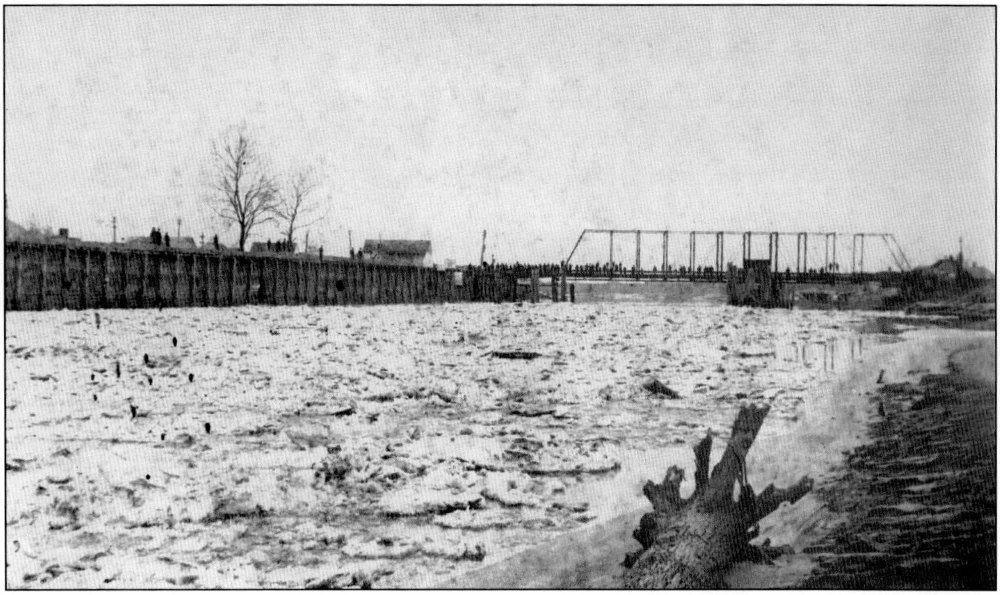

This photograph, taken on February 15, 1890, shows Bayou Lafourche clogged with ice. It is taken with the river behind the photographer. The bridge in the photograph is the footbridge that spanned the bayou that would open for boat traffic. Notice how the Donaldsonville side of the bayou had been built up to protect it. The timber from the old statehouse in Donaldsonville was used as part of this project. (Courtesy of the Landry family.)

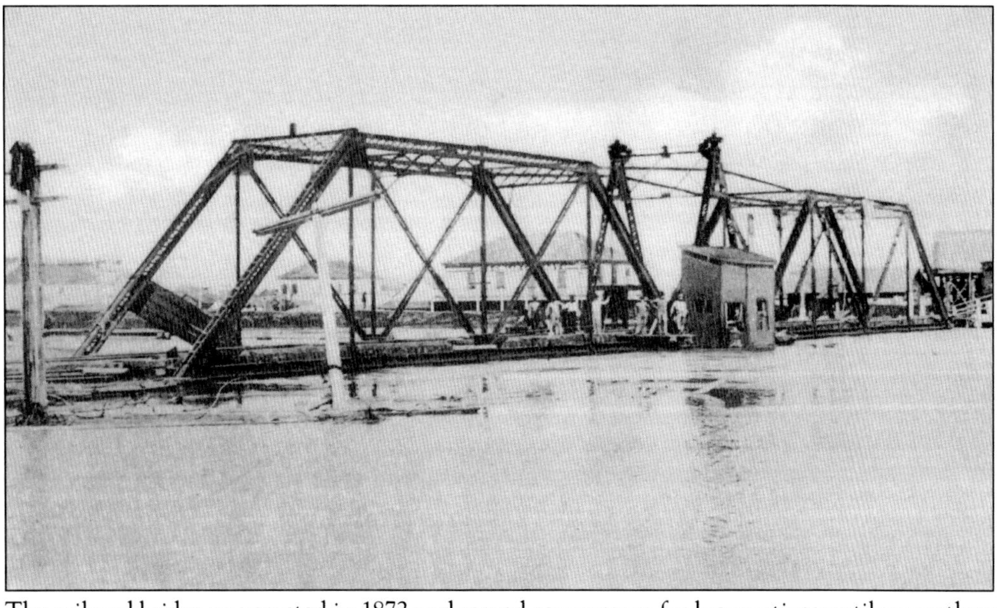

The railroad bridge was erected in 1872 and served as a passage for locomotives until an earthen dam was built in 1934–1945. From the *Donaldsonville Chief* newspaper, dated March 13, 1872: "The pile driver is at work at the site of the railroad bridge to be built across Bayou Lafourche, and we infer the work of constructing the bridge had been commenced in good earnest. We hope it may be steadily continued, and our railroad extended somewhere or other, we are not very particular where." The bayou was at flood stage when this picture was taken. (Courtesy of the Landry family.)

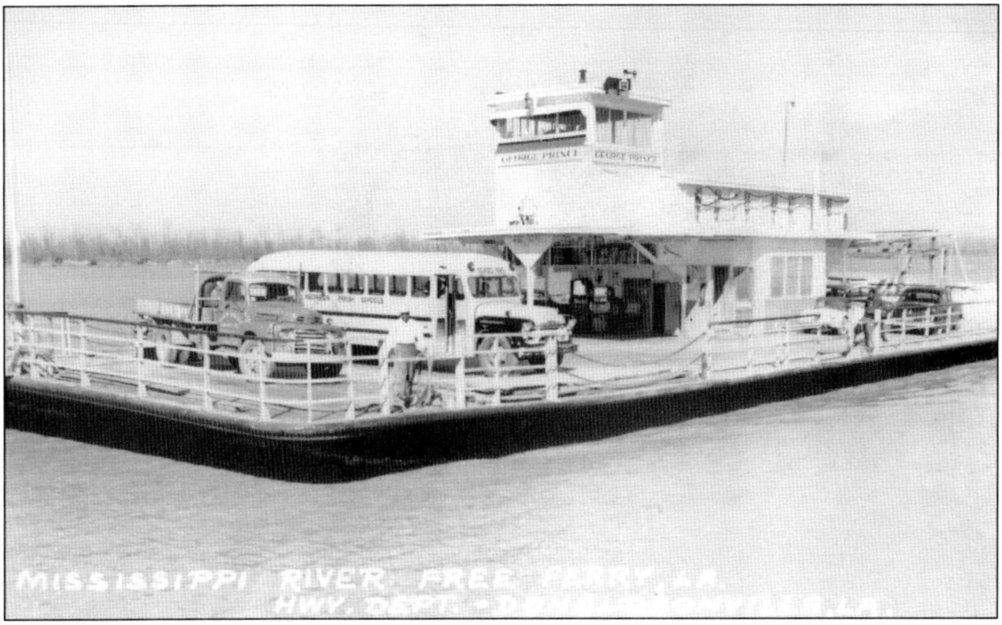

The *George Prince* was a ferry owned and operated by the Louisiana Department of Highways, originally built in 1937 in Slidell, Louisiana, and converted for its final use in Avondale, Louisiana. In 1969, the US Coast Guard ceased inspection and certification of the vessel at the request of the State of Louisiana. Since it was a free ferry and was not carrying passengers "for hire," the Coast Guard complied with the request. (Courtesy of the Kocke family.)

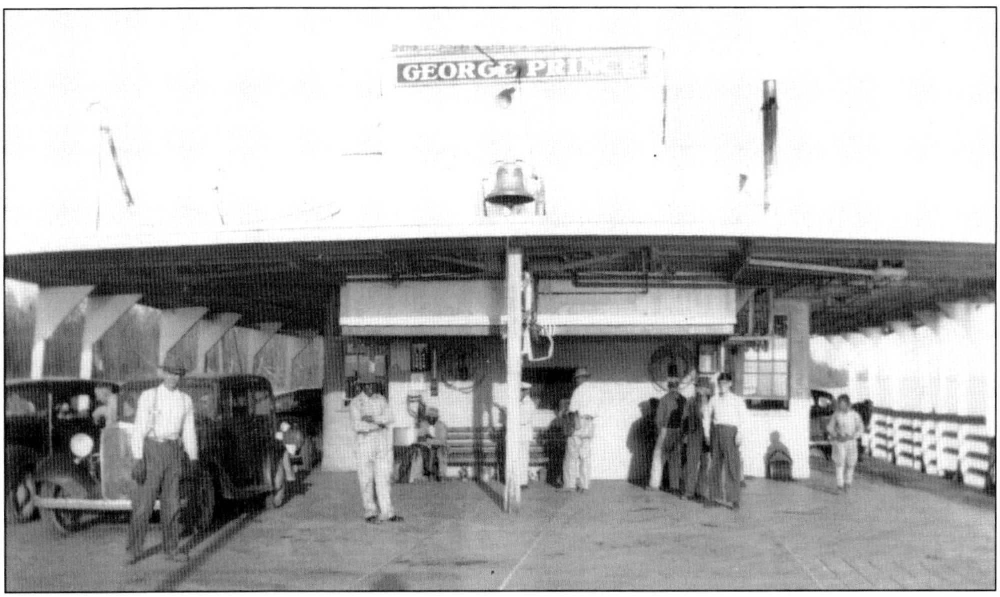

The MV *George Prince* ferry disaster was a nautical disaster that occurred on the morning of October 20, 1976. The Norwegian tanker SS *Frosta*, which was traveling upriver, struck the ferry *George Prince*. The collision occurred at milepost 120.8, less than three-quarters of a mile from the construction site of the Sunshine Bridge, which would replace the ferry seven years later. This image was taken in April 1946 on board the *George Prince* in Donladsonville. (Courtesy of the Marchand family.)

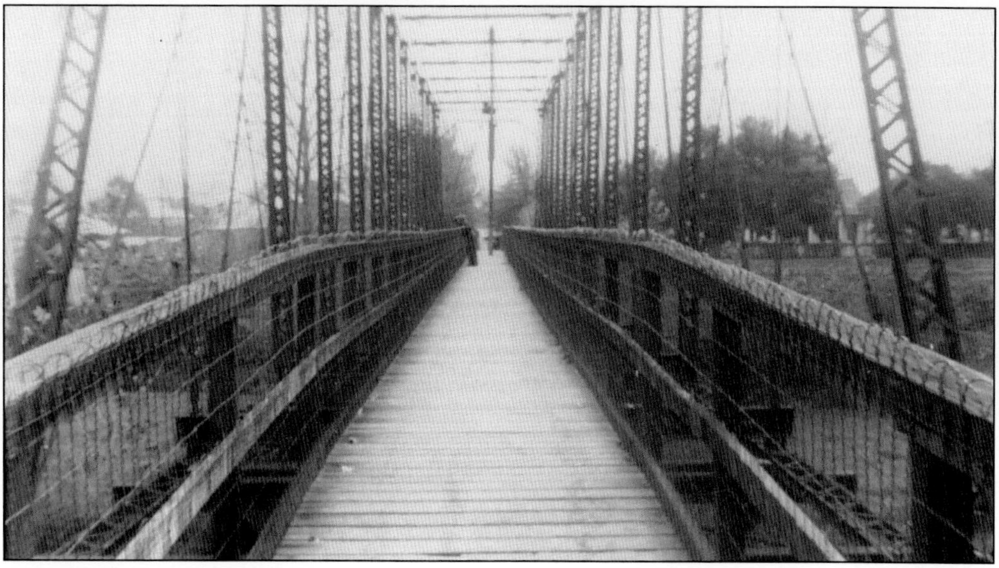

Crossing the bayou was accomplished by boat for many years. About 1818, the police jury contracted Louis Bringier to construct a bridge across the bayou at a cost of $8,000. It was used until 1846. A ferry service at the mouth of the bayou provided tow service with different sized flatboats, tow skiffs, and a "man handy both day and night" to handle the traffic. In 1854, Maxwell Briggs and Company was contracted to build a Howe truss-type drawbridge of pitch pine in alignment with Attakapas Street. It cost $17,000 and opened to permit the passage of boats by means of a windlass, powered by a mule. When this bridge deteriorated and was abandoned, a rope-pulled ferry replaced it. In 1881, the Donaldsonville Bridge Company was organized to build and operate a toll bridge. Tolls were collected for 20 years. Prosper Bernard Rodrigue and two family members were employed to operate the bridge 24 hours a day. It took six men to operate and turn the bridge's "key." Rodrigue placed benches on the Port Barrow side of the bayou, and as many as 15 men could be seen gathered under the trees. At the sound of a steamboat whistle, two groups of three men would push in opposite directions on the key to open the bridge. As sailors passed, they were greeted and received news from the six men. (Courtesy of the Kocke family.)

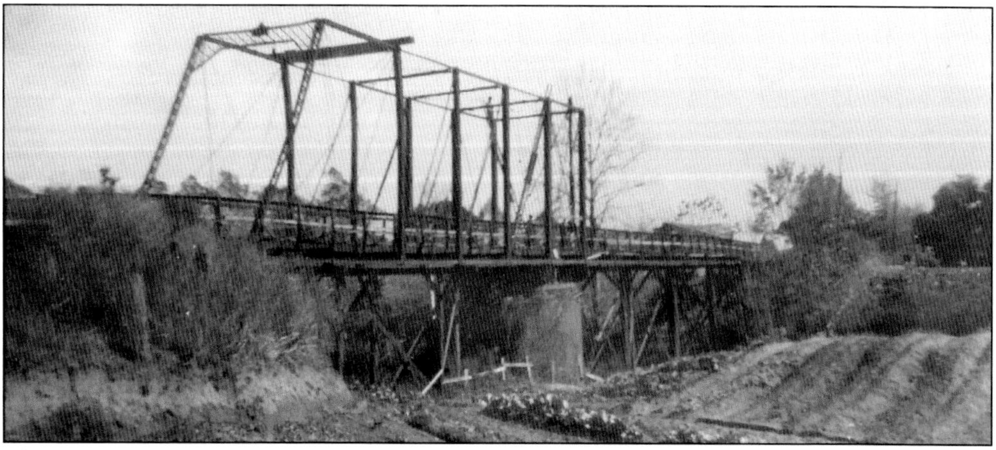

The US Army Corps of Engineers dammed the mouth of the bayou in 1903, and many people began walking across the bayou over the dam. The bridge remained in use until 1916 and was demolished during World War II to be used as scrap metal. Bayou Lafourche footbridge demolition is seen on December 9, 1942. (Courtesy of the Kocke family.)

Bayou Lafourche was the fork in the Mississippi River that flowed to the Gulf of Mexico. It was an important waterway for Native Americans, as well as pirates and early traders. After the damming of the bayou in 1904, the importance of Bayou Lafourche diminished. In the 1950s, a pumping station was built to supply water from the Mississippi River to the once glorious bayou. This photograph shows the pumping station with the Mississippi River in the background. (Courtesy of the Marchand family.)

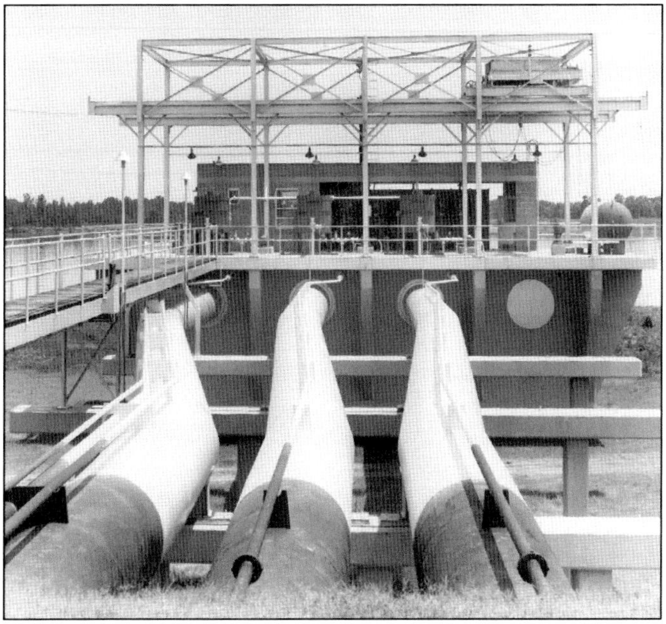

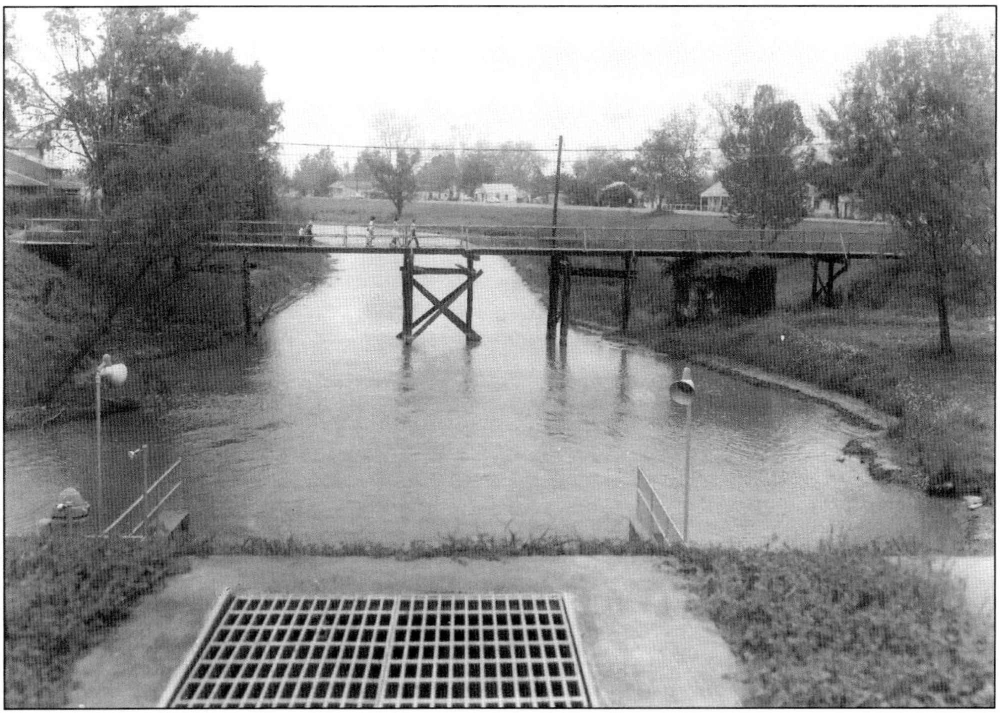

Even though Bayou Lafourche was no longer a transportation route from the Mississippi River, it still supplied drinking and agriculture water needed for the five-parish area leading to the Gulf of Mexico. The large amounts of silt that used to travel down the bayou and be deposited in the marshes protected the coast of Louisiana from hurricanes and storms. The closing off of the bayou has significantly decreased the amount of silt, as is evident by the amount of erosion over the last century. This is a view of the bayou at the point where the water is being pumped into it from the river. (Courtesy of the Marchand family.)

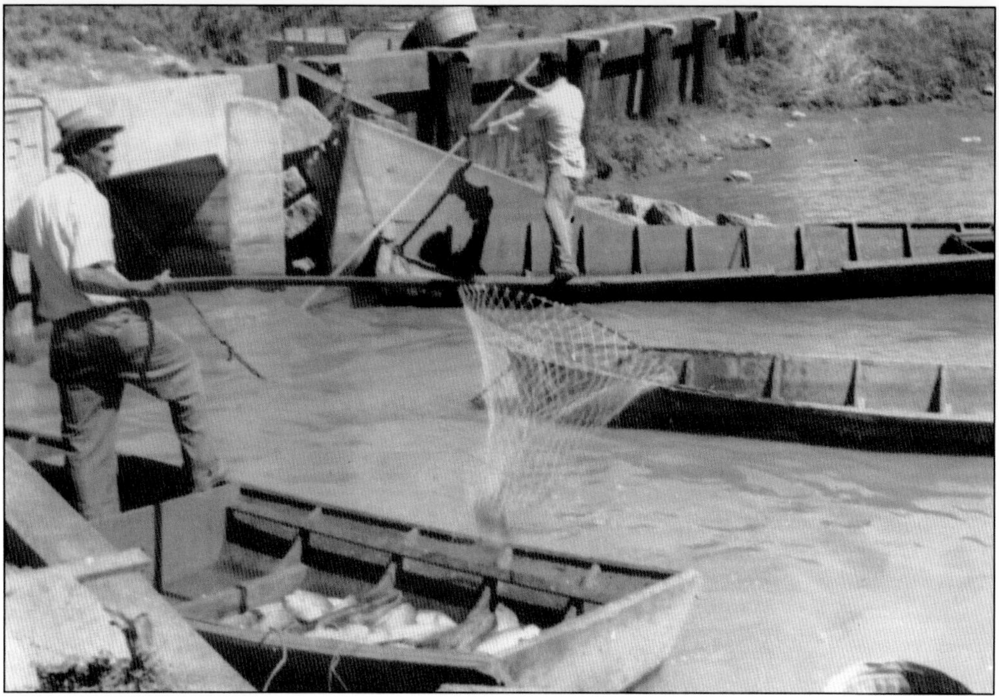

After the bayou was dammed and the pumping station put in place, culverts were constructed to allow highways to be built over the bayou. This also offered a restricted point in the bayou for fishing and the catching of sardines as baitfish. Since the sardines swam upstream, the fishermen would dip the nets in the water and let the current do the work for them. (Courtesy of the Marchand family.)

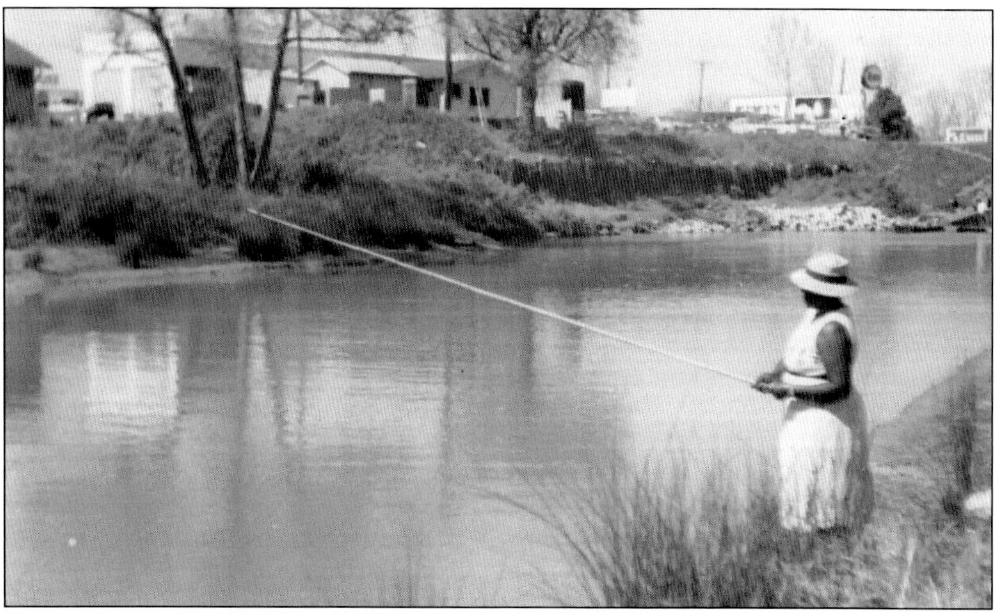

On any day, one could see locals with a fishing pole along Bayou Lafourche trying to catch that next big catfish. Shrimp boxes were also set out using sardines that were caught in the bayou for bait. (Courtesy of the Marchand family.)

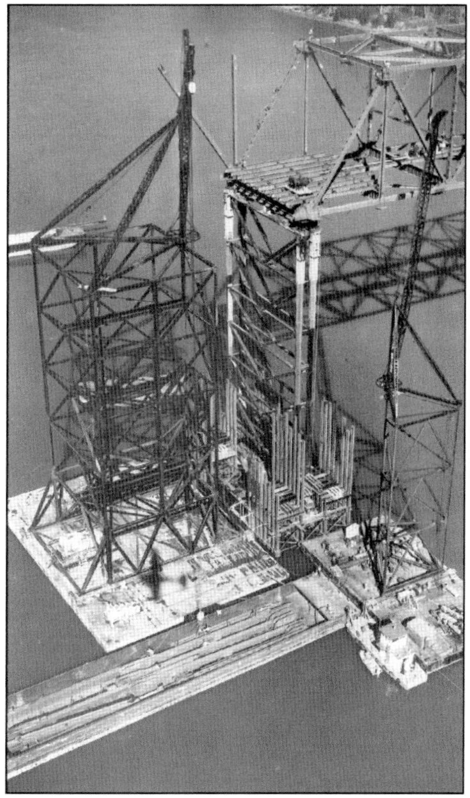

The Sunshine Bridge is a cantilever bridge over the Mississippi River in St. James Parish. Completed in 1963, it carries LA 70, which connects Donaldsonville on the west bank of Ascension Parish with Sorrento on the east bank of Ascension Parish as well as with Gonzales on the east bank of Ascension Parish. The approach roads on the east and west banks begin in Ascension Parish before crossing into St. James Parish. At the time of construction, it was the only bridge across the Mississippi between New Orleans and Baton Rouge, but for some time after its construction, while awaiting funds to connect it to LA 70 and other roads, the south end of the bridge emptied into a swamp. During that time, the term Sunshine Bridge entered satirical usage. The bridge had been "built under the administration of" Governor Davis, who had twice picked and sung his way into the Governor's Mansion with hits like "You Are My Sunshine" and whose horse, which he rode into the governor's office at his second inaugural, was named Sunshine. (Both, courtesy of the Capone family.)

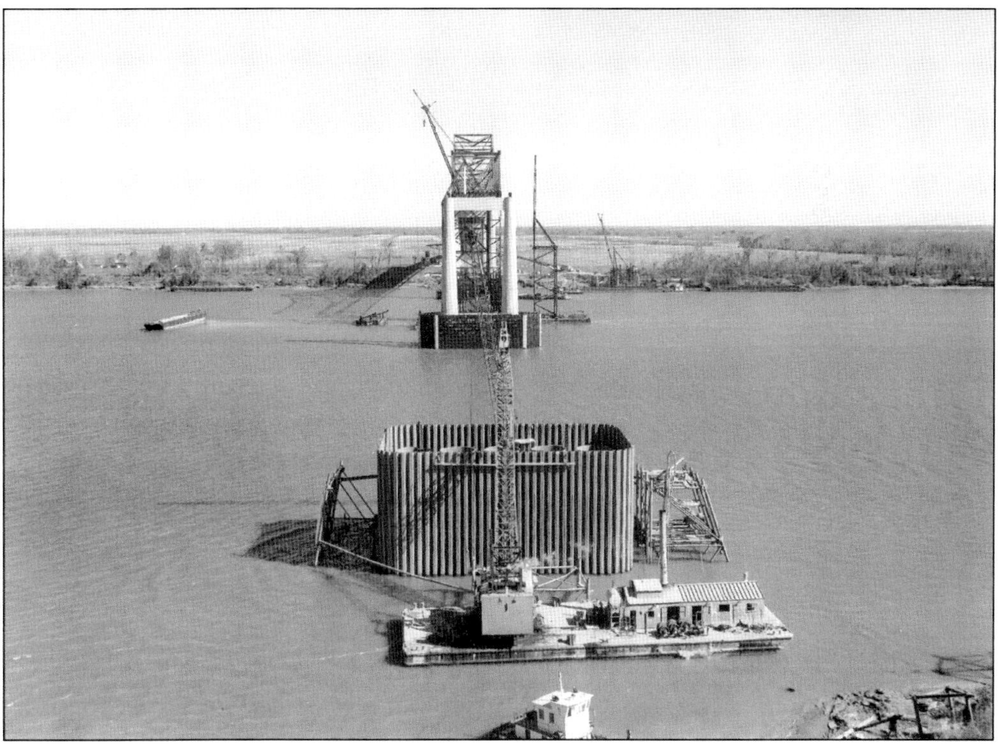

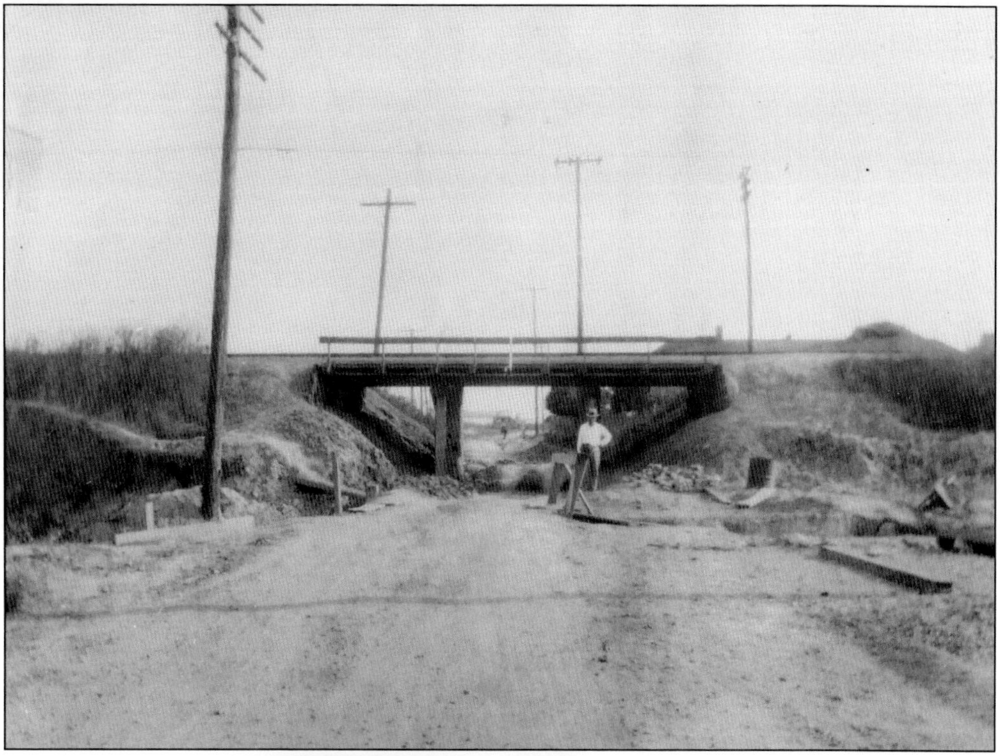

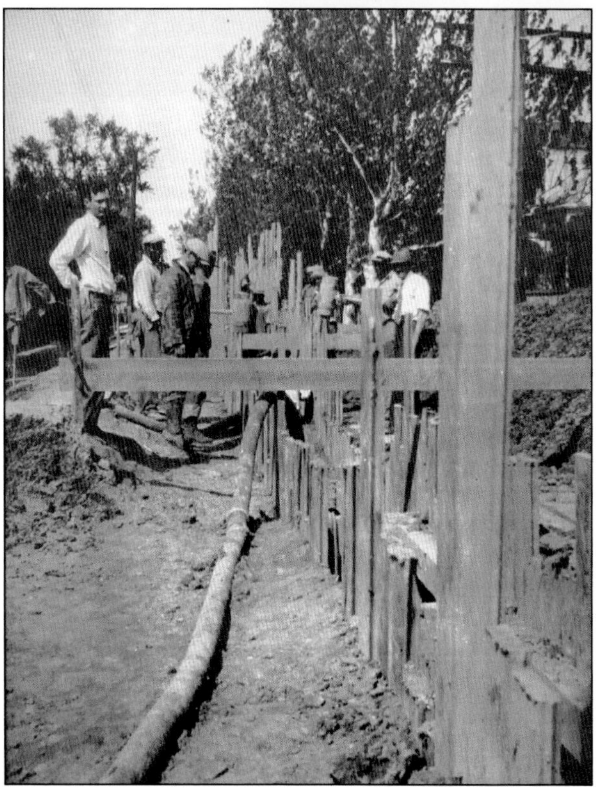

This image shows the Texas & Pacific underpass of Highway 1 south going down the bayou. Notice the bayou in the background through the dugout area. (Courtesy of the Marchand family.)

As the city of Donaldsonville grew, infrastructure needed to keep pace. This photograph shows sewer construction on Lafourche Street near Claiborne Street in April 1931. (Courtesy of the Marchand family.)

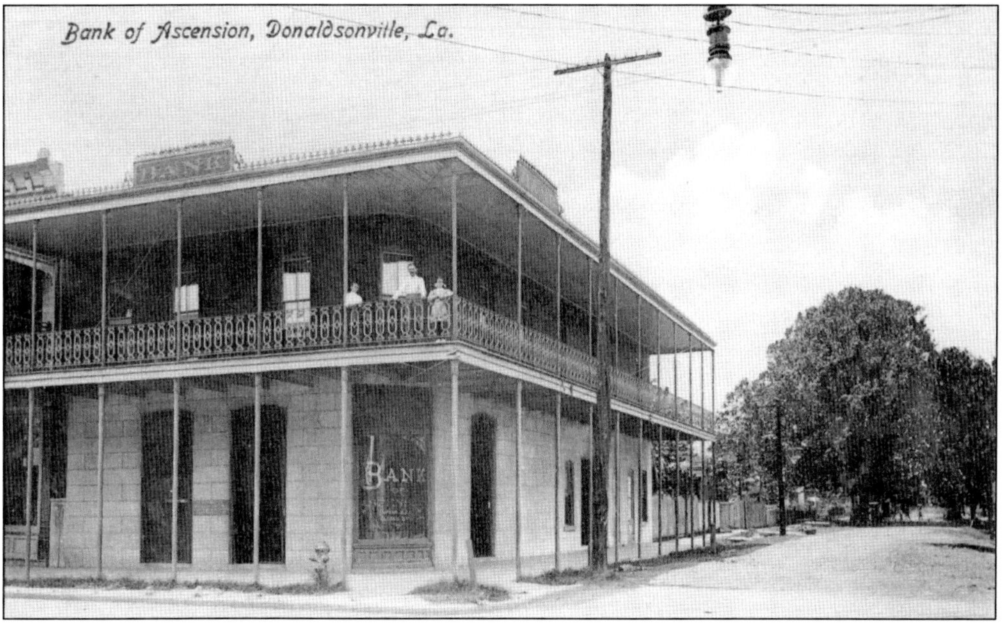

The "old" Bank of Ascension, originally located at the corner of Lessard and Mississippi Streets where the Ascension Parish Library stands today, burned in the great fire of 1911. After the fire, it was rebuilt across the street. In 1923, the name was changed to Ascension Bank and Trust. It was closed in 1933 because of bad loans; in 1935, it was opened as the First National Bank. (Courtesy of the Landry family.)

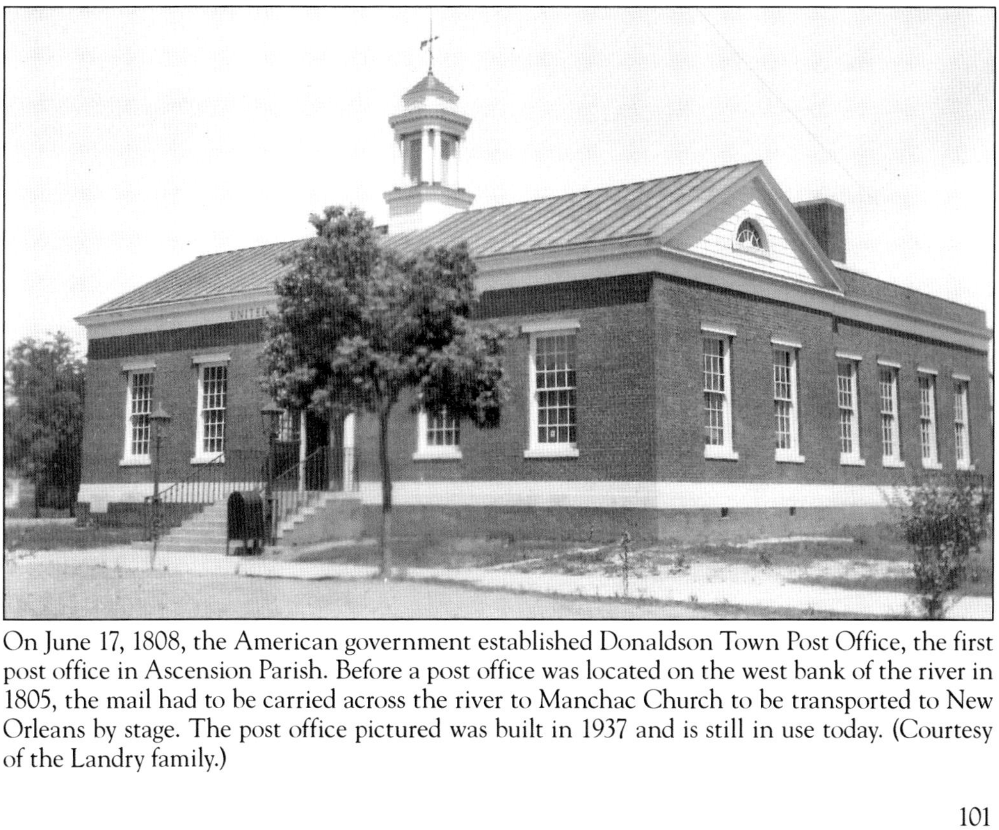

On June 17, 1808, the American government established Donaldson Town Post Office, the first post office in Ascension Parish. Before a post office was located on the west bank of the river in 1805, the mail had to be carried across the river to Manchac Church to be transported to New Orleans by stage. The post office pictured was built in 1937 and is still in use today. (Courtesy of the Landry family.)

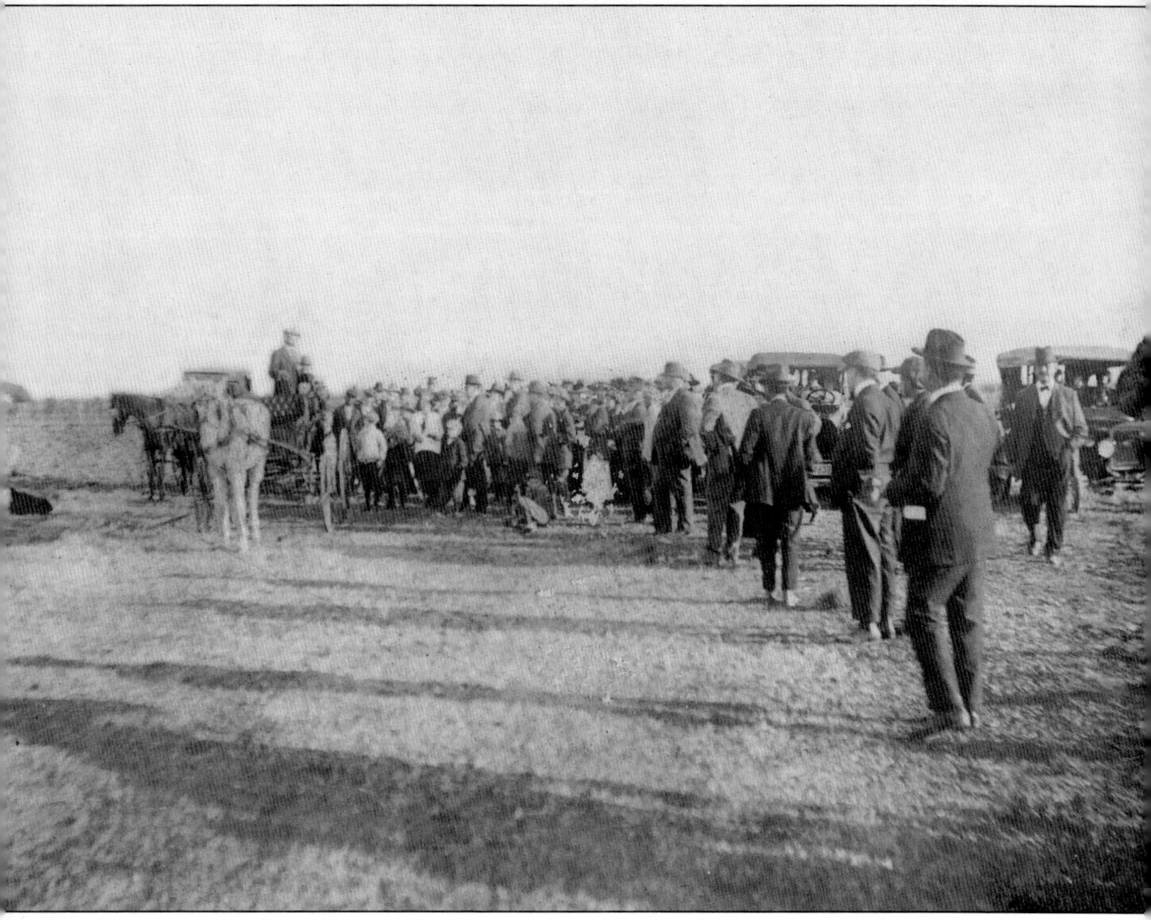

Hoping to be elected to public office, politicians would regularly visit farms, ranches, and communities, making stump speeches and promising the people whatever it took to get them elected. Here is a gathering at Palo Alto Plantation where such a speech is being delivered. (Courtesy of the Lemann family.)

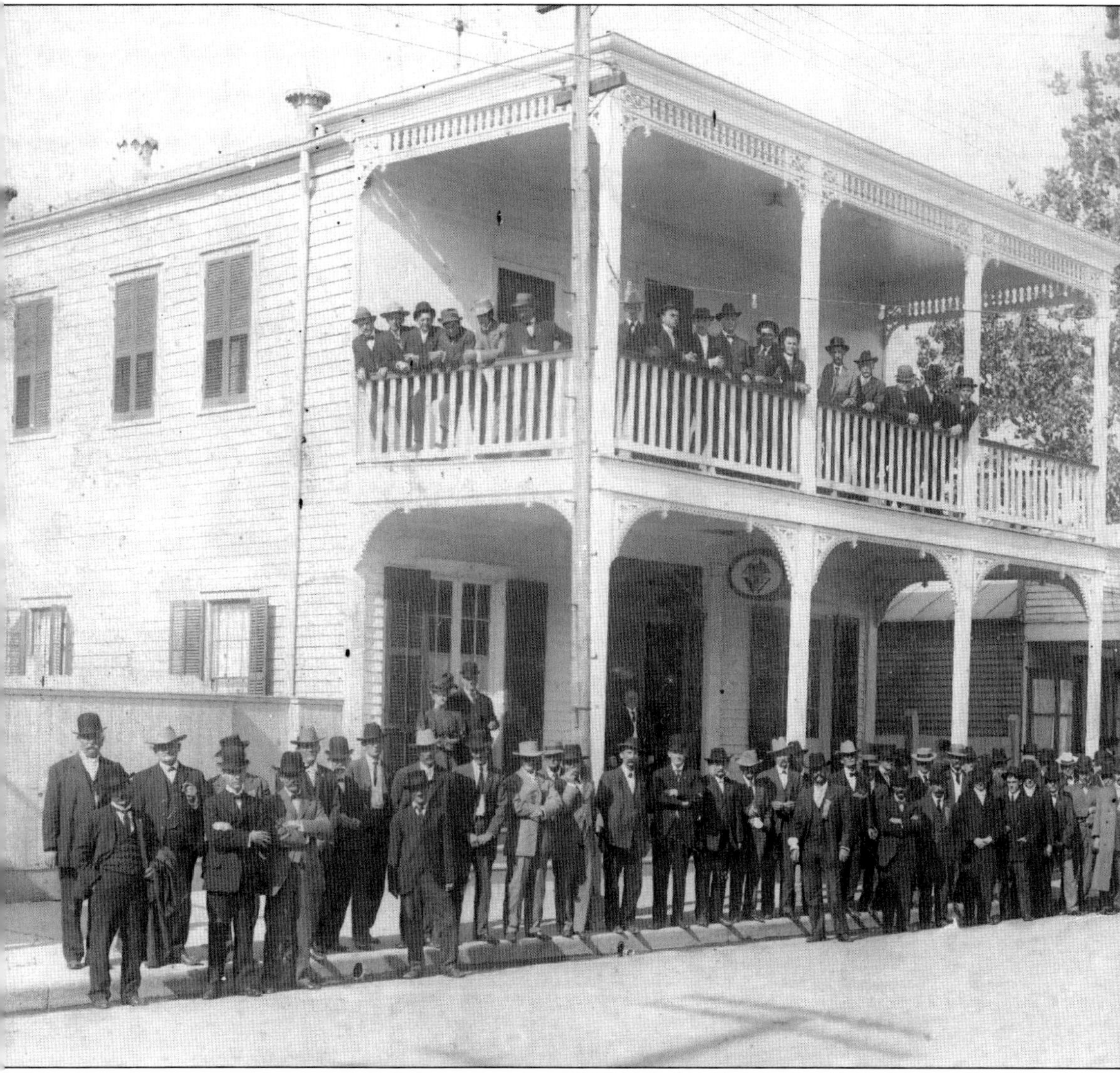

The Knights of Columbus, founded in 1882, is the world's largest Catholic fraternal service organization with more than 1.8 million members. While business meetings and all of the order's ceremonials are private, the public is welcome to all other events. To be a member, one must be a practicing Catholic man of 18 years or older and must promise not to reveal the details of any ceremonials to anyone who is not a qualified Knight. Shown is a gathering of the Knights of Columbus at the building across from Elray Kocke Service; the building is no longer there. (Courtesy of the Marchand family.)

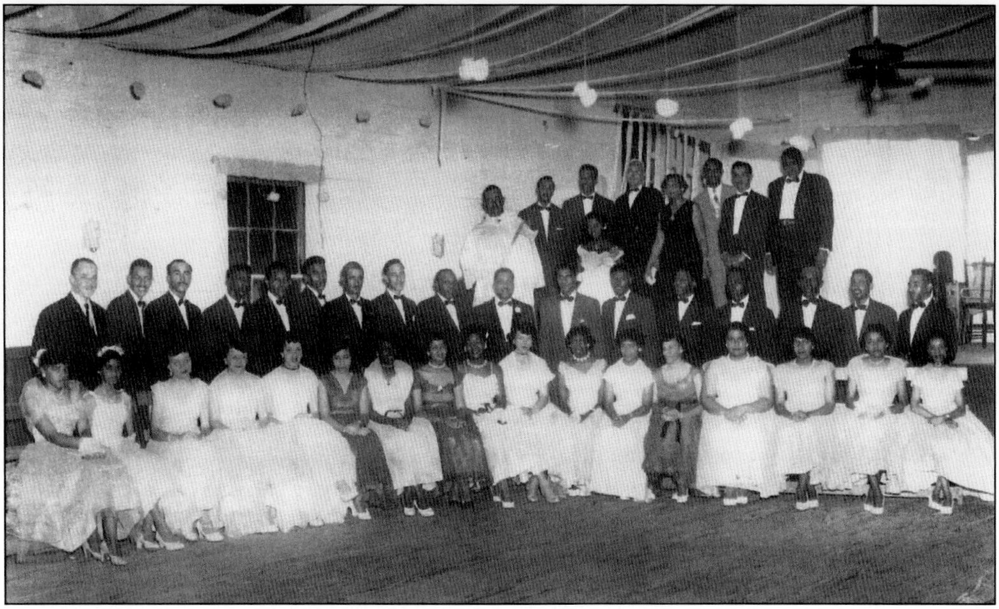

In 1883, five newly freed African American men started The True Friends Benevolent Society. White-owned insurance companies refused to insure the black community after emancipation and The True Friends Benevolent Society provided medical and burial insurance, aid to fire victims and orphans, and support to college students. True Friends Hall was the center of the African American social life in Donaldsonville and was used for meetings, social activities, weddings, and balls. Noted musicians who performed there were Claiborne Williams, Ike and Tina Turner, James Brown, Joe Tex, Fats Domino, Reynald Richard, and Plas Johnson. This is an image of the Easter Monday Ball at the True Friends Hall on April 11, 1955. (Courtesy of Kathy Hambrick Jackson.)

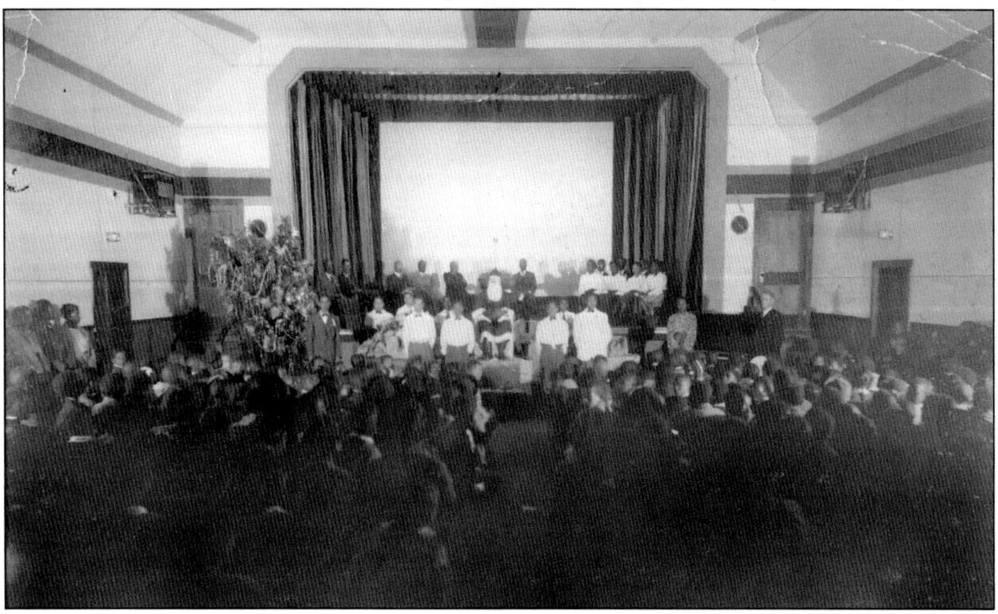

The Harlem Theater was located next door to the True Friends Hall and was home to motion pictures, special events, and this Christmas performance on its stage. (Courtesy of Kathy Hambrick Jackson.)

This is the fire alarm board that was located in the fire station. It lists the location of all of the fire alarms around the city. If the alarm were pulled, a siren would blow to alert the firemen and the residents that a fire was burning in a specific area. The combination of five short blows followed by four short blows was for No. 54 or Orange Street at West Third Street, Shirley's Grocery. (Courtesy of the LeBlanc family.)

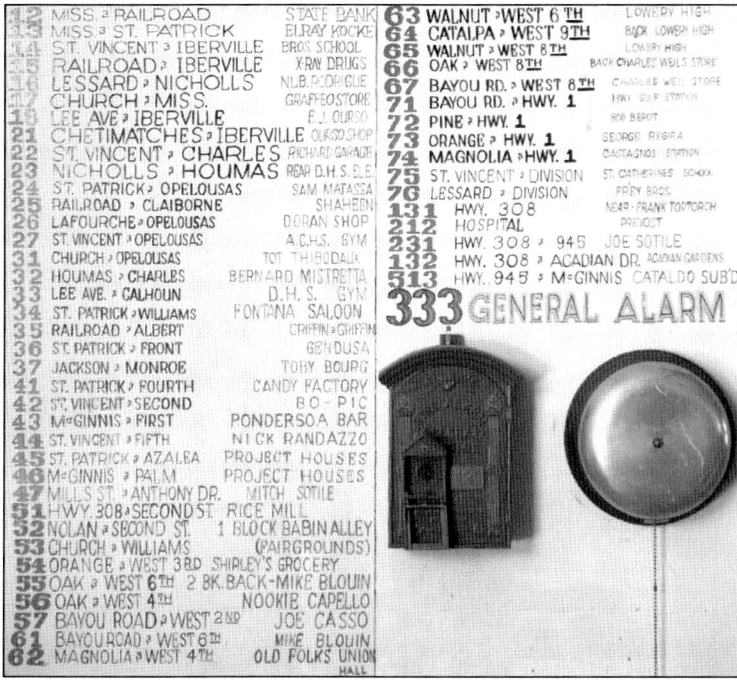

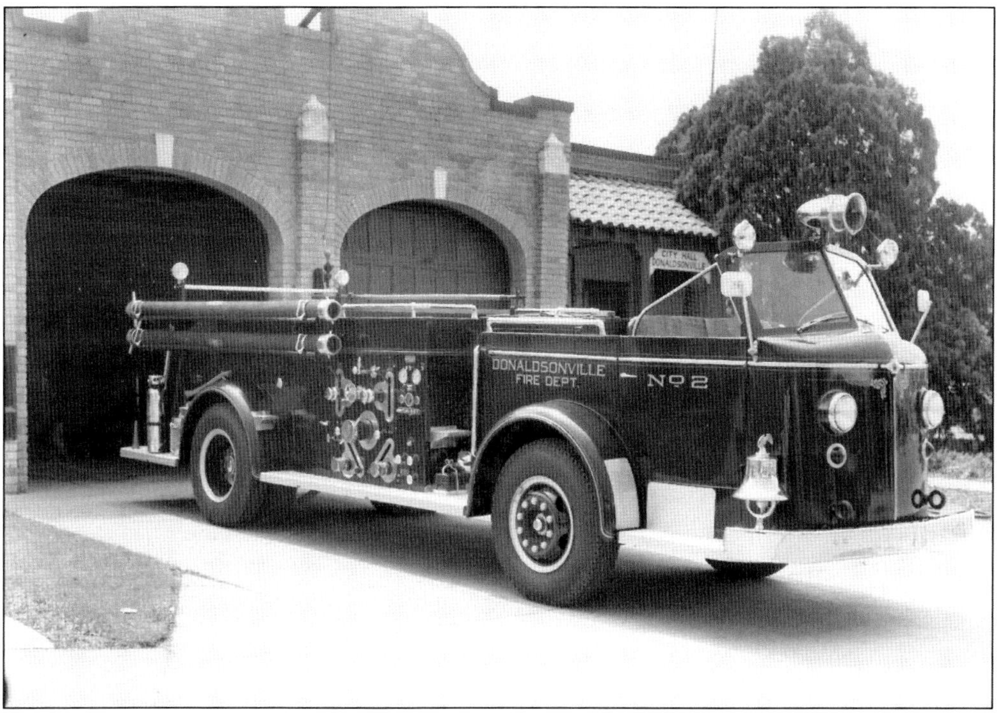

This American Lafrance fire engine was purchased in 1960 and is pictured in front of the old fire station on Railroad Avenue. City hall now occupies this spot. (Courtesy of the Landry family.)

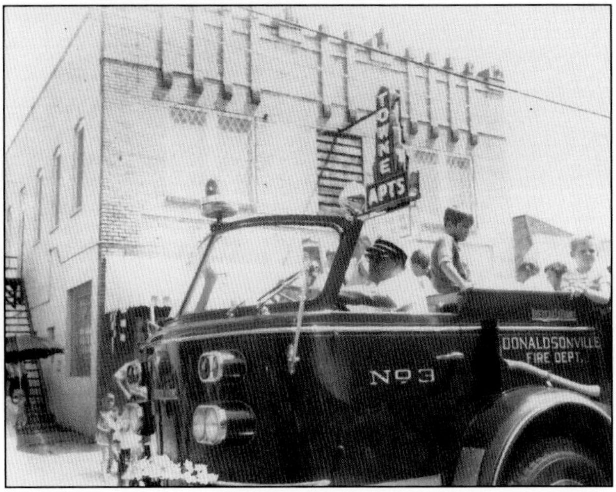

Fire chief Pasqual Fontana is driving the American Lafrance fire engine down Railroad Avenue during a parade. The Town Apartment behind him is now the home of The Grapevine Restaurant and Gallery. (Courtesy of the Marchand family.)

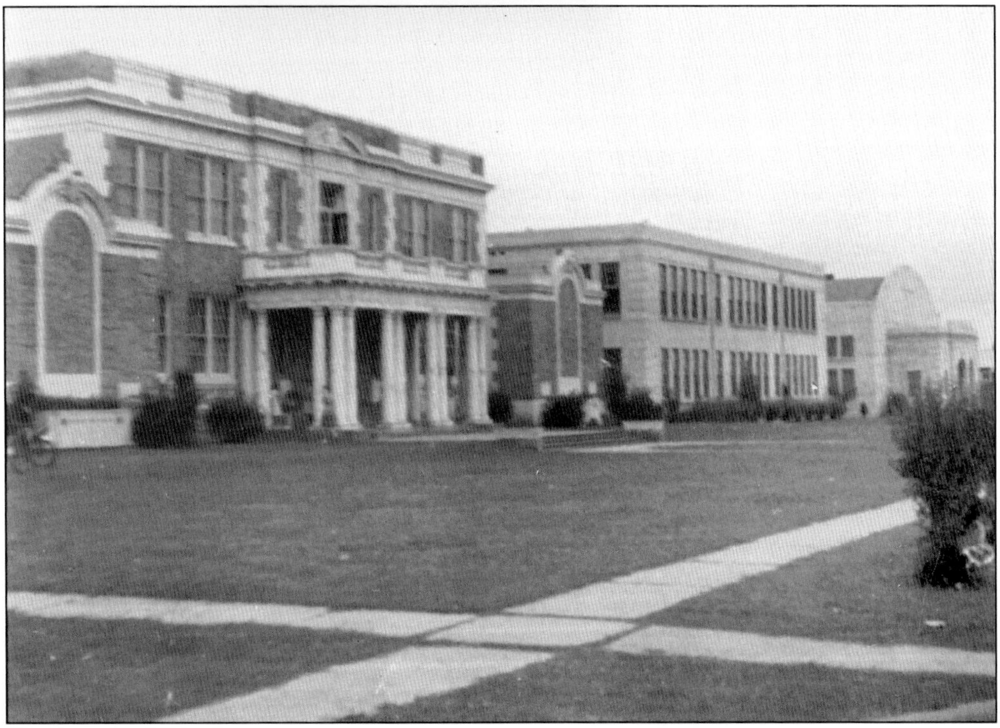

The first Donaldsonville High School began construction in 1906 and was completed in 1907. A parade in celebration of the school's completion originated at the Nicholls Hotel on Mississippi Street and proceeded down Railroad Avenue to the site of the school, which was located in Louisiana Square. Governor Blanchard addressed the crowd of 700 that had gathered for the ribbon-cutting ceremony. Also addressing the crowd was school superintendent E.N. Pugh, nephew of former governor and then Supreme Court justice Francis Nicholls, who was born a block away. Pugh read a letter of regret from Nicholls regarding his inability to attend. The new school was touted as one of the most modern in the state. A new high school was constructed around 1925 on Lee Avenue. The Lemann family donated the property for the facility. Later, around 1932, the construction of additional classrooms and a gymnasium took place. (Courtesy of the Marchand family.)

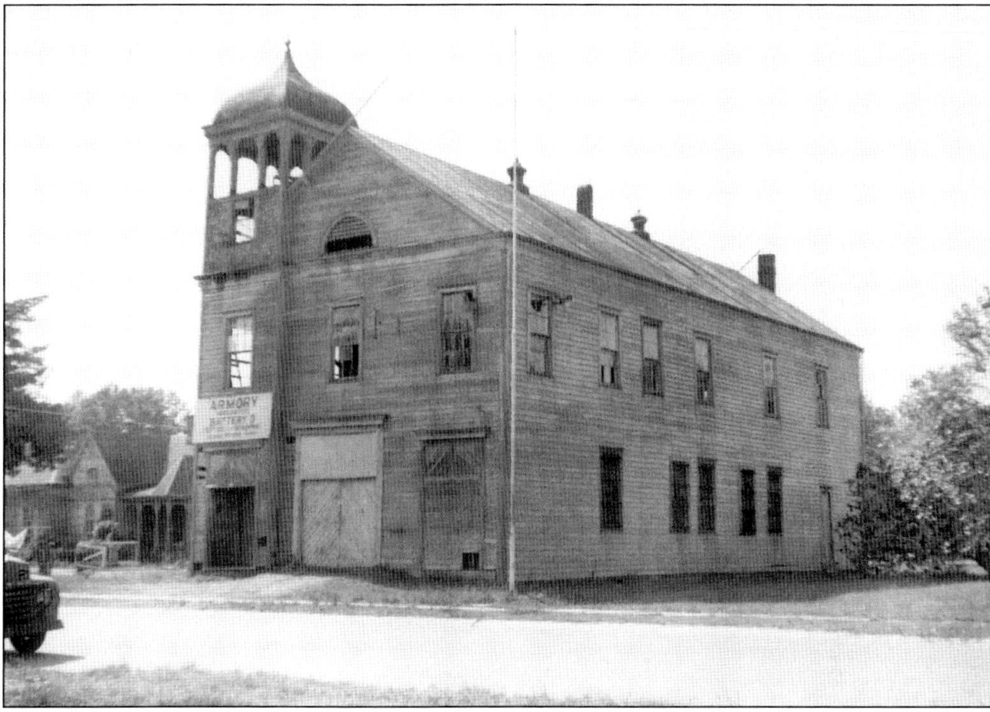

Located next to the courthouse, this magnificent building witnessed much of Donaldsonville's history. In 1875, it was the home of the hook and ladder fire department. From 1939 to 1947, it was the home of M. Trelles Tobacco Company, the makers of Keep Moving Cigars. In 1948, it became the Louisiana National Guard Armory. It has since been torn down, and a wing of the courthouse now occupies the space. (Courtesy of the Marchand family.)

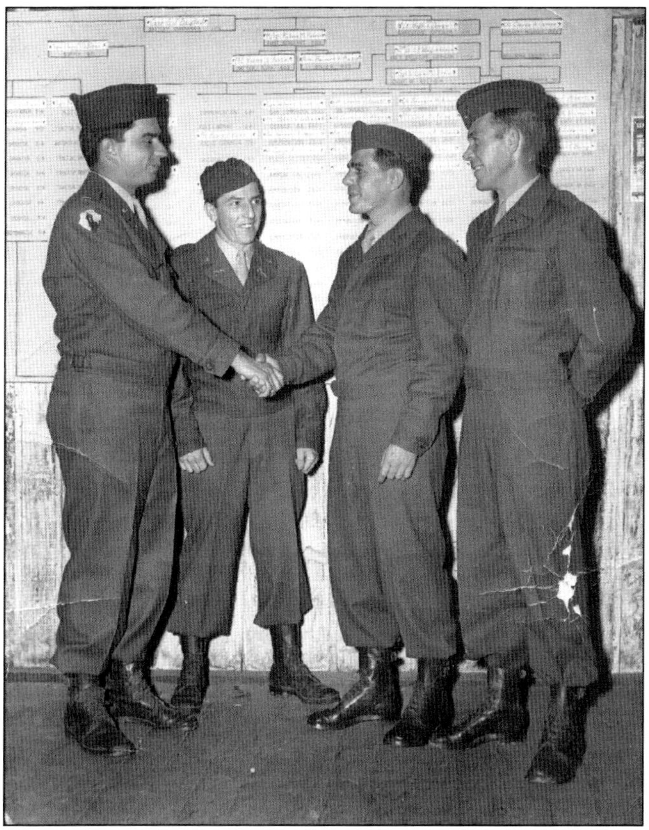

The original local officers of the Louisiana National Guard are seen inside the National Guard Armory in June 1948. Pictured are, from left to right, Capt. O.J. Daigle, Lt. Hugh T. Doran, 2nd Lt. Lynn Waguespack, and 1st Lt. Edward Delatte. (Courtesy of the Doran family.)

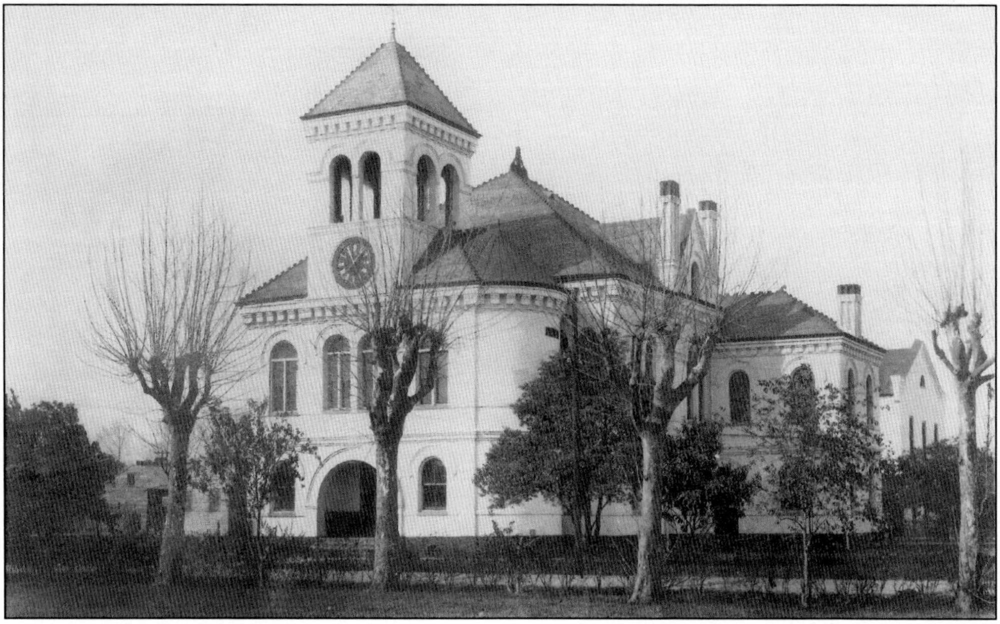

The Ascension Parish Courthouse is located in Donaldsonville, the parish seat. The first courthouse was constructed in 1806. The second one, constructed in 1810, was destroyed by fire in 1846. The third courthouse, built in 1847, was burned during the bombardment of Donaldsonville in August 1862. The structure just behind this courthouse is the "old" jail. Built as the fourth courthouse in 1867, just after the Civil War, it served as the courthouse for 10 years. It was also the site of many public hangings. (Courtesy of the Rodrigue family.)

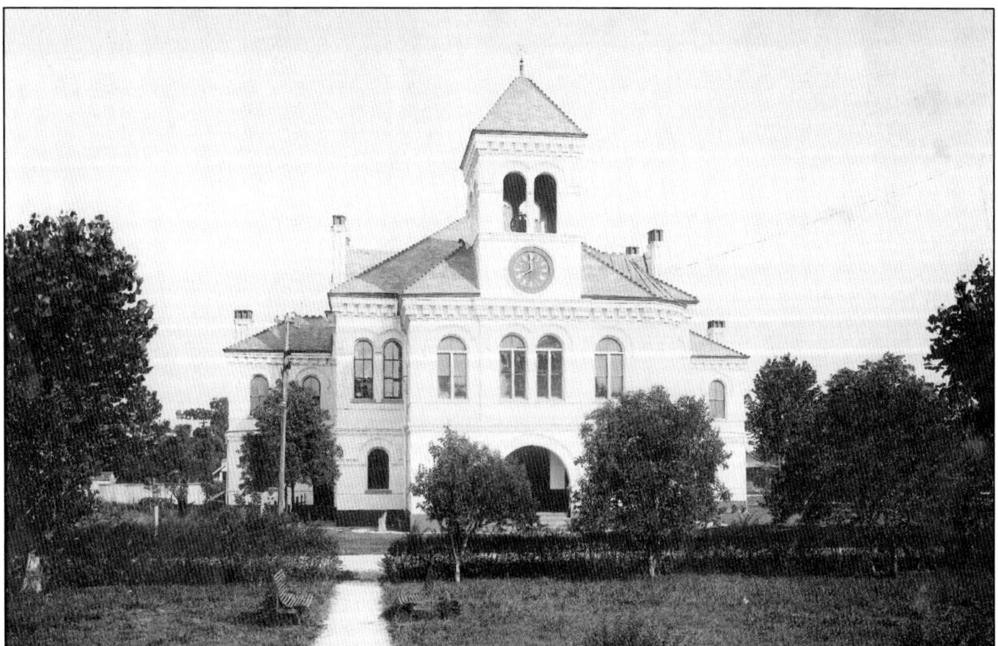

The fifth courthouse, completed in 1888, was consumed by fire in 1889, which led to the construction of the courthouse that still stands today. (Courtesy of the Kocke family.)

Six

WHO ARE YOU?

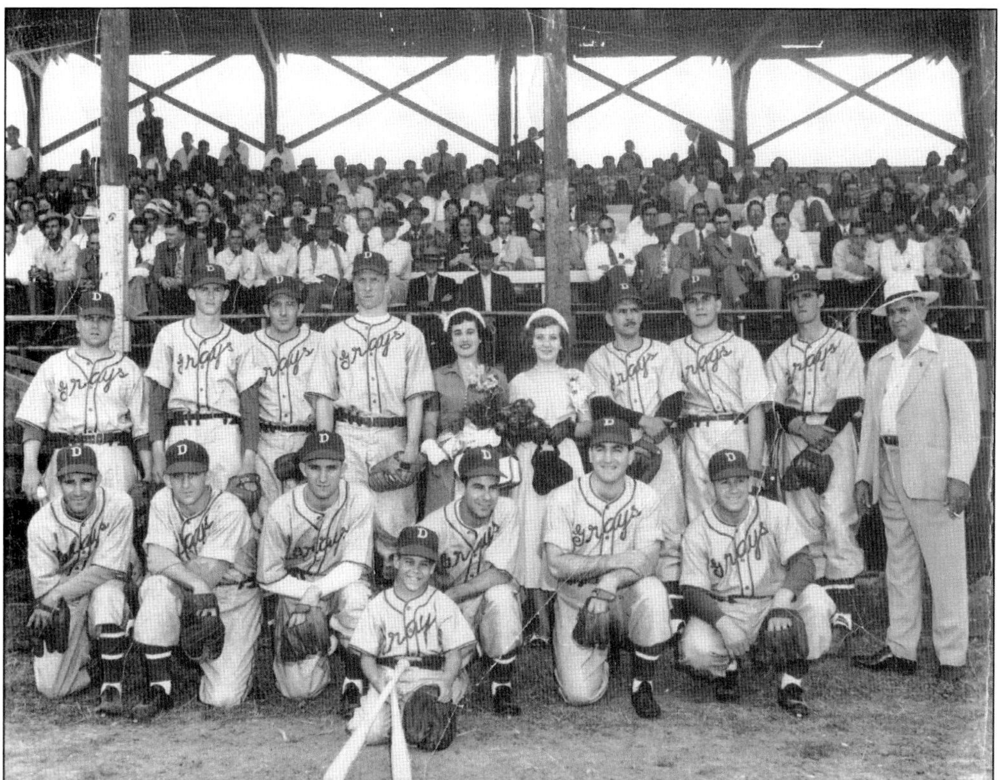

The Donaldsonville Greys are pictured in this image. Members are, from left to right, (first row) Arthur Capello, Bertis Robert, Frank Sotile, Batboy Larry Dugas, Jerry Marhcand, Tony Falsetta, and LaLa Regira; (second row) Clyde Didier, Fred Mitchell, Mel Didier, Marian Savoie, Elmo Landry, Claude Songy, Harry Smith, and Nick Romero. (Courtesy of the Dugas family.)

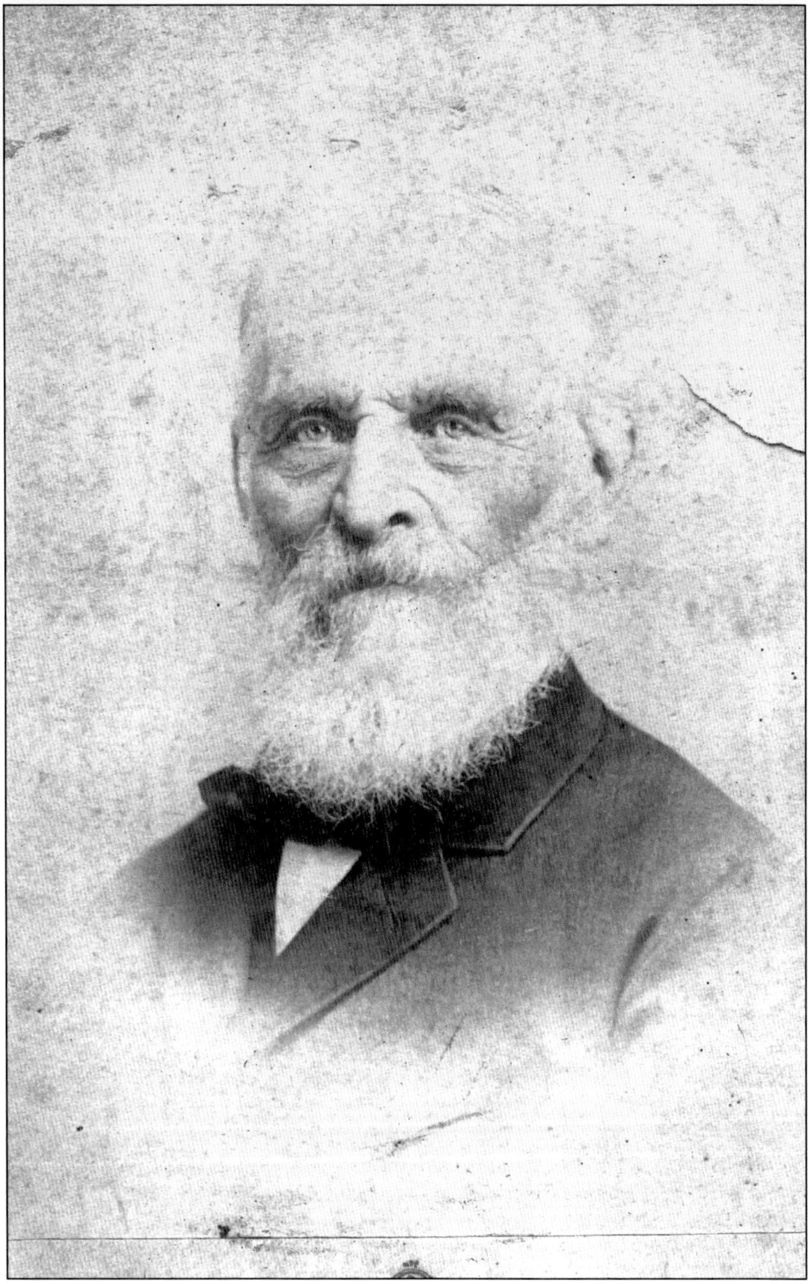

Born in 1809, Jacob Lemann left his homeland in 1836 for New Orleans. He became a peddler of dry goods and moved to Donaldsonville in 1840. During the two decades preceding the Civil War, the young Lemann was listed in 20 purchases of property in and around the Donaldsonville area. During the Civil War, Jacob moved his wife and four children to Paris. Upon returning to Donaldsonville after the war, Lemann acquired a number of sugarcane plantations, starting with the Peytavin Plantation and then the Palo Alto Plantation. In 1877, Jacob's oldest son, Bernard, purchased the site of today's store jointly with his brother Myer and opened what would become known world wide as B. Lemann & Brothers. Jacob Lemann died in February 1887. (Courtesy of the Lemann family.)

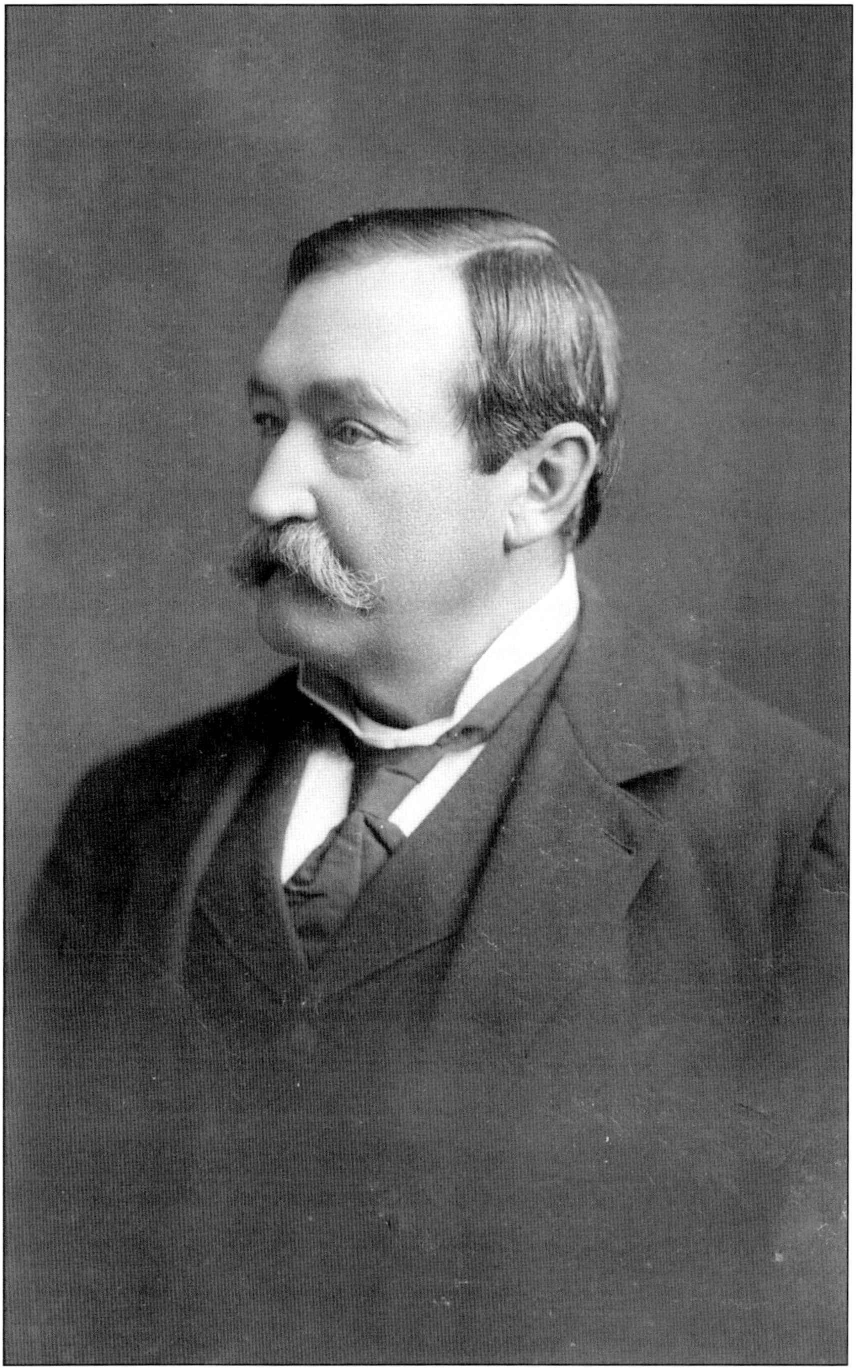

R.N. Sims was a native of Donaldsonville and a graduate of the University of North Carolina at Chapel Hill in 1860, graduating as valedictorian of his class. When the call for troops by the Confederate States of America was made, he immediately joined. After the Civil War, he studied law and was admitted to the bar in 1866. In 1896, he was elected to the Louisiana Senate. The Sims family has had a strong and distinguished presence in Donaldsonville's history ever since. (Courtesy of the Hanson family.)

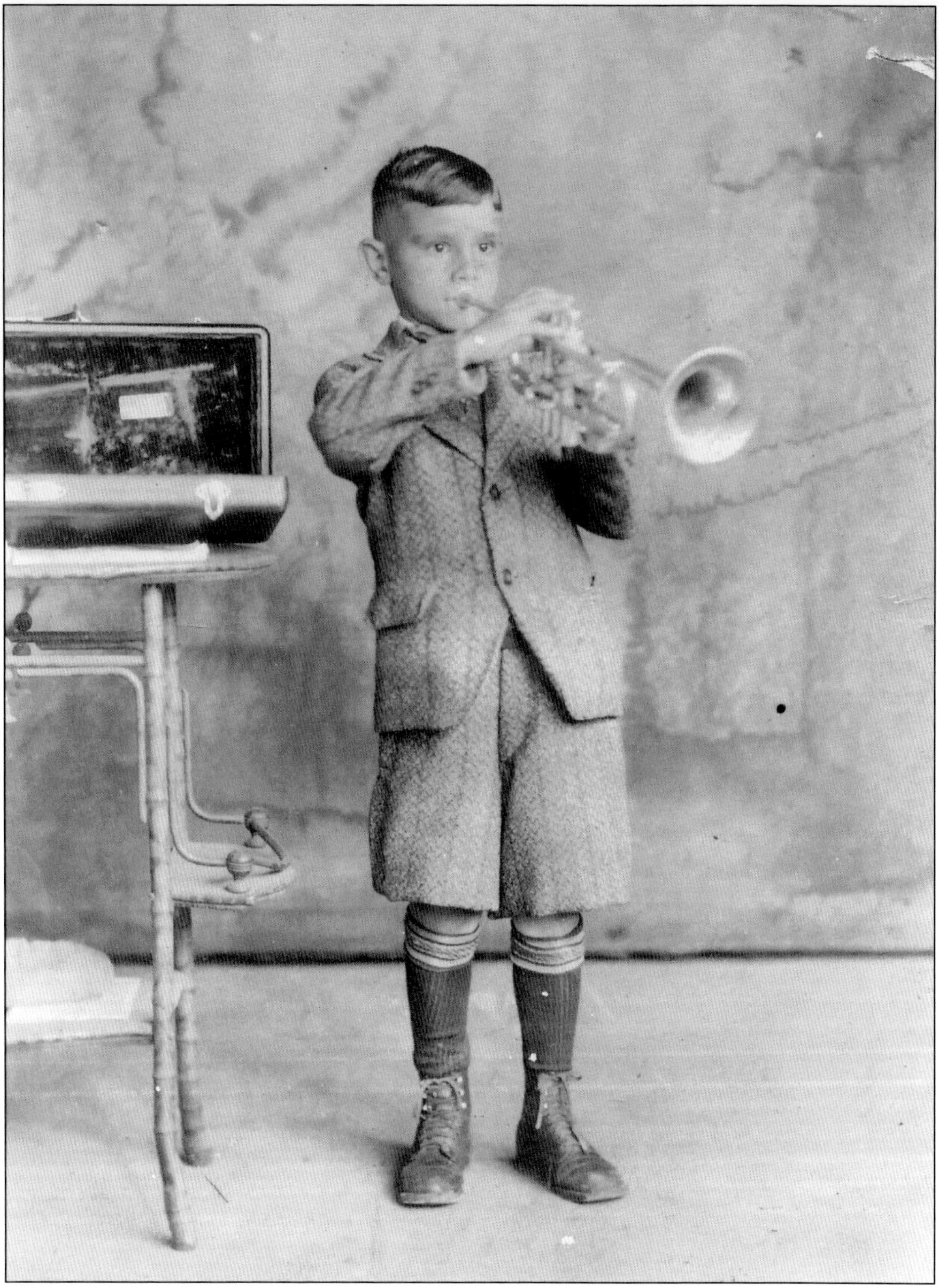

Donaldsonville was blessed with several different versions of Vincent Sotile throughout the years. Many remember Vincent Sotile as the city manager under Mayor LaLa Regira; however, a few know him as a professional musician for 30 years. He was also a first cousin to world-class musician Mitch Sotile. As a young boy, he played in the "Hot Cha Band." Vincent worked at Home Gas and Appliance and later became a partner in the candy factory. He was also on the Ascension Savings and Loan board of directors. (Courtesy of the Sotile family.)

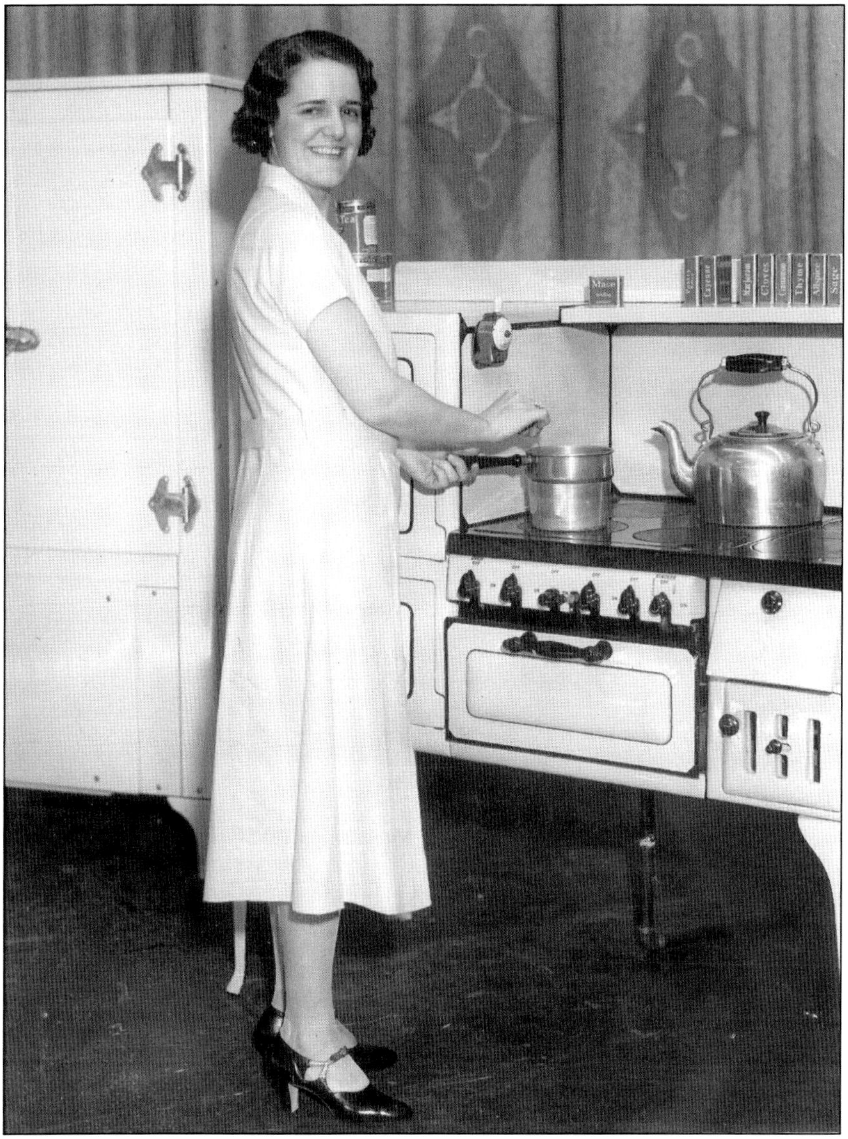

A funny thing happened to Alice Sims of Donaldsonville. She assumed the stage name of Miss Virginia Randolf and became the Julia Childs of the South and the West. She was exceptionally successful in her year and a half of conducting cooking schools in the West. Born in 1904 in Donaldsonville, she specialized in home economics in her hometown high school and then got her bachelor of science degree in home economics from the Southwestern Louisiana Institute in 1927. She went on the staff of the National Association of Ice Industry and lectured throughout nine Southern states on household refrigeration. In 1929, she received an offer from the Federal Electric Company in Chicago to conduct cooking schools in Texas, Arkansas, and Oklahoma. In 1931, she held her first cooking school in Hanford, California, and put on another 35 cooking schools in the West. Her larger cooking schools include those for the *Oakland Tribune*, the *Fresno Republican*, the *Sacramento Bee*, and the *Modesto News-Herald* in California. She also worked with the *Elpaso Herald-Times* in Texas and the *Medford Mail-Tribune* and the *Roseburg News-Review* in Oregon. The advantages of being such a celebrity is that she got to cook on all of the latest and greatest kitchen equipment, as shown in this photograph. (Courtesy of the Hanson family.)

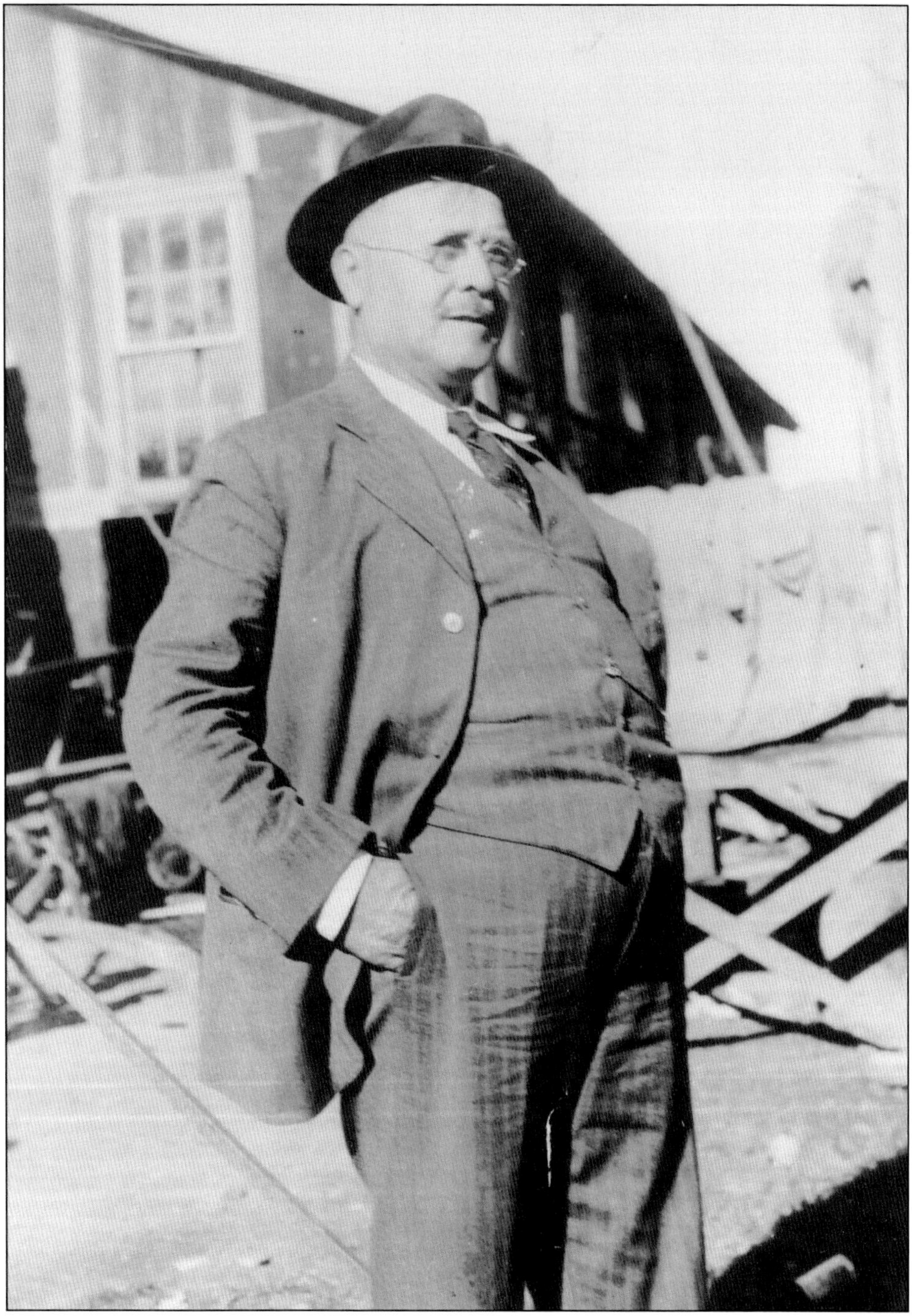

Frank Milano came to Donaldsonville from Sorrento, Italy, in 1897. His specialty was woodworking. He designed and built cabinets out of his shop for Donaldsonville kitchens and decorated the front of many homes with his unique fretwork (gingerbread) designs. Milano was called upon to build the pulpit, side altars, and communion rail at the Ascension Catholic Church. Frank Milano Sr. is shown here in the back of his house. The building behind him was used for storage of lumber used to build buses. (Courtesy of the Milano family.)

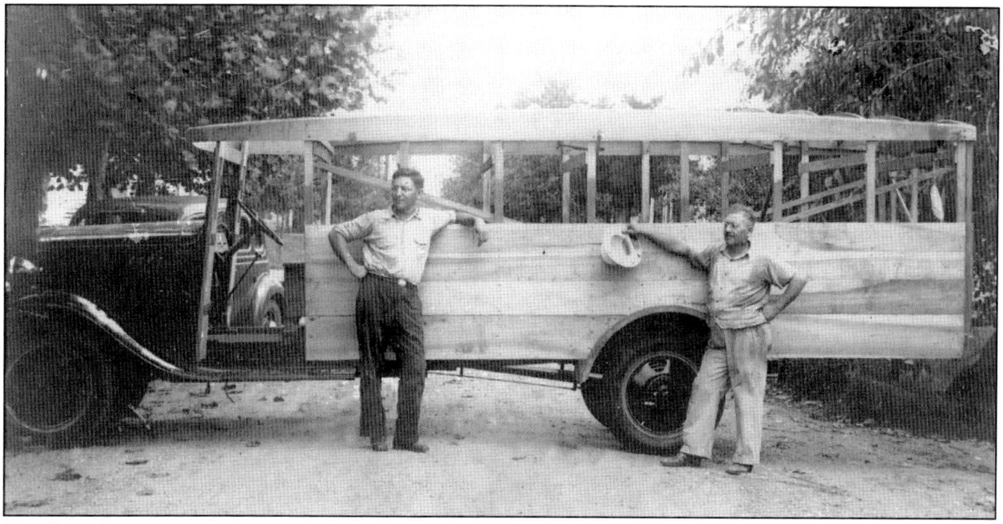

Frank Milano Sr. was a master carpenter. When Milano was not designing patterns for sugar mills in Donaldsonville as well as several in the Los Angeles area, he was building bodies for school buses, refrigerated trucks for Frey Brothers, and cattle trucks for area farmers. Mike Milano Sr. (left) and Frank Milano Sr. are shown here with a bus in progress. They would buy the truck frame and custom build the body. (Courtesy of the Milano family.)

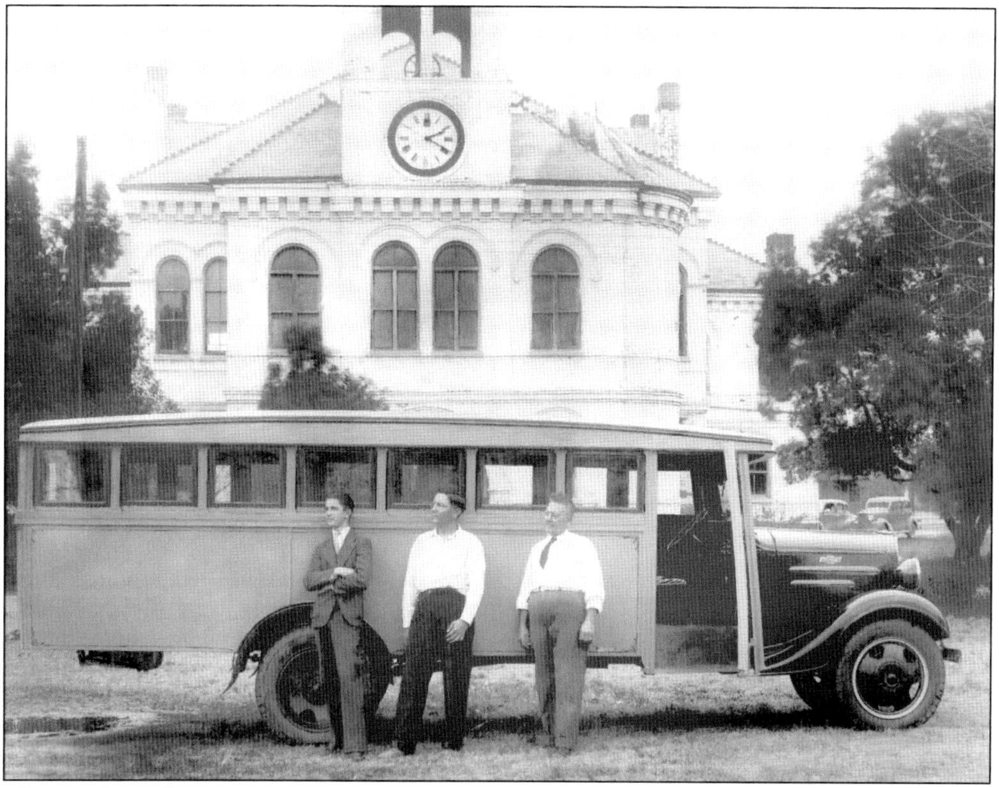

This is why Milano was in such high demand. From left to right, Wilbert Blanchard, Mike Milano Sr., and Frank Milano Sr. show off their handiwork in this photograph in front of the Donaldsonville Courthouse. (Courtesy of the Milano family.)

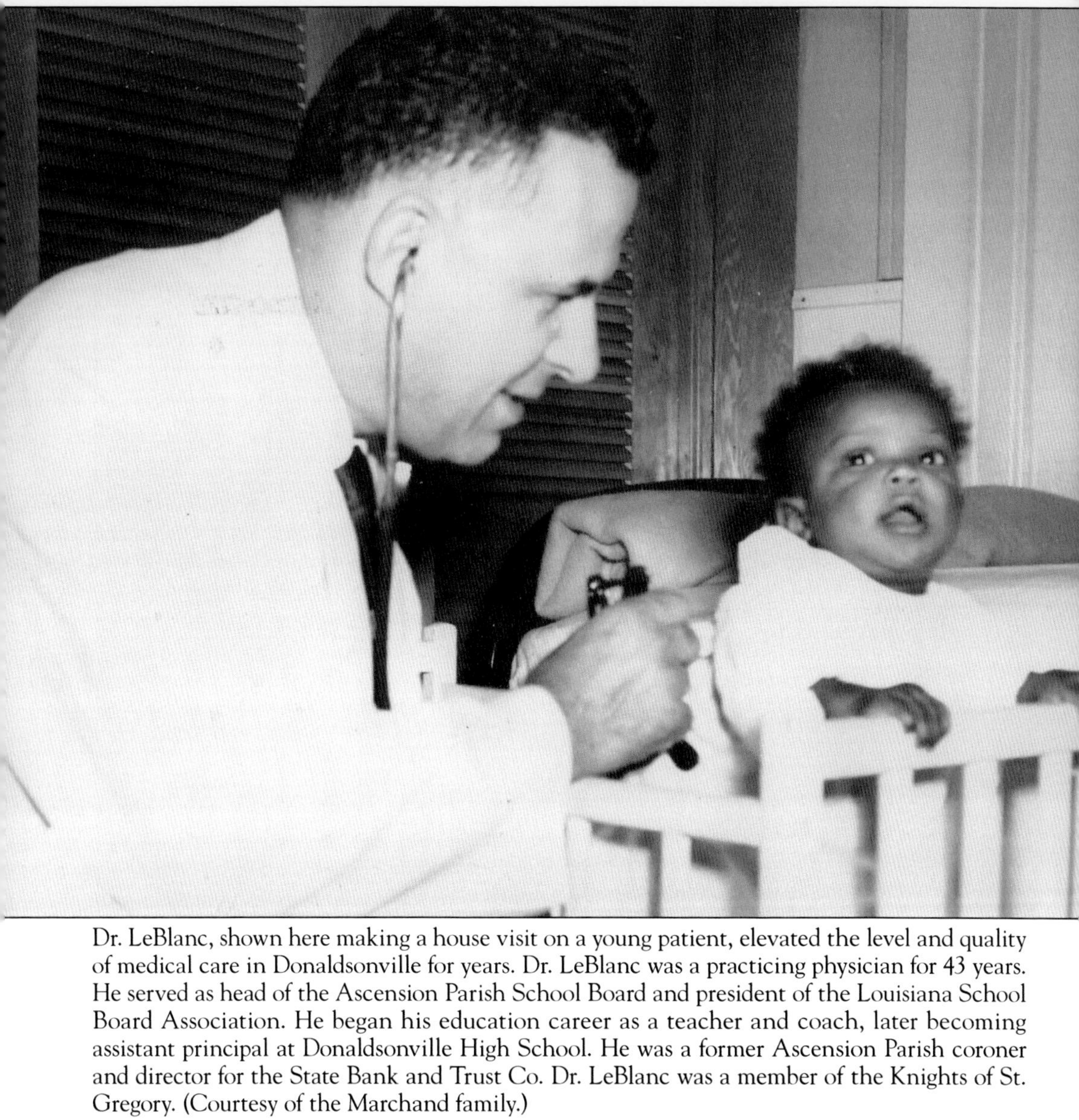

Dr. LeBlanc, shown here making a house visit on a young patient, elevated the level and quality of medical care in Donaldsonville for years. Dr. LeBlanc was a practicing physician for 43 years. He served as head of the Ascension Parish School Board and president of the Louisiana School Board Association. He began his education career as a teacher and coach, later becoming assistant principal at Donaldsonville High School. He was a former Ascension Parish coroner and director for the State Bank and Trust Co. Dr. LeBlanc was a member of the Knights of St. Gregory. (Courtesy of the Marchand family.)

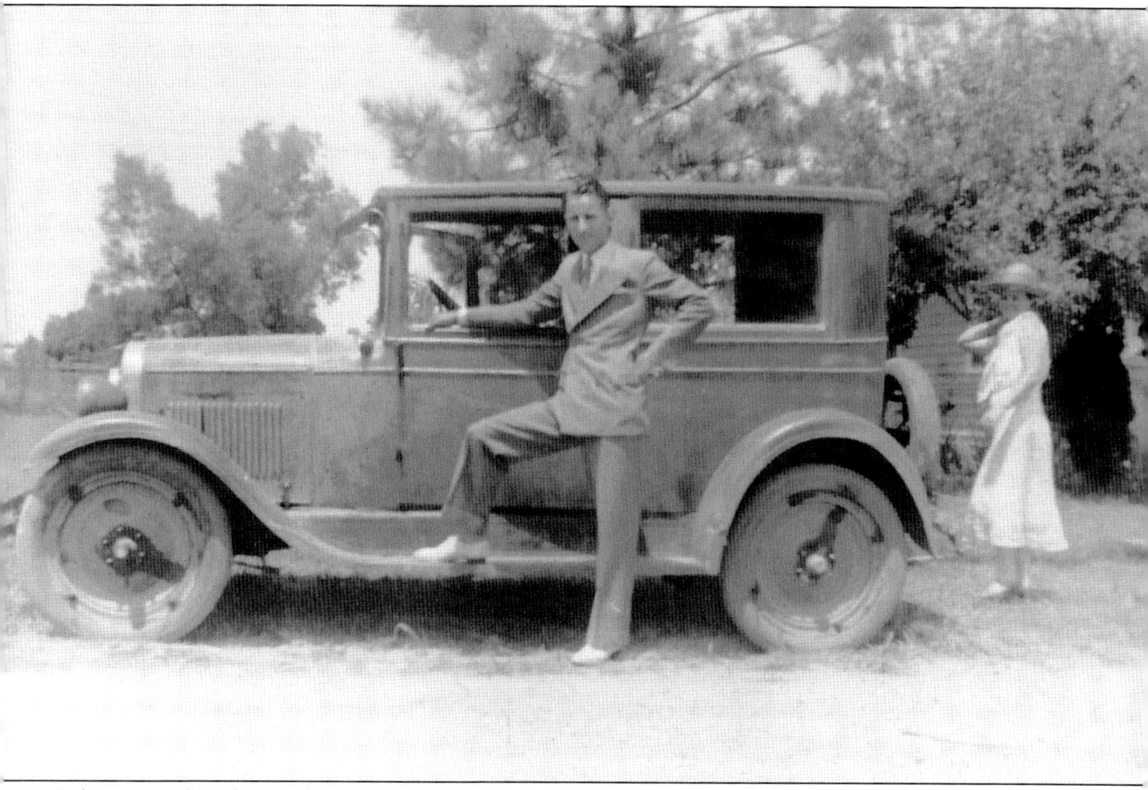

Sidney Marchand was a historian, mayor, legislator, and attorney. As a state senator, Marchand was a contemporary of Huey Long. It was during the mayoral administrations of Sidney Marchand Sr. and Sidney Marchand Jr. that significant infrastructure was constructed in Donaldsonville, including about 12 miles of paving and the extant sewerage system. Here, Sidney Marchand models his Deluxe Chevrolet while a friend models behind him. (Courtesy of the Marchand family.)

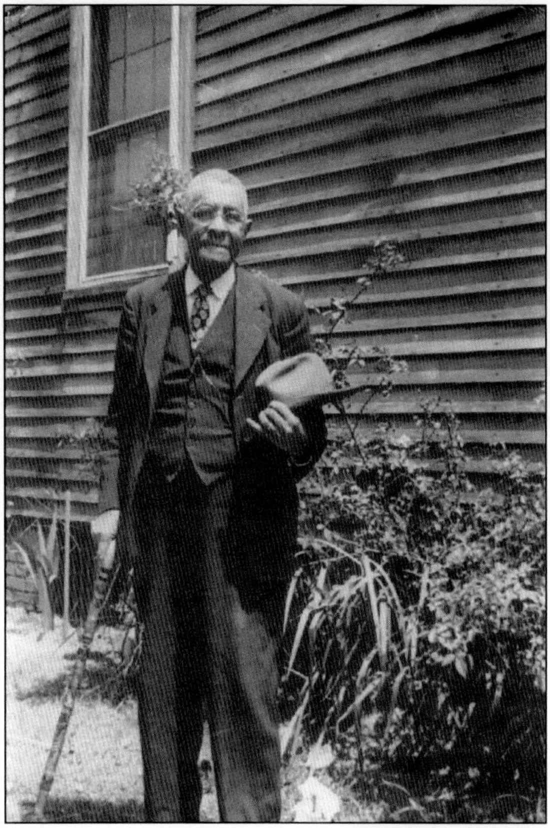

Born Claiborne Williams in 1868 on the Valenzuela Plantation, this local jazz great is regarded as a musical genius and widely respected music teacher who played a pivotal role in the evolution of jazz music. With a gifted and natural aptitude for music, he made his first violin out of a cigar box. At age 18, he played with the St. Joseph Brass Band of Donaldsonville. From there, he began the Claiborne Williams String Band and became one of the first bandleaders to incorporate a saxophone into his act. Williams traveled extensively but eventually came back home to Donaldsonville. For years, he attracted crowds to Donaldsonville's Grand Theatre and the True Friends Hall. He became a community treasure and made a great cultural impact on the area, teaching music to innumerable people of all ages, races, social status, and talent. The Claiborne Williams String Band is shown below in True Friends Hall. (Both, courtesy of Kathy Hambrick Jackson.)

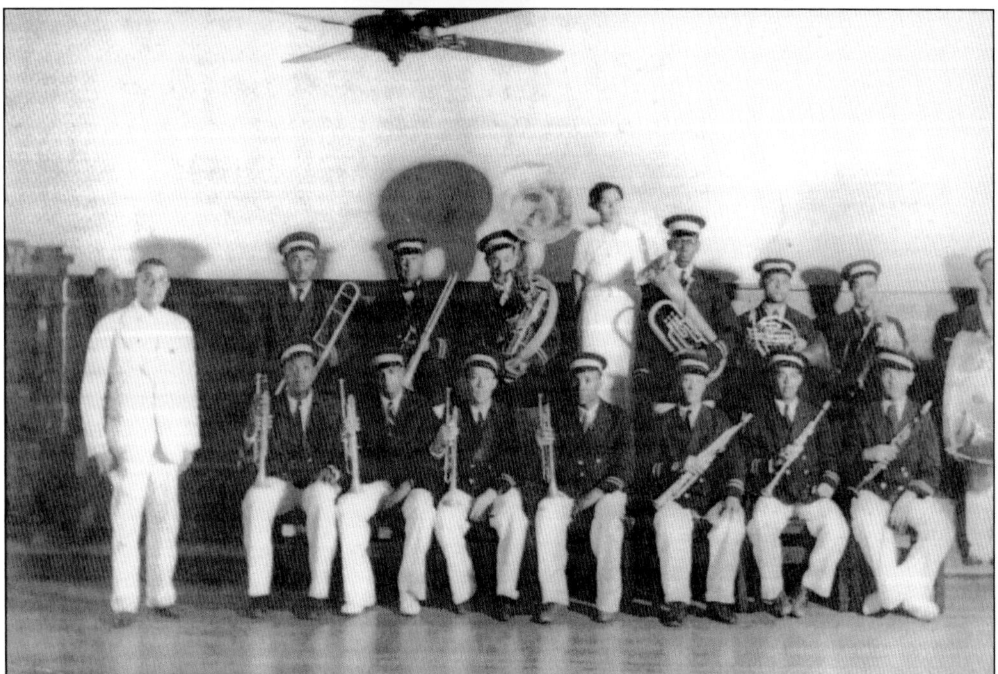

Best known for his bee business just down the bayou from Donaldsonville, Emile Garon was a Western Union telegraph agent for the railroad prior to becoming a beekeeper. Emile met his wife, Jeanne Rodriguez, while working for Western Union, and it was actually his father-in-law, Prosper Rodriguez, who introduced him to honey bees. Here he is at the depot with his very young daughter Jeanne Marie in May 1932. (Courtesy of the LeBlanc family.)

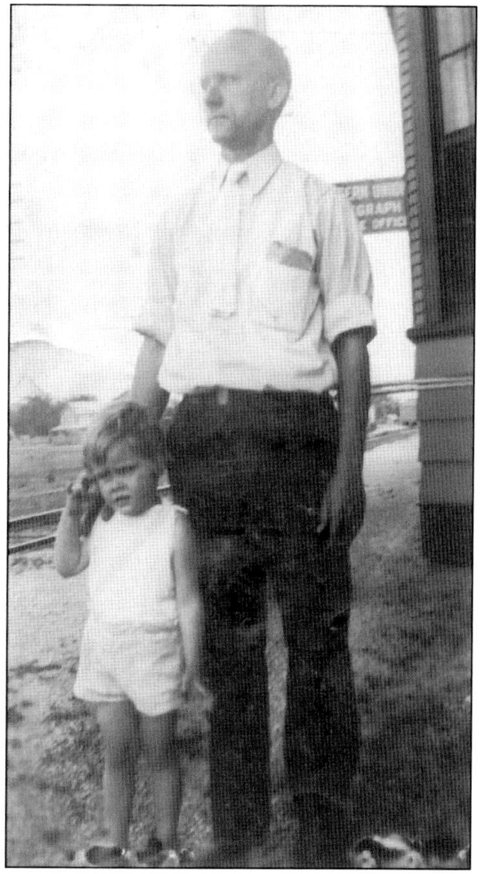

The well-known site of the Garon Bee Company, located along Bayou Lafourche, was a frequent stop for anyone who wanted fresh honey. Eventually, Garon concentrated on the raising and selling of queen bees over honey production. He ended up shipping his queens all over the world in his custom-made bee-shipping containers. (Courtesy of the LeBlanc family.)

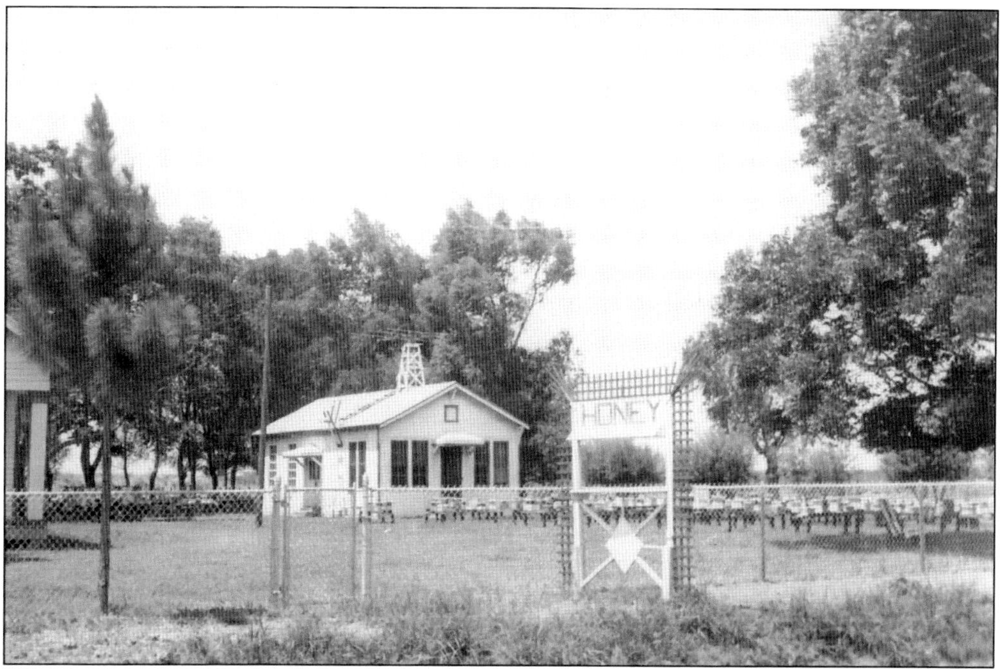

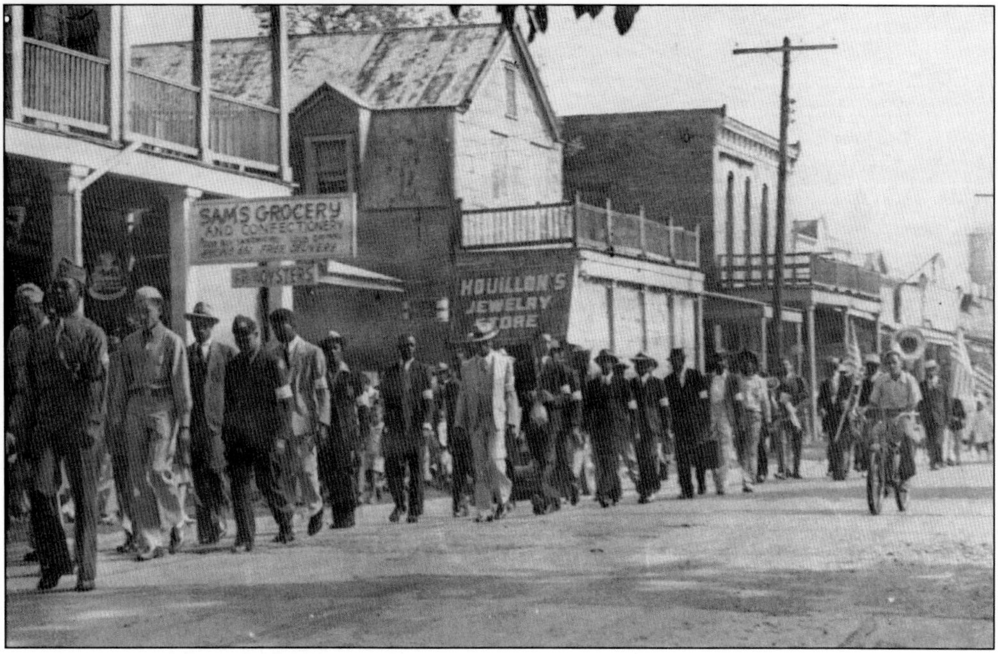

During World War II, Donaldsonville did not spare its patriotism. As the community pulled together to find scrap metal for the war, many would volunteer to make the ultimate sacrifice. This is a parade down Railroad Avenue for the young black men who are on their way to enlist in the service of their country. (Courtesy of Kathy Hambrick Jackson.)

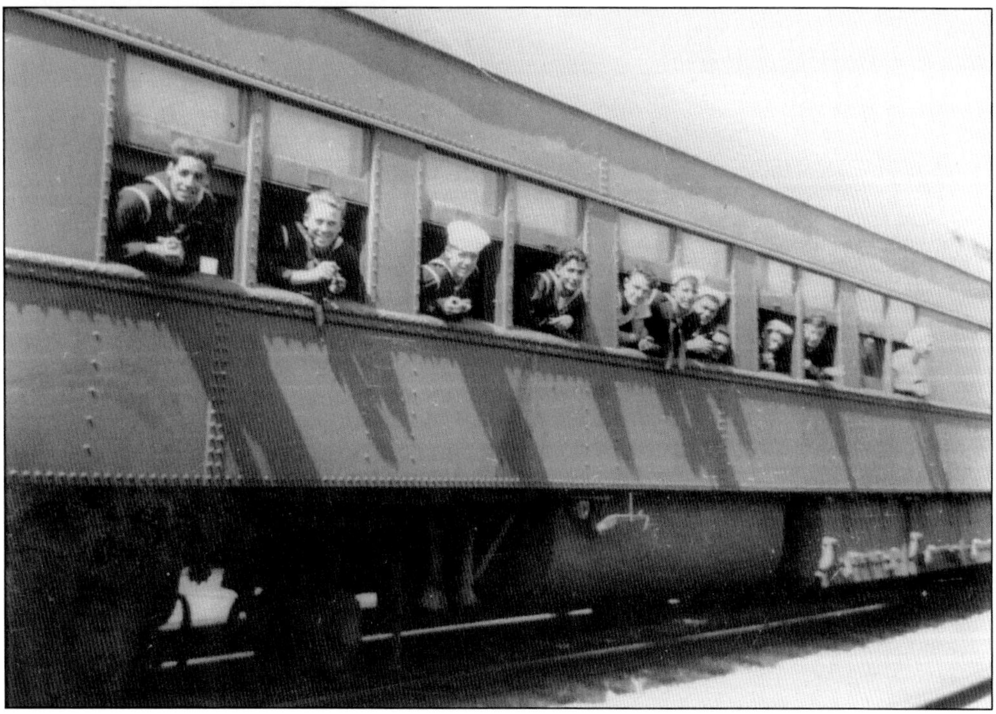

This photograph of servicemen passing through Donaldsonville on their way to war was taken at the train depot at the end of Railroad Avenue. (Courtesy of the Rodeillat family.)

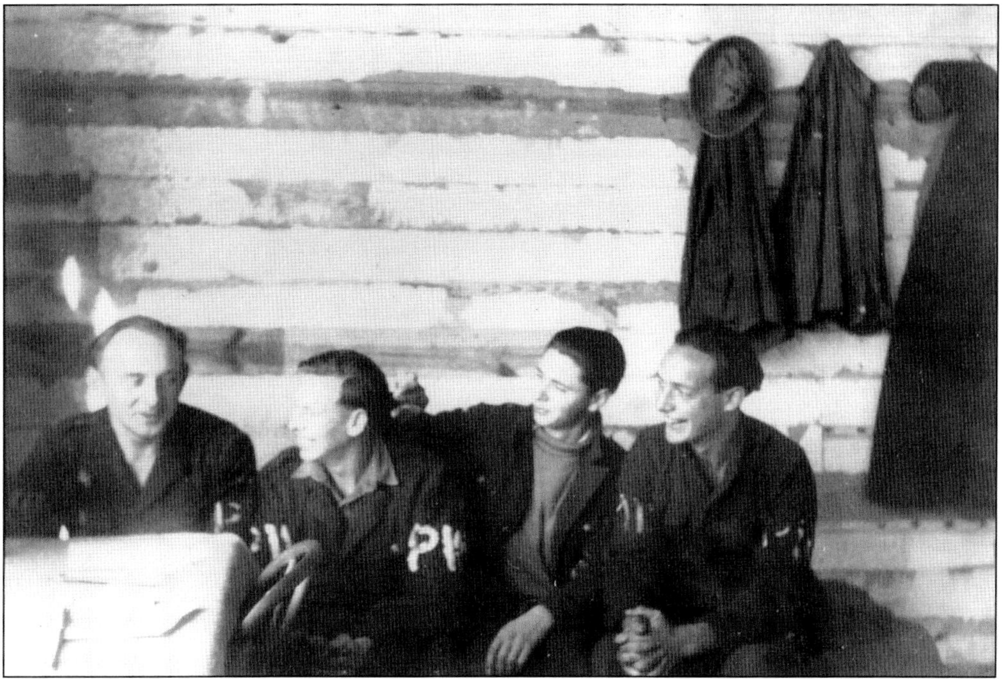

During World War II, many of the young men who would normally be working in the fields planting and harvesting sugarcane and rice were off to war. German prisoners of war were brought to farms all around Louisiana to help harvest the crops. (Courtesy of the Marchand family.)

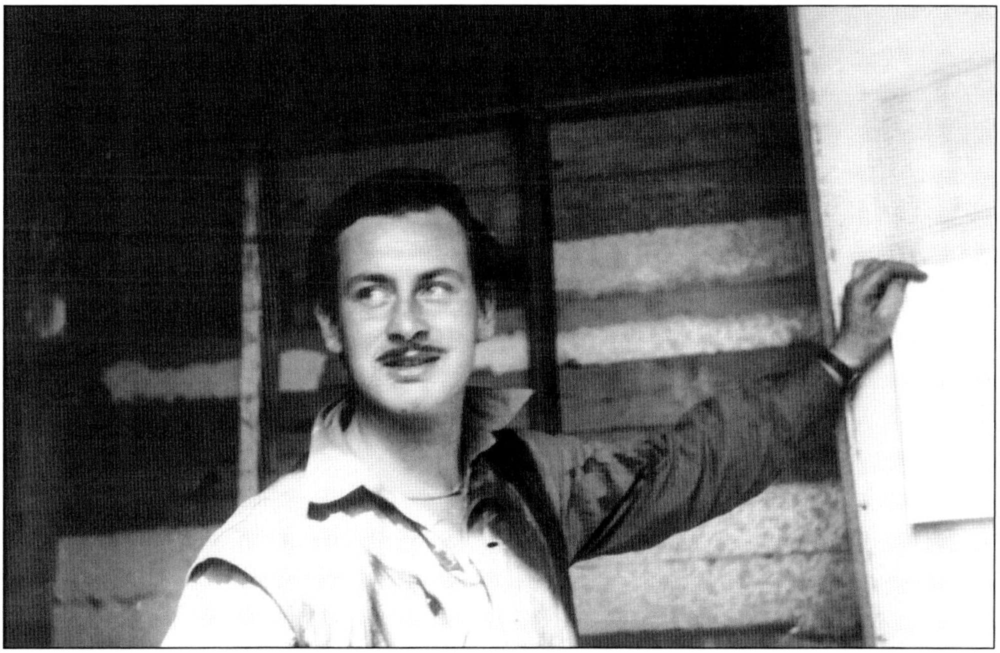

The POW camp in Donaldsonville was located at the end of Church Street near the fairgrounds. Stories of a prisoner escaping the camp and living in the woods circulated for some time. The relationship with the prisoners and the locals seemed to be good as the young Germans tended to be hard workers. (Courtesy of the Marchand family.)

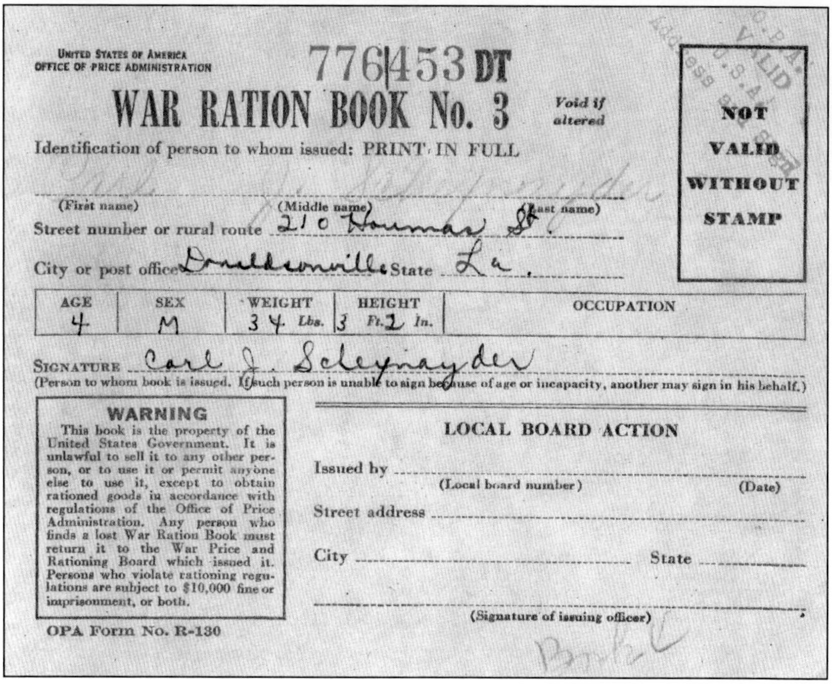

UNITED STATES OF AMERICA
OFFICE OF PRICE ADMINISTRATION

776453 DT

WAR RATION BOOK No. 3

Void if altered

NOT VALID WITHOUT STAMP

Identification of person to whom issued: PRINT IN FULL

(First name) (Middle name) (Last name)

Street number or rural route 210 Houmas St.

City or post office Donaldsonville State La.

AGE	SEX	WEIGHT	HEIGHT	OCCUPATION
4	M	34 Lbs.	3 Ft. 2 In.	

SIGNATURE Carl J. Scheynayder

(Person to whom book is issued. If such person is unable to sign because of age or incapacity, another may sign in his behalf.)

WARNING

This book is the property of the United States Government. It is unlawful to sell it to any other person, or to use it or permit anyone else to use it, except to obtain rationed goods in accordance with regulations of the Office of Price Administration. Any person who finds a lost War Ration Book must return it to the War Price and Rationing Board which issued it. Persons who violate rationing regulations are subject to $10,000 fine or imprisonment, or both.

OPA Form No. R-130

LOCAL BOARD ACTION

Issued by ______ (Local board number) (Date)

Street address ______

City ______ State ______

______ (Signature of issuing officer)

During World War II, one could not just walk into a shop and buy as much sugar or butter or meat as he or she wanted, nor could cars be filled all the way up with gasoline. All these things were rationed, which meant people were only allowed to buy a small amount (even if they could afford more). The government introduced rationing because certain things were in short supply during the war, and rationing was the only way to make sure everyone got their fair share. Pictured are the front and back covers of the war ration book belonging to four-year-old Carl Schexnayder. (Both, courtesy of the Schexnayder family.)

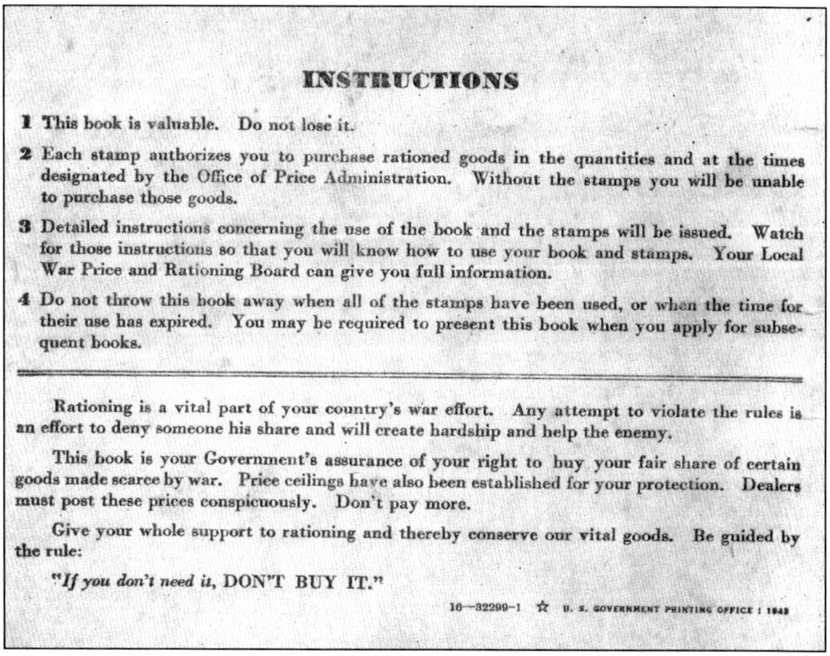

INSTRUCTIONS

1 This book is valuable. Do not lose it.

2 Each stamp authorizes you to purchase rationed goods in the quantities and at the times designated by the Office of Price Administration. Without the stamps you will be unable to purchase those goods.

3 Detailed instructions concerning the use of the book and the stamps will be issued. Watch for those instructions so that you will know how to use your book and stamps. Your Local War Price and Rationing Board can give you full information.

4 Do not throw this book away when all of the stamps have been used, or when the time for their use has expired. You may be required to present this book when you apply for subsequent books.

Rationing is a vital part of your country's war effort. Any attempt to violate the rules is an effort to deny someone his share and will create hardship and help the enemy.

This book is your Government's assurance of your right to buy your fair share of certain goods made scarce by war. Price ceilings have also been established for your protection. Dealers must post these prices conspicuously. Don't pay more.

Give your whole support to rationing and thereby conserve our vital goods. Be guided by the rule:

"*If you don't need it,* DON'T BUY IT."

16—32299-1 ☆ U. S. GOVERNMENT PRINTING OFFICE : 1943

This is an actual partially used page of stamps from the war ration book of Carl Schexnayder. Sugar stamps always seemed like the first to go. (Courtesy of the Schexnayder family.)

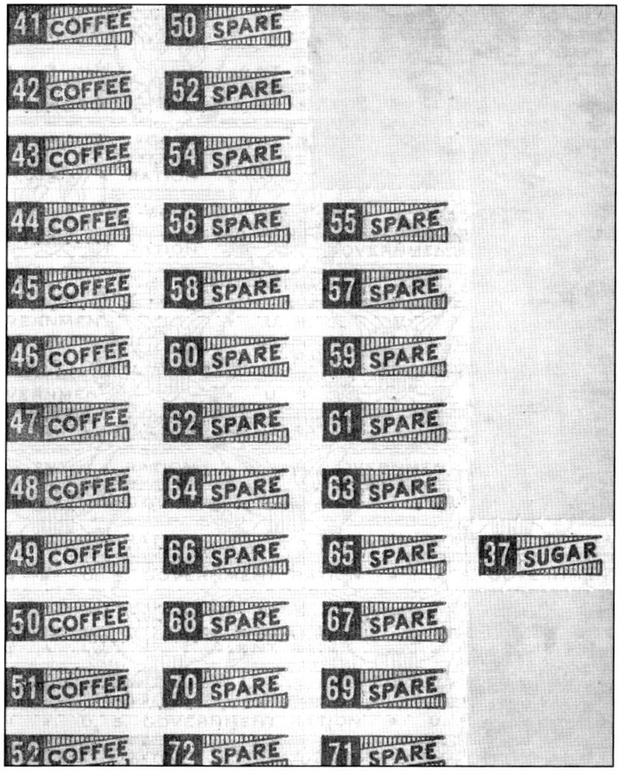

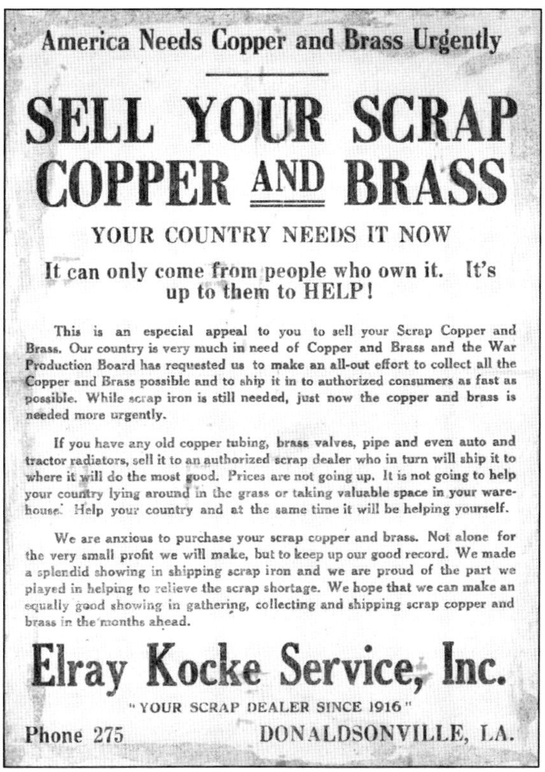

America Needs Copper and Brass Urgently

SELL YOUR SCRAP COPPER AND BRASS

YOUR COUNTRY NEEDS IT NOW

It can only come from people who own it. It's up to them to HELP!

This is an especial appeal to you to sell your Scrap Copper and Brass. Our country is very much in need of Copper and Brass and the War Production Board has requested us to make an all-out effort to collect all the Copper and Brass possible and to ship it in to authorized consumers as fast as possible. While scrap iron is still needed, just now the copper and brass is needed more urgently.

If you have any old copper tubing, brass valves, pipe and even auto and tractor radiators, sell it to an authorized scrap dealer who in turn will ship it to where it will do the most good. Prices are not going up. It is not going to help your country lying around in the grass or taking valuable space in your warehouse. Help your country and at the same time it will be helping yourself.

We are anxious to purchase your scrap copper and brass. Not alone for the very small profit we will make, but to keep up our good record. We made a splendid showing in shipping scrap iron and we are proud of the part we played in helping to relieve the scrap shortage. We hope that we can make an equally good showing in gathering, collecting and shipping scrap copper and brass in the months ahead.

Elray Kocke Service, Inc.

"YOUR SCRAP DEALER SINCE 1916"

Phone 275 DONALDSONVILLE, LA.

Since salvage was how Elray Kocke Service started its business, helping secure scrap metal, copper, and brass came naturally for the company. This was an actual poster used to solicit scrap metals. (Courtesy of the Kocke family.)

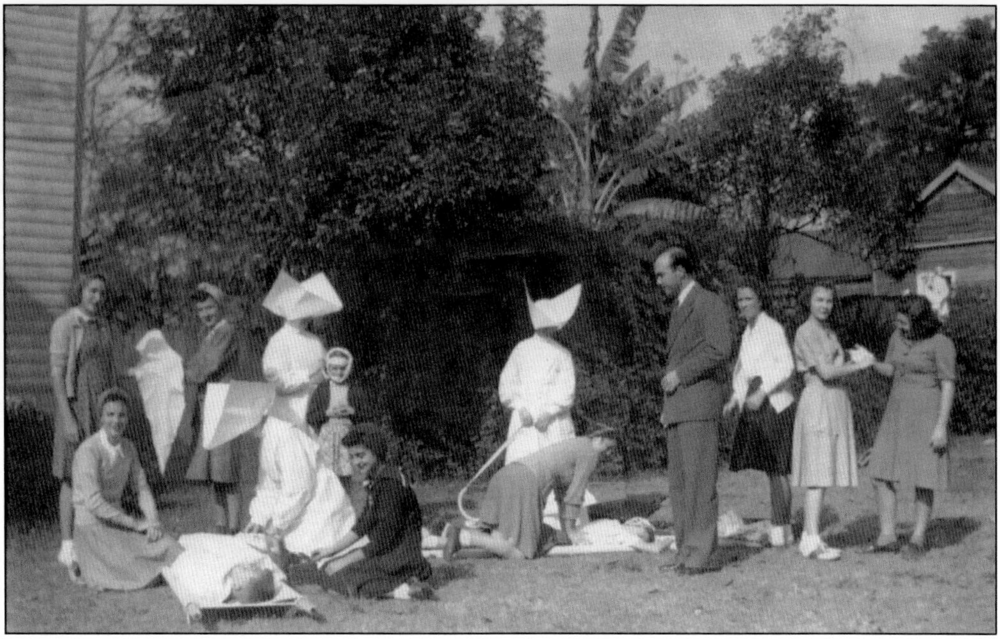

Dr. E.A. Schexnayder (standing) gives lessons on first aid to local residents and nuns. This was a common event during World War II. (Courtesy of the Mistretta family.)

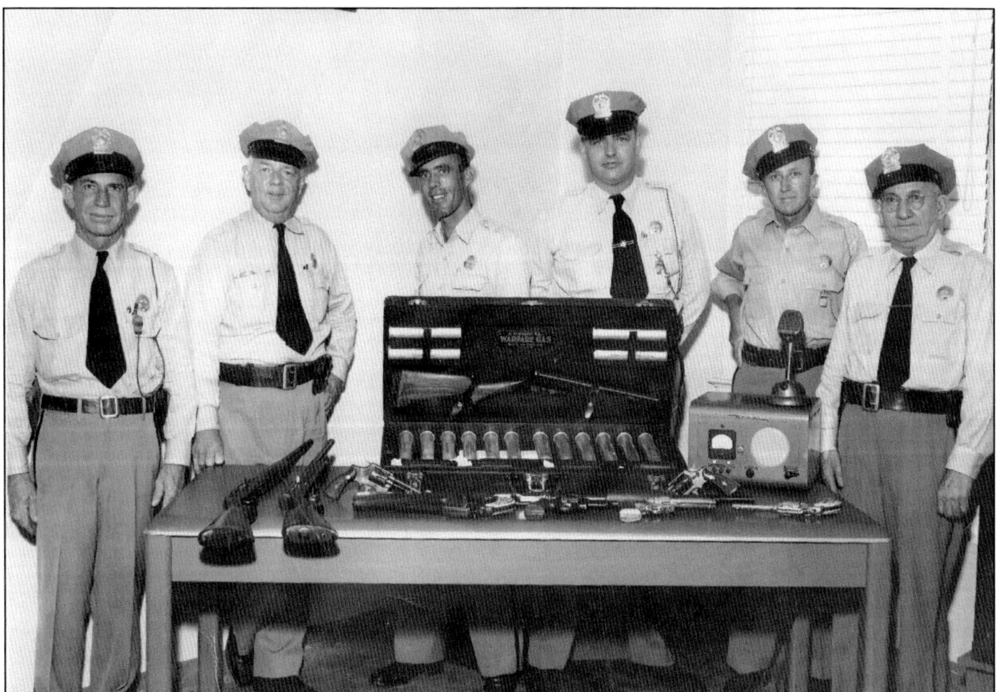

Keeping the peace, the Donaldsonville Police Department showed off the latest in law enforcement technology. Pictured are, from left to right, Carlo Pizzalotta, Leo Mattingly, Bob LeBlanc, Tony Milano, George Rodeillat, and Sam Solar around 1950. (Courtesy of the Falcon family.)

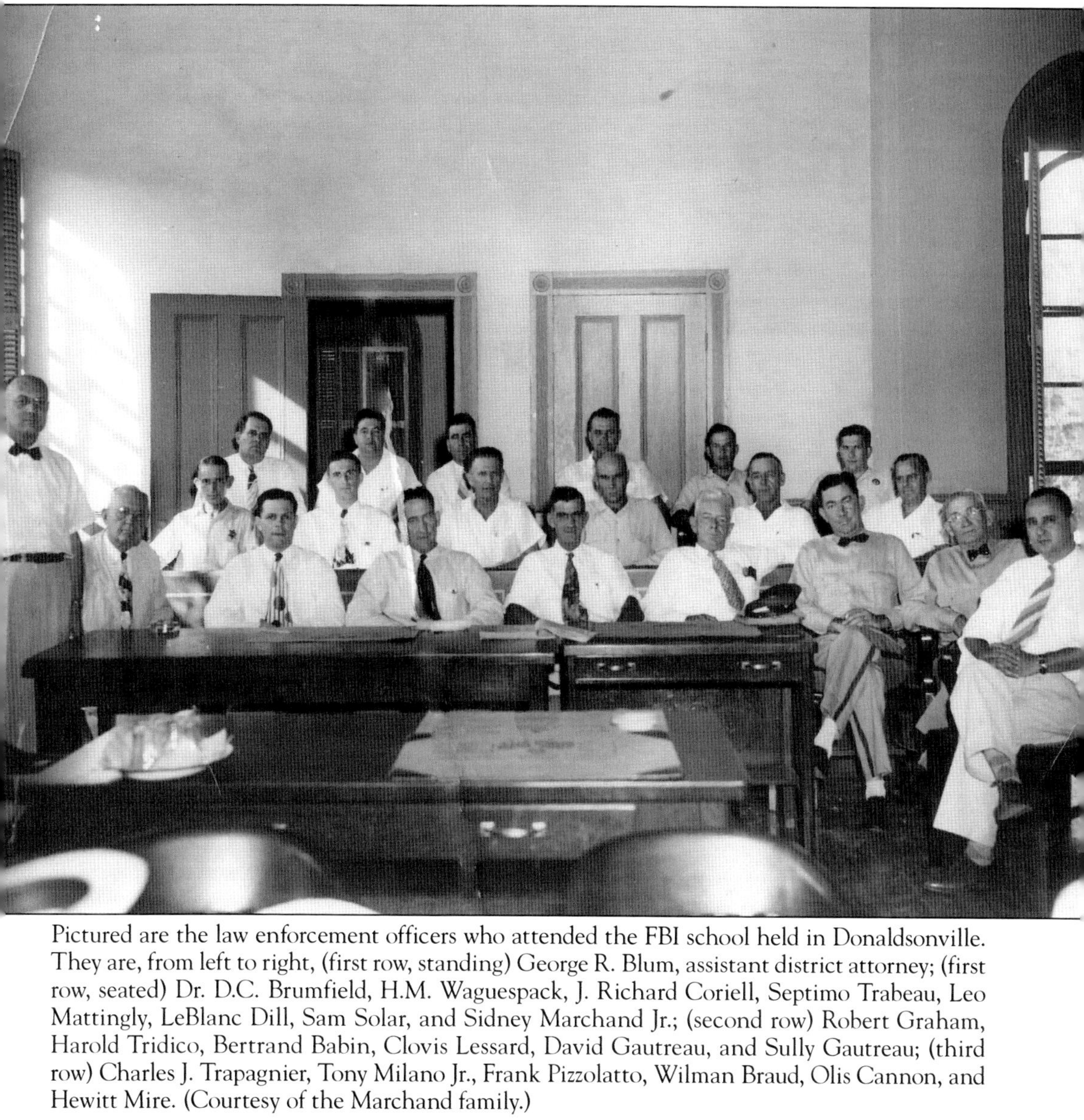

Pictured are the law enforcement officers who attended the FBI school held in Donaldsonville. They are, from left to right, (first row, standing) George R. Blum, assistant district attorney; (first row, seated) Dr. D.C. Brumfield, H.M. Waguespack, J. Richard Coriell, Septimo Trabeau, Leo Mattingly, LeBlanc Dill, Sam Solar, and Sidney Marchand Jr.; (second row) Robert Graham, Harold Tridico, Bertrand Babin, Clovis Lessard, David Gautreau, and Sully Gautreau; (third row) Charles J. Trapagnier, Tony Milano Jr., Frank Pizzolatto, Wilman Braud, Olis Cannon, and Hewitt Mire. (Courtesy of the Marchand family.)

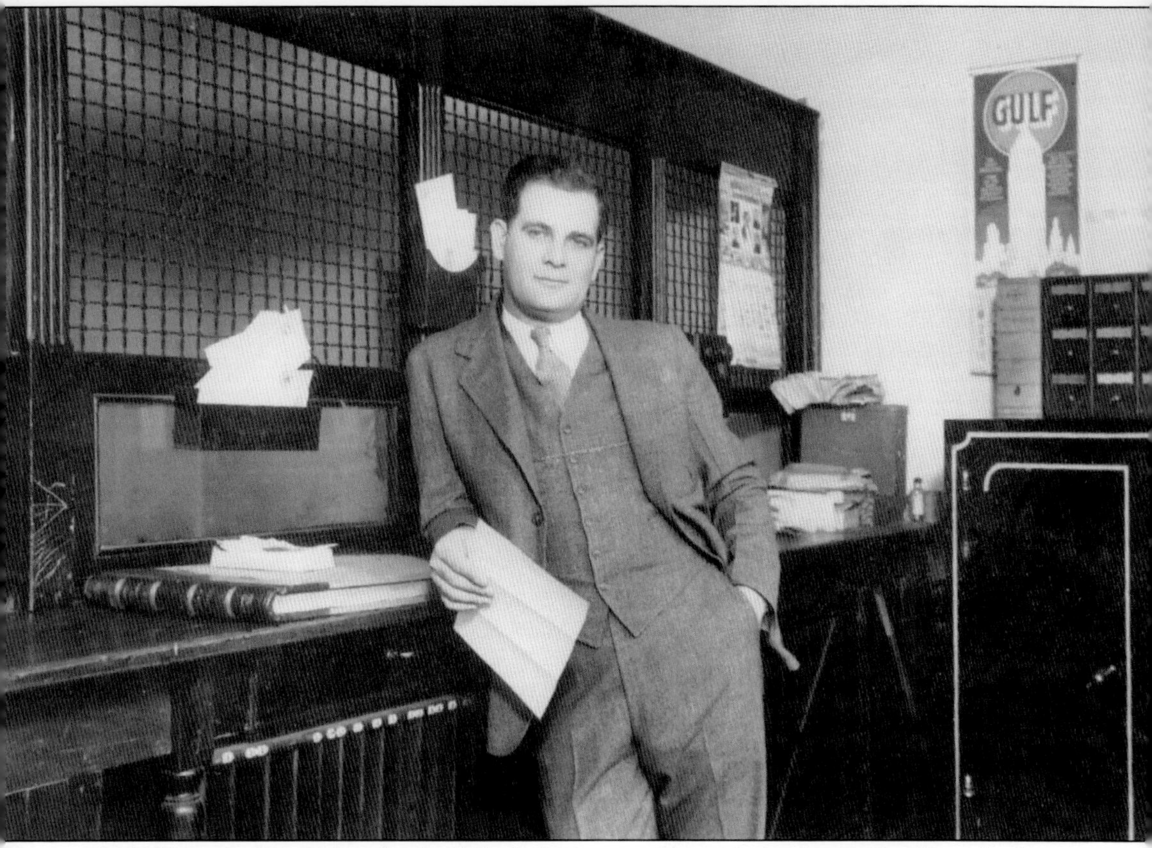

In 1924, at the age of 18, Charles "Chalou" Trepagnier was the youngest sheriff in the history of Ascension Parish. At the time, he was six feet, two inches tall and weighed 220 pounds. His career spanned 51 years, but he never used the gun on his hip. His cool demeanor and presence of mind under the most dangerous situations served to disarm those he came into contact with. (Courtesy of the Trepagnier family.)

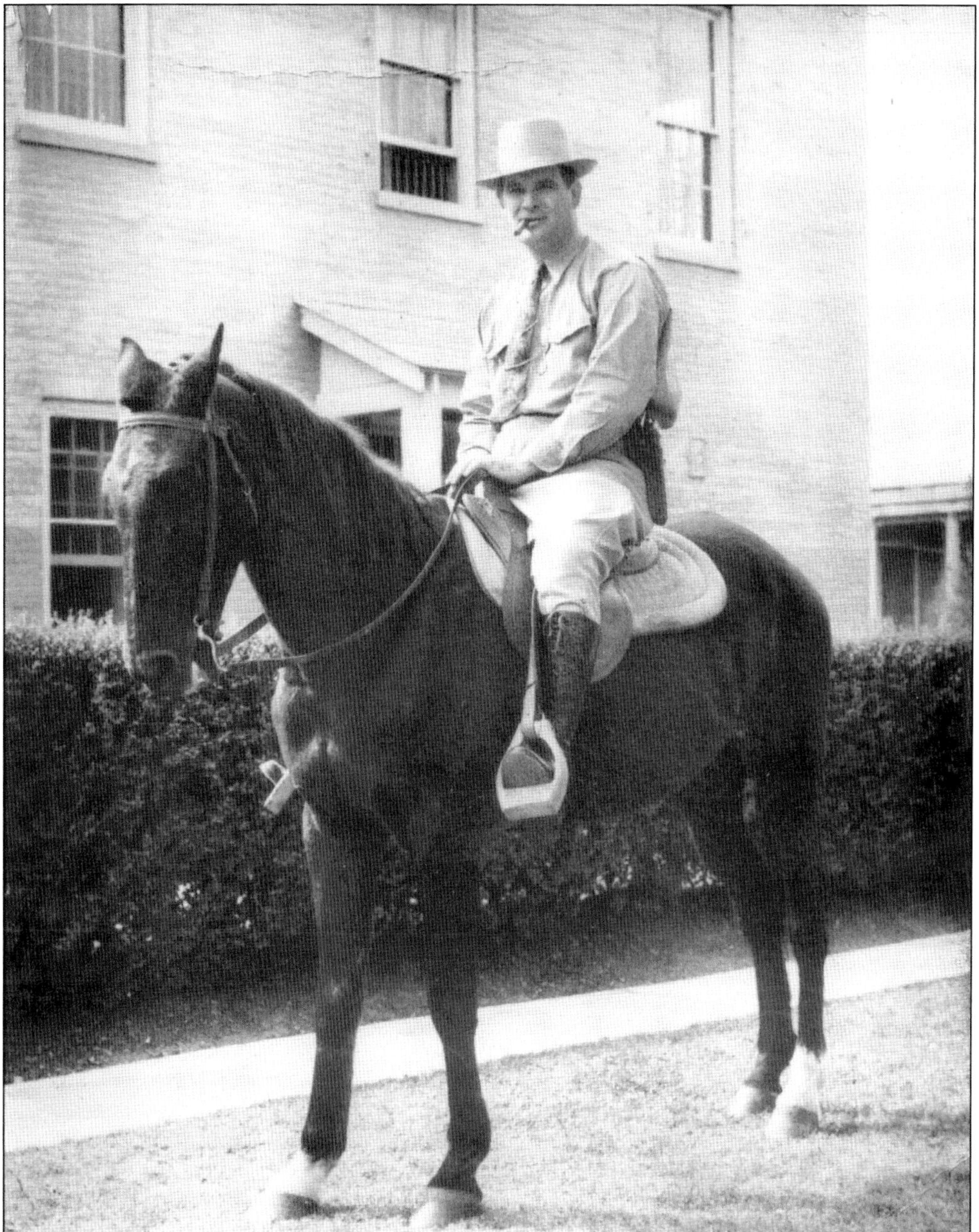

Chalou grew up in the black section of Donaldsonville and was quite well known in the black community. After the death of Dr. Martin Luther King, a march was planned down Railroad Avenue to the courthouse. When Chalou heard of it, he instructed his deputies to stay away from the parade route, met the organizers, and led the parade peacefully through town. (Courtesy of the Trepagnier family.)